THE UNITED NATIONS
LIBRARY

THE UNITED NATIONS LIBRARY

ITS ORIGIN AND DEVELOPMENT

Doris Cruger Dale

American Library Association

Chicago 1970

International Standard Book Number 0-8389-0090-9 (1970)
Library of Congress Catalog Card Number 74-132060
Printed in the United States of America

*To my parents and husband;
their encouragement made
this book possible.*

Contents

CONTENTS

Illustrations

Organizational charts and Tables

Preface

Although many books, articles, and dissertations have been written on the United Nations, on the Secretariat of the United Nations, and on the documents of the United Nations, no full-length study has ever been made either of the United Nations Library, the League of Nations Library, or any of the other international libraries in the world. There have been a few shorter studies of seminal importance, however, on the United Nations Library.

Recently the United Nations Library compiled a pioneer work entitled *The Libraries of the United Nations: A Descriptive Guide*, which includes information on both the Dag Hammarskjöld Library in New York and the United Nations Library in Geneva.[1]

At the dedication of the Dag Hammarskjöld Library on 17 November 1961, Verner W. Clapp presented a paper entitled "The United Nations Library 1945–1961," which was later published both in the dedication book and in *Libri*.[2] He had previously written about the establishment of the library at the United Nations Conference on International Organization at San Francisco in 1945.[3] S. Hartz Rasmussen kept a diary, in English and in Danish, while he was director of the United Nations Library. At one time he had started to write the history of the library during its early years.[4] Carl H. Milam also kept a diary during his two-year tenure as director and after his retirement wrote a long article on the library for *The Library Quarterly*.[5] A four-part diary written by Dr. Josef Stummvoll, director of the library at the time of the dedication of the new building, has been published in *Biblos*.[6] This is the extent of the major historical writings on the United Nations Library. As the library celebrates its twenty-fifth birthday, a more detailed historical analysis of those important early years seems appropriate.

This study is based on the author's doctoral dissertation.[7] Although it does include some recent events, major emphasis has been placed on the period from the library's inception in 1945 until the dedication of the new library building on 16 November 1961.

The bulk of the data presented in this study is derived from official documents, archival materials, and primary published sources. Official documents include those of the United Nations, especially the debates of the Fifth Committee of the General Assembly, the resolutions of the General Assembly, the annual reports of the Secretary-General on the work of the organization, and the annual reports of the library.

Archival materials include the minutes of the meetings of the Permanent Advisory Library Committee, official correspondence in regard to library policy, the surveys and studies of the operations of the library, Mr. Milam's papers while he was director, the working files of the office of the director from 1948 to 1961, and administrative correspondence and working papers on the policy of the Department of Public Information and the other departments under which the library was organized.

Other primary sources include the private papers and diary of Carl H. Milam; letters to the author, which have been used to clarify troublesome points; and personal and contemporary records from a number of people closely associated with the United Nations Library. Finally, the author has conducted interviews with persons connected with the library.

The bibliography is divided into two parts. The first part deals with the United Nations Library in New York. The author has attempted to make this an exhaustive bibliography of all items relating to the library and to the documents of the United Nations. Only individual memoranda and letters from archives and private sources have been omitted. The second part of the bibliography deals with the League of Nations Library and the United Nations Library in Geneva. This bibliography is more selective, since the author has not had access to the archives in Geneva, although it does include most items of major importance.

Acknowledgments

Without the patience and generous assistance of many persons, this study of the United Nations Library could not have been completed. A special word of appreciation and gratitude is due Dr. Oliver L. Lilley, Professor of Library Service in the School of Library Service at Columbia University, who served as the supervisor of the dissertation on which this book is based.

The Deputy Director of the United Nations Library, Mr. Joseph Groesbeck, offered the full support of the library during all phases of the study and graciously supplied the author with copies of the library's annual reports, a copy of the beautiful dedication book, and numerous other items.

Most of the research was undertaken at Columbia University and the United Nations Archives, and the author would like to acknowledge the assistance of both the various librarians of the School of Library Service Library at Columbia University and the following personnel of the United Nations Archives: Mr. Marjan Stopar-Babsek, Archivist; Mr. Vincent G. Hyland, Associate Archivist; and Miss Freda Abramowitz, Senior Archives Clerk.

Mr. Albert C. Gerould and Mr. S. Hartz Rasmussen (former librarians of the United Nations Library), as well as Mr. Verner

ACKNOWLEDGMENTS

W. Clapp, consultant and former president of the Council on Library Resources, graciously answered the author's many questions about the United Nations Library and provided her with material from their personal files.

Mrs. William A. Seidler, Jr., very kindly lent the author the papers of the late Carl H. Milam, her father, as well as the diary written while he was librarian of the United Nations.

Southern Illinois University provided both research funds and research time during the academic year of 1969/70 so that the dissertation could be extensively revised for publication.

Thanks are due the Author's Office in Carbondale, Illinois, which undertook the labors of typing the manuscript; Mrs. Regina Shelton, who provided the author with accurate translations of several articles; and Betty Ruth Wilson Marrero, who graciously consented to read the manuscript and proofread the final copy.

Even though considerable assistance has been rendered by the aforementioned persons and by other individuals too numerous to mention, the judgments and conclusions are solely the responsibility of the author.

THE UNITED NATIONS LIBRARY

chapter 1

Historical evolution of the United Nations Library

Parent organization

The origins of the United Nations lie far back in history. As early as 1693, William Penn published an essay suggesting that the deputies of the sovereign princes of Europe meet, in a round room at least every three years, as a general parliament and establish rules of justice. The benefits of this parliament would be not only to prevent the spilling of blood but also to increase personal friendship between princes and states.[1] Although Penn did not provide his parliament with a library, surely if this essay had been written fifty years later by his compatriot Benjamin Franklin, a library would have been advocated as being essential to the success of the parliament.

Similarly, the League of Nations and the United Nations were agencies designed for peace, war having provided the impulse to organize in both instances. Both organizations consisted of a parliament of the deputies of the sovereign states in the world – the Assembly of the League of Nations, the General Assembly of the United Nations. Smaller bodies, consisting of the major powers plus representatives of the other powers, were an added refinement – the Council of the League of Nations, the Security Council of the United Nations. The League

3

of Nations Covenant, which went into effect 10 January 1920, and the Charter of the United Nations, signed 24 October 1945, also provided for a permanent Secretariat with a secretary-general and a supporting staff. The only major difference in provisions for the Secretariat staff was that appointments to the League staff required formal approval of the Council, while appointments to the United Nations Secretariat were made on the sole authority of the secretary-general.[2]

The Secretariat, one of six principal organs of the United Nations, was designed to serve all member nations, to remain independent of political changes in those nations, and to provide administrative unity and continuity in the United Nations. The Secretariat was also charged with aiding the United Nations to fulfill the purposes assigned to it by the Charter: (1) to maintain international peace and security, (2) to develop friendly relations among nations, based on respect for the principle of equal rights and self-determination of peoples, (3) to achieve international cooperation in solving problems of an economic, social, cultural, and humanitarian character, and (4) to be a center for harmonizing the actions of nations in the attainment of these common ends.[3]

The United Nations Secretariat plays various roles. It acts as a parliamentary clerk—furnishing translation services for the debates and meetings, providing legal and procedural assistance, providing services for the various conference activities, and offering library facilities for the delegates and for its own staff. It also provides information. It has the responsibility for interpreting the United Nations to the public by providing information services for the press, the nongovernmental organizations, and the scholarly community. It performs the executive tasks necessary to carry out the various technical-assistance programs. It has the responsibility of recruiting staff and providing various personnel services. It also has a diplomatic or political function, because the secretary-general is charged with the responsibility of bringing to the attention of the Security Council any matter which in his opinion may threaten international peace and security.[4]

As can be seen from this list of functions, the library plays an important role in two major instances. It must provide library services not only to delegates but also to the Secretariat staff;

and it must provide services to the press, the nongovernmental organizations, and the scholarly community. The purpose of the library, as of the Secretariat, is to aid the parent organization in fulfilling its goals.

The library, however, is not only a part of the United Nations, but is also a member of the international library community. As such, it should be committed to carry out the principles enunciated in the Library Bill of Rights and the Freedom to Read statement issued by the American Library Association and the American Book Publishers Council. This stand is especially important in an organization such as the United Nations, where all points of view are represented. Dr. Víctor Belaúnde, at the dedication of the Dag Hammarskjöld Library, stated the position of the library: "The Library represents the principle of objectivity, the principle of impartial research, the principle by virtue of which we must let the facts speak for themselves, without passion."[5]

One of the responsibilities of the Secretariat is the provision of an international, impersonal civil service acting only in the interests of the United Nations. "By accepting appointment, they [the members of the Secretariat] pledge themselves to discharge their functions and to regulate their conduct with the interests of the United Nations only in view."[6] Besides being international and impersonal, the staff members of the library must be multilingual and conversant with all aspects of international affairs.

Little has been written about the role of the library in fulfilling the functions enumerated above, yet it is an important role. The proliferation of publishing in all languages, the need for research materials and primary documents in many fields, the need to classify and catalog an international collection and to provide reference services to an international clientele, in addition to providing the key through indexes to all of the United Nations documents, require a library organized in the most efficient manner and providing a high level of public service.

Libraries in the League of Nations and in the United Nations were not given much attention when organizational plans for these two agencies were in progress. Yet, of necessity, libraries were established in both instances.

League of Nations Library

The library of the League of Nations grew out of a series of sectional libraries attached to the various divisions of the League. One of these was the Economic and Finance Library, which was started in a small room of Sunderland House on Curzon Street in London on 25 June 1919, under the direction of Marguerite E. Day. This room soon became too small; so the sectional library was removed in September 1919 to a larger room at 117 Piccadilly, where it continued to expand. In January 1920, when the League of Nations officially came into being, all of the sectional libraries were merged with the Economic and Finance Library. This unit then became the League of Nations Library. In the fall of 1919, Miss Florence Wilson, an American, began her duties as the first librarian of the League. Later in 1920 the Secretariat, including the library, was moved to Geneva to the Hôtel National on the Quai Woodrow Wilson. In Geneva the library occupied a few offices, the old dining room, and the cellars of the hotel.[7]

Miss Wilson, who was born in Lancaster, Pennsylvania, was educated at the Drexel Institute, the University of Pennsylvania Extension Division, and Columbia University, and was graduated from the Drexel Institute Library School in 1909. She was employed by the Columbia University Libraries from 1909–17. After the war she went to the Peace Conference in Paris as a liaison officer of the American Library Association and the Library of Congress. Later she was elected to the Peace Commission. She was the chief librarian of the League of Nations Library for the first seven years, from 1920 until 1927, being one of two women in the Secretariat to have the status of Chef de Service.[8]

Before Miss Wilson took up her duties as League librarian, she prepared a report in which she carefully outlined the scope of the library, her plan of operation, and the library methods she wished to adopt.[9] Miss Wilson admitted to having a definite national bias in regard to the question of library methods, favoring American techniques. When she arrived in London a delegation presented to her a criticism of the classification scheme she had suggested. This scheme was presumably the Library of Congress Classification system, for the delegation insisted that the international aspects of the League had to be considered in determining the classification scheme. Letters of the alphabet, they suggested, were not international, while numbers were. It was agreed that Miss Wilson should immediately visit France, Belgium, and Holland to study European library techniques, as the League had to have an international library rather than an American one. As a result of this trip, the Universal Decimal Classification scheme was adopted. Although this system was based on an American scheme (the Dewey Decimal Classification), it had been expanded in Belgium by bibliographers and had been translated into French.[10]

There were no objections to the other library methods that Miss Wilson suggested, which were generally those in use in American libraries. The main public catalog was a dictionary catalog with Library of Congress printed cards. Subject headings were in English.[11]

Miss Wilson prepared three supplementary catalogs: (1) a *catalogue systématique*, arranged according to the classification numbers (providing a classed subject index to the collection) with a subject index in French to the classification numbers; (2) an alphabetic subject index of all important articles in journals since January 1920 (this was used as the basis for the compilation of published lists); and (3) a dictionary catalog of government publications, begun with 300,000 entries provided by the Library of Congress.[12] The classed catalog was an excellent attempt to provide access in French to the library collection, since both French and English were working languages of the League.[13] The official languages of the United Nations are Chinese, English, French, Russian, and Spanish.[14] This increase in number compounds the problem of providing suitable indexes and catalogs in the United Nations Library.

Miss Wilson was also responsible for initiating a journal index, published weekly, which appeared in two parts: one part covering economic and finance journals, and the other part, political and social science journals. This short list was circulated to sections of the Secretariat. It was expanded in 1929 into the *Monthly List of Selected Articles* and is still being published by the library of the United Nations Office in Geneva.

In 1927, Miss Wilson's services were terminated, and Dr. T. P. Sevensma of Holland became the chief librarian.

League of Nations Library/United Nations Library, Geneva

The League Library occupied the same quarters in the Hôtel National until 1936, when it was moved into a new building made possible by a gift from John D. Rockefeller, Jr. Early in 1920, Miss Wilson had realized that to make the library a truly international one, she had to have sufficient funds to carry out her work. For several years she appealed to various foundations and organizations for an endowment which would provide these funds; she traveled to the United States a number of times to make personal appeals. She remembers "Mrs. Andrew Carnegie saying that her husband would have liked very much to do it for it was a combination of his ideals Peace and Libraries."[15]

However, it was not until Miss Wilson had left the League that her idea became a reality. On 9 September 1927 the secretary-general of the League submitted the following memorandum to the fifth meeting of the forty-sixth session of the League Council (the counterpart of the United Nations Security Council):

> The Secretary-General has pleasure in informing the Council that, following certain tentative discussions, a group of American citizens would be willing, should the competent authorities of the League desire to accept funds from outside sources for the construction and endowment of a League Library, which would provide full and adequate facilities for research work and for students, to furnish such funds up to the amount of two million dollars.[16]

Immediately thereafter the president of the Council, Enrique Villegas of Chile, proposed a draft resolution accepting the gift. After some discussion, especially in regard to the effect this donation would have on the construction of the new buildings which the League was then planning, the draft resolution was adopted, and the Council accepted the gift.

The news broke in the *New York Times* on 11 September 1927, and the dispatch stated that this was the largest gift ever made to the League.[17] The negotiations were carried on through Arthur Sweetser, an American member of the League's Information Section; a man who was later to be of service to the United Nations Library. An editorial of 13 September 1927 noted that:

9

America will be permanently represented, though unofficially, in the League of Nations through Mr. ROCKEFELLER's gift, for out of the library which he is helping to build and maintain will come much of the information upon which the decisions of the League will be based.[18]

The League of Nations Assembly (the counterpart of the United Nations General Assembly) on 12 September 1927 unanimously confirmed the Council's acceptance of the gift. At that time, Alberto N. Guani of Uruguay, president of the Assembly of the League, announced that John D. Rockefeller, Jr., was the sole donor of the $2,000,000 gift.

In 1923 a committee of experts appointed by the Assembly of the League had begun discussing the usefulness of establishing at Geneva a world center for international research. The munificent Rockefeller gift made this world center possible. "It was Rockefeller's idea that the library would serve as an information center for the Secretariat of the League and other international organizations and also as a center of study for scholars doing research work on questions within the League's field of interest."[19]

Soon after the gift was announced, the League Assembly authorized the secretary-general to invite several library experts, including some Americans, to visit Geneva for consultation relative to the best possible use for the gift.

A Library Planning Committee was organized and held its first meetings in Geneva on 12, 13, and 14 March 1928. The committee was composed of the following men: Mr. Vittorio Scialoja, representative of Italy on the Council (chairman); Mr. William Warner Bishop, the librarian of the University of Michigan; Mr. Raymond B. Fosdick, former undersecretary-general of the League of Nations and in 1928 the president of the Rockefeller Foundation, New York; Dr. Hugo Andres Krüss, director-general of the Preussische Staatsbibliothek, Berlin; Mr. Pierre Roland-Marcel, administrateur général of the Bibliothèque Nationale, Paris; Sir James Rennell Rodd, who had served as the British representative to the General Assembly of the League in 1921 and 1923; Dr. T. P. Sevensma, the librarian of the League of Nations; and Mr. A. de Maday, the librarian of the International Labour Organisation.[20] Of the eight members of the committee, five were librarians. However, Mr. Bishop was the only American librarian on the committee. Unfortunately, Mr. Bishop and Mr. Fosdick were unable to be present at this first meeting. The committee studied the architectural plans which had been submitted to them and argued that the original site, consisting of three properties at Sécherondessous on Lake Geneva between the Parc Mon Repos and the Villa Barton, was not large enough to accommodate the new League buildings and the new library. "The Committee therefore came to the unanimous conclusion that it was unable to recommend to the Secretary-General the adoption of the proposed site."[21]

The Library Planning Committee held its second session at Geneva on 4 and 5 June 1928, reaffirming the recommendation of its first report. Although the New Building Committee, in charge of planning all of the new buildings for the League, approved this recommendation, negotiations for purchasing the additional land needed for the library were unsuccessful.[22] Because the League was unable to purchase additional contiguous property, it exchanged the three lakeside properties it did own (Bartholoni, Perle du Lac, and Moynier) for a larger site in Ariana Park, about one and one-quarter miles north of the Pont du Mont-Blanc, the center of Geneva. The agreement to purchase the Ariana site was signed on 26 March 1929, clearing the way for the approval of the architectural plans.[23]

The plans finally adopted were the results of the combined efforts of several architects: Mr. H. P. Nénot of Paris, Mr. J. Flegenheimer of Geneva, Mr. C. Broggi of Rome, Mr. Camille Lefèvre of Paris, and Mr. Joseph Vago of Budapest. The foundation stone was laid on 7 September 1929, although additional construction was delayed until 1 March 1931.

The Library Planning Committee held three other sessions (all of which Mr. Bishop attended) to discuss and approve the detailed plans for the new library. The third meeting was held on 17 July 1929, again in Geneva. In the morning there was general discussion on the use of the endowment fund money (the Rockefeller gift had been placed in an endowment fund), the capacity of the bookstacks, the height of the stacks, and whether smoking should be allowed in the library. In the afternoon discussions were continued, and the committee paid a visit to the new site, which was viewed with complete approval.[24]

At the fourth session of the committee, on 6-8 June 1932, the members again visited the site to see how construction was progressing. Discussions centered on the costs of construction and on the furnishing of the library.[25] At the close of this session, on 8 June 1932, Mr. Bishop wrote to Mr. Sweetser:

> The Library itself has begun at last to show positive evidence of becoming that great library of reference in the social and political sciences, particularly in their international aspects, which from its beginning has been its "manifest destiny."[26]

The last meeting of the committee was held on 8-9 February 1934, and again there was general discussion of construction costs, budget, and the planning of the move to the new building. The committee visited the new library building, and all members were impressed with the dignity of its appearance.[27] At this meeting Mr. Bishop represented not only himself but also Mr. Fosdick, for he had been charged by the Rockefeller Foundation to hasten the acceptance of the balance of the gift. Writing later about his experience in Geneva, Mr. Bishop stated that although he had never approved of the layout of the library building and had especially disliked the position of the reference desk and the location of the catalogs, he felt that functionally it was "a workable building, if not an American one."[28]

The ceremony of the crowning of the roof tree with flowers, which marked the structural completion of the building, was held on 6 November 1933.[29] But it was not until 17 September 1936 that the new reading room of the library was opened for service.[30]

An inscription cut in stone at the main entrance to the library commemorates the name of the donor, John D. Rockefeller, Jr. It also states that the purpose of the library is "to serve as a center of international research and an instrument of international understanding."[31]

Throughout all this planning William Warner Bishop served as a consultant, just as Verner Clapp later served the United Nations Library. Their generous advice and guidance proved invaluable to both libraries. Mr. Bishop's chief contribution to the League of Nations Library lay in the stress he placed on the service that a well-organized international library could give not only to the League delegates and to the Secretariat staff, but also to the scholarly community. The service rendered by the League Library set an example which the United Nations Library in New York was to follow, but in a somewhat different manner. Rudolph Gjelsness eulogized Mr. Bishop's international contribution in these words:

> In no area of library relations did he contribute more than in that of international relations. Few men have had a clearer vision of the values to be derived from international library co-operation.[32]

Political events during the late 1930s adversely affected the work of the League but did not immediately lessen the activities of the library. Many international institutions transferred their headquarters to Geneva at this time, and many scholars sought refuge there. In the period from September 1939 until May 1940 the work of the library continued with only slight changes. From 15 May to 1 July 1940 the library was closed, and arrangements were made to reduce its activities to what was feasible with the small remaining staff and the severe budgetary restrictions. During the rest of the war most of the expenditures for acquisitions were spent for keeping the most essential serial sets intact.[33]

During the summer of 1940 the major part of the Economic, Financial, and Transit Department of the League Secretariat was sent on mission to Princeton, New Jersey, to continue its work on world economic problems. A joint invitation from Princeton University, the Rockefeller Institute for Medical Research, and the Institute for Advanced Study made this move possible.

In January 1941, Sigurd Hartz Rasmussen was sent to the United States to organize the documents for this department and to acquire other publications required for its work. Mr. Rasmussen, who was born in Denmark, had been trained in library science at Columbia University School of Library Service. He served as head of the Geographical Department of the League of Nations Library for ten years, 1931–40.

Mr. Rasmussen, writing of his experiences, hoped that at the end of the war the collections of the Princeton branch and the

13

deposits collected in many other countries would be transferred to Geneva so that the League Library would continue to have a strong collection.[34] However, the Princeton collection of League of Nations documents and other publications and the documents which had been collected by the Woodrow Wilson Foundation in New York were donated to the United Nations Library in New York. After the war Mr. Rasmussen became librarian of the United Nations Library.

The League Library has been directed by an American – Miss Florence Wilson (1920–27); a Dutchman – Dr. Tietse Pieter Sevensma (1927–38); and an Austrian – Dr. Arthur C. Breycha-Vauthier (deputy librarian from 1939–45 and chief librarian from 1946–64). There was no chief librarian during the war years. In 1946, Mr. Norman S. Field, formerly with the Bodleian Library at Oxford University, became the deputy librarian. He served as acting chief librarian from 1964–69, at which time he was named associate chief librarian. In January 1969, Mr. György Rózsa, a Hungarian, became the chief librarian. In 1946 the League of Nations Library was officially designated as the United Nations Library in Geneva. It was in London during the first session of the General Assembly that plans were made to transfer certain functions, activities, and assets of the League of Nations to the United Nations. The League of Nations Committee, in discussing the transfer, made several references to the use of the League of Nations Library by the International Labour Organisation and in the plan for the transfer agreed that the International Labour Organisation could use the library.[35] The committee did not envisage at this time the transfer of the League of Nations Library to the permanent site of the United Nations.

The report of the League of Nations Committee to the General Assembly proposed the adoption of a resolution, which in part read:

> The General Assembly requests the Secretary-General to make provision for taking over and maintaining in operation the Library and Archives.[36]

During the next two years the role of the League of Nations Library was frequently discussed by officials at the United Nations. Mr. S. Hartz Rasmussen, the librarian of the United Nations Library in New York, and Mr. A. C. Breycha-Vauthier, the librarian of the newly named United Nations Library in Geneva cooperated in several endeavors. Copies of League of Nations documents in English and French were sent to New York. The duplicate collection of approximately 20,000 volumes in Geneva was made available for selection by the library in New York. Bibliographies similar to the *Monthly List of Selected Articles* and the *Monthly List of Books Catalogued* issued by the Geneva library were initiated by the library in New York (these are now called *Current Issues: A Selected Bibliography on Subjects of Concern to the United Nations* and *New Publications in the Dag Hammarskjöld Library*).[37]

In a memorandum to Adrian Pelt, who was assistant secretary-general for Conference and General Services, and under whose department the library was administratively placed, Mr. Rasmussen suggested that the library in Geneva be transferred to the permanent site of the United Nations. He listed two very cogent reasons for the transfer: (1) the 350,000 volumes in the library in Geneva would provide adequate library service for the Secretariat, and (2) it would involve an economy of over $1,000,000 and would also cut future expenditures because it would then be necessary to maintain only one library instead of two.[38]

Although this idea was proposed informally by the librarian, a memorandum dated 14 July 1948 indicated that it was not to be the solution to the growing pains of the United Nations Library in New York:

> The Secretary-General asked me this morning to make it clear to all concerned that under no circumstances would he at present contemplate any suggestion that the United Nations Library at Geneva be transferred to Lake Success.
>
> He would be willing to consider this only when a new headquarters at Manhattan has been built, and even then it does not follow that he would agree to such a transfer.[39]

A working paper prepared by the headquarters library for the International Advisory Committee of Library Experts (see chapter 4 for a more detailed study of this committee), which was convened in August 1948 to discuss library policies, presented the following arguments for maintaining the library in

15

Geneva: (1) the Geneva library served the United Nations European office, commissions, conferences, and specialized agencies, (2) the library, because of the widespread destruction in Europe caused by the war, was the only remaining research center in Europe where complete collections of laws and many other unique documents were available, (3) the library assisted other libraries in Europe to obtain collections of League of Nations and United Nations publications, (4) the library, almost completely self-supporting, did not have available nearby any large collections of special and research libraries from which to draw, and (5) since the library was a gift of John D. Rockefeller, Jr., it was believed that there was a moral obligation to maintain the library as a unit.[40]

The role of the Geneva library was also discussed at the 7 July 1948 meeting of the Permanent Advisory Library Committee, which was composed of representatives of the various departments of the Secretariat. Mr. P. J. Schmidt, the representative of the Department of Security Council Affairs, "expressed the opinion that the main library of the United Nations should be at Lake Success [the temporary location of the United Nations on Long Island] inasmuch as the research work necessary for meetings of committees and commissions is carried on at Headquarters of the organization."[41] Various viewpoints continued to be offered, but the recommendations of the International Advisory Committee of Library Experts were finally accepted. The committee adopted nine resolutions regarding the Geneva library, of which three deserve to be quoted in full:

> 56. Having considered the present status of the United Nations Library at Geneva, its present and probable future use and obligations for service in Geneva to the United Nations Secretariat, international conferences and organizations, specialized agencies and individual specialists, and taking into account that a major change in the situation would involve the establishment of new library facilities which might prove to be much more costly than the maintenance of the existing library service, the Committee recommends that the Geneva Library be continued for these purposes.

> 58. The Committee recommends that requests for the transfer of portions of the Geneva Library to other libraries,

even of the United Nations and the specialized agencies, be not acceded to. The Geneva Library as an articulate whole has an important function to perform in furthering the work of the United Nations, which would be seriously impaired if portions of the Library were detached.

59. The Committee recommends that the activities of the United Nations Libraries and those of the specialized agencies be further co-ordinated with the object of providing an efficient library service in all fields covered by those libraries. In view of the circumstances at Geneva, the Committee is impressed by the possibility open to the United Nations Libraries and the related libraries to provide an example of co-ordinated service which would be an inspiration to libraries all over the world.[42]

These recommendations were in direct conflict with those made previously by Ralph Shaw in his 1947 management survey (see chapter 4 for a full discussion of this survey). Mr. Shaw's two recommendations regarding the Geneva library were:

It is recommended, therefore, that the Geneva collection should not be further developed by the United Nations and that it should be kept on a maintenance basis until arrangement for its transferral to suitable sponsorship, preferably UNESCO, can be made.

It is recommended that all publications issued by international organizations, whether official or unofficial, and regardless of the method of reproduction, be transferred immediately from the Geneva Library to the United Nations Library to form the basis for its complete research collection in the field of documentation of international organizations.[43]

The recommendations of the International Advisory Committee were not only accepted by the library but were also endorsed by the Economic and Social Council and the Netherlands delegation, always a strong exponent of good library service. The first annual report of the United Nations Library, which was sent to the members of the Permanent Advisory Library Committee, reported that the Division of Library Services and the Department of Public Information endorsed the recommendations of the International Advisory Committee of Library Experts in regard to the Geneva library.[44]

17

The Economic and Social Council passed a resolution on 6 July 1949 that expressed "its approval of the Secretary-General's plan [which was drawn up on the basis of recommendations of the International Advisory Committee of Library Experts], it being understood that the works in the Library shall continue to be housed in the European office of the United Nations."[45]

To Dr. W. H. J. van Asch van Wijck, the permanent representative of the Netherlands to the European Office of the United Nations, it was very "important that nothing should be done to hamper its work or disperse the collection."[46]

The United Nations Library, bereft of the resources of the Geneva library, had to develop its own philosophy, policies, and procedures. It was a long and agonizing task, which began before the United Nations Charter was officially signed.

UNCIO Library at San Francisco

Unlike the League of Nations Library, the United Nations Library had a precursor in the Conference Library established in San Francisco by the Library of Congress for the United Nations Conference on International Organization (UNCIO).

The conference convened on 25 April 1945, to draw up the Charter of the United Nations. It was an auspicious day not only in the macrocosm of international organizations and world peace but also in the microcosm of books and libraries, for on that day the conference library also opened its doors. To emphasize the importance of the library to the conference, it was featured in the first issue of the daily *Journal*, a spot garnered for it by the conference librarian. For the benefit of delegates and Secretariat staff the article furnished the vital statistics concerning the library: location and hours of service, type of collection, the reference and research services to be extended, the facilities of the reading room, and the names of the administrative and service personnel.[47]

This momentous statement not only announced the inception of a United Nations library, but also described the character of the conference library as an active agent of information services. It was specifically designed to provide reference and information services on agenda topics to all the delegations and staff of the international conference. Verner W. Clapp, the conference librarian, definitively described the library for the *Library Journal*, in addition to filing his official report with the executive secretary of the International Secretariat of the United Nations Conference on International Organization.[48] Jerrold Orne and Paul Kruse, library staff members, also wrote of their experiences in San Francisco.[49]

Credit for the original idea of a library in San Francisco belongs equally to Archibald MacLeish, assistant secretary of state for Cultural and Public Relations and former librarian of Congress, and Robert Rea, head librarian of the San Francisco Public Library; but it was Mr. MacLeish's proposal which came to fruition in the conference library.[50] Early in March 1945 he suggested such a library to Luther H. Evans, then acting librarian of Congress, and discussions between the two agencies immediately began. Durward Sandifer, Clyde Eagleton, Denys P. Myers, and Alice Bartlett participated on behalf of the Division of International Organization Affairs of the Department of State; Dr. Evans, Robert C. Gooch, and Paul Kruse on behalf of the Library of Congress. By 17 March agreement had been reached on all the details of the operation of the library, and the proposals submitted by Dr. Evans and Dr. Eagleton were formally accepted for the Department of State by Mr. MacLeish on 26 March.[51]

While the books were being selected from a list compiled by the Library of Congress in conjunction with the State Department, Mr. Kruse was sent to San Francisco on 2 April to supervise arrangements there. He wisely negotiated for the conference library so that it could be strategically situated in room 226 in the Veterans' War Memorial Building in quarters adjacent to the principal committee room of the conference. The library consisted of a reading room of about 1,000 square feet, two offices, storage space, and a reception foyer.

The collection included 2,877 volumes, exclusive of current subscriptions to periodicals and newspapers, and consisted of publications in the following categories: League of Nations documents, international relations and organizations, international law, treaties, indexes to periodicals and newspapers, encyclopedias, dictionaries, biographical dictionaries, statistical yearbooks, and a vertical file of pamphlets and miscellaneous

19

materials. The books in the collection were borrowed for the conference from the following sources: Los Angeles Public Library; Mills College Library; Stanford University Library; Hoover Library of War, Peace and Revolution; United Nations Information Office; University of California (both the University Library and the Bureau of International Relations Library); and individual publishers. Twenty-six volumes were given to the library by the Carnegie Endowment for International Peace. It was necessary for the Library of Congress to send to San Francisco 879 volumes, or only 30.6 percent of the total collection.[52]

The books came from many libraries and bore a variety of classification numbers; therefore, the staff arranged them on the shelves in large subject categories and issued a *Short Title Classified Catalog* for use with the collection.[53] The library also compiled an author card catalog and a card shelflist which held the record of books borrowed from the local libraries. The library was open for sixty-five days between 23 April and 26 June 1945. A total of 973 people visited the library between 25 April and 20 June, of whom 573 could be identified as readers.[54]

Since the conference library was reserved for the exclusive use of the delegates and the staff of the Secretariat, the San Francisco Public Library opened its facilities to the public and press in addition to the delegates, and a special conference room for their use was inaugurated on 23 April.[55] Robert Rea, head librarian of the San Francisco Public Library, had decided early in March 1945 to organize a service for the delegates. Besides supplying information Mr. Rea planned to give the delegates an idea of the operation and services of a public library in a large American city.[56] Each of the delegates was issued a conference library card entitling him to the privileges of the public library. The cards were printed by the Grabhorn Press, one of San Francisco's finest, making them automatically collectors' items.[57]

The public services of the conference library were organized on three levels: (1) services which were available within the library itself, either from materials or personnel, (2) services available in the immediate San Francisco Bay area, and (3) services available outside this area, in Washington primarily, where the entire resources of the Library of Congress and other Washington libraries were instantly available by a direct tele-

21

phone line to Washington.[58] Mr. Clapp graphically illustrated the third type of service, which, although expensive and novel for its time, proved to be most valuable:

> A regular telephone call at eight in the morning (San Francisco time) found Washington with two hours still to go before lunch; and the requested material (if it was material that was wanted) could usually be assembled and placed on the special cargo plane leaving Washington at two in the afternoon, to be in San Francisco in time for business the next morning.[59]

The functions of the library were organized into three main areas under the administrative officer: procurement, general reference, and special reference. The administrative staff was responsible for contact with the Secretariat, for the establishment of policies, for direction, and for security. The procurement staff was responsible for liaison with information sources in the San Francisco area, for short-term interlibrary loan, and for the maintenance of the catalog and shelflist. The general reference staff was responsible for reading room service, for answering general reference inquiries, and for keeping statistics and the records of loans. The special reference consultants handled all difficult inquiries requiring extensive and precise knowledge of the literature and documentation of international affairs, inquiries requiring considerable time, and inquiries demanding an answer in the form of a report or memorandum.[60]

Examples of special reference services extended include two memoranda prepared by Denys P. Myers for the Brazilian delegation, one on the employment of women in international secretariats and the second on the veto at Vienna and Geneva, and two bibliographies, one on postwar economic and banking policies and the second giving current references on the USSR.[61]

An ancillary responsibility which was assumed voluntarily by the library was to collect and collate the nearly 6,000 separate documents produced in the ten weeks of the conference. Mr. Clapp devoted much of his time to making arrangements whereby fifty sets of the unrestricted and unclassified documents would be collected, held in reserve, and later distributed by the Library of Congress to other libraries.[62] Because of this foresight the complete documentation of the conference was available for later publication by the United Nations Information tion Organization in cooperation with the Library of Congress.

In less than a week after the final signing of the Charter, Mr. Kruse had the satisfaction of closing all loan accounts without a single loss.[63] Each employee of the conference library was selected for his expertise. Verner W. Clapp, who was the conference librarian, was director of the Acquisitions Department of the Library of Congress. He later became chief assistant librarian of Congress and in 1956 became president of the Council on Library Resources. Lewis Hanke, his associate at San Francisco, was director of the Hispanic Foundation of the Library of Congress. Paul Kruse, who served as one of the executive officers, was assistant in charge of Reference Collections at the Library of Congress. Ruth Savord, a reference consultant, was chief librarian of the Council on Foreign Relations, a position she held from 1930 until her retirement in 1960. The other reference consultant, Denys P. Myers, was a student of the League of Nations and a specialist in documentation in the field of world peace and international organizations in the Division of International Organization Affairs of the Department of State. He had previously served with the World Peace Foundation from 1910 to 1942. The two reference librarians were Mrs. Mary L. Hurt (now Mrs. Mary Hurt Richmond) from the University of California Library at Berkeley and Nona K. Doherty from the Department of State Library.

Jerrold Orne, the other executive officer, had been a fellow at the Library of Congress in 1940–41 and before the war had been librarian of Knox College. In 1945 he was an instructor in the Naval Training Center at San Diego. Yeoman Orne was directed on 19 April 1945 to report to the Twelfth Naval District, San Francisco, "for temporary duty in the office of Mr. Alger Hiss in connection with the United Nations Conference."[64] He was allowed to wear civilian clothes during this assignment. He writes amusingly of his transfer to the conference library, speaks glowingly of this short period of his life as a "life within a life," and sums it up in these words:

> Working with a professional staff including every needed capacity and the best person for each need, strategically located and publicized to all concerned, and provided with

23

> every physical asset a librarian could want, what could be
> finer? Where could any librarian be faced with extremes of
> potential need, yet have such narrow limits of time and
> precedent to prepare? Where, finally, could one be placed in
> better professional comradeship, or enjoy the numerous
> evidences of appreciation from such a heterogeneous com-
> pany of patrons?[65]

Both Mr. Kruse and Mr. Orne have continued their interest in international and foreign libraries. Mr. Kruse has served as a library adviser to the University of Teheran, Iran, and has lectured at the Library School of the University of Ceylon.[66] Mr. Orne has been a delegate to many conferences abroad and, at the request of the State Department, visited Vietnam for three months in 1965 to study library resources and services.[67]

The conference library fulfilled a threefold function, the first assigned and the next two assumed: (1) the establishment of a genuine reference service to all delegations and Secretariat staff, (2) the renewal of contact with representatives from nearly all the civilized countries of the world to facilitate the acquisition of publications from these countries for the Library of Congress, and (3) the development of a keen cooperative relationship among professional librarians on the West Coast.[68] The library's paramount function, however, was the first: to serve as an information source for the delegates and the research staff of the Secretariat. By providing this specialized type of service, it set the pattern which was to be followed in the development of the United Nations Library. The conference library depended chiefly on interlibrary loan to assemble its collection, as the fledgling United Nations Library was to depend on the cooperation of libraries in the New York area during its infancy.

Preparatory Commission Library in London

Another precursor of the United Nations Library was the small library established in London, where the Preparatory Commission was meeting to make arrangements for the first session of the United Nations and the establishment of the permanent Secretariat. The library in London was temporarily organized under the Documents Section, headed by Waldo Chamberlin as documents officer (he had served in this same position in San Francisco). The library was, however, under the nominal supervision of the archivist, Richardson Dougall.[69]

In August 1945 a suggestion was made that a library might be set up in the lounge on the east side of Church House, where the meetings were being held, since there were "indications that an opportunity to consult the publications of the League of Nations would be specially welcome to the members of the Delegations."[70] The small reference library was opened to the delegates and the members of the staff on 17 September. A small room called the Lords Lounge on the first floor of Church House was used as a reading room, and room 129 off the lounge was used for an office. The librarians at that time were Miss Ruth Partington of the United Kingdom and Mrs. M. E. Bury, probably also of the United Kingdom.[71] Mrs. E. F. Alvarez of the United Kingdom later replaced Mrs. Bury.

The collection consisted of a small stock of specialized documents, including British government white papers, texts of international agreements, documentation of various conferences, and League of Nations publications. Special requests were met by interlibrary loan from the various official and private libraries in London. Both the Royal Institute of International Affairs at Chatham House and the United Nations Information Organization in London invited delegates to use their libraries for reference.[72]

The same pattern which had developed at San Francisco appears evident, and three trends repeat themselves: (1) the acquisition of a small reference collection, (2) service limited to delegates and Secretariat staff, and (3) extensive use of interlibrary loans.

Although the library was small and not significant as far as the actual development of the United Nations Library is concerned, it was in London that the basic organization of library services for the United Nations was instituted. In the *Report of the Preparatory Commission* two statements in particular applied to library services:

> 38. The main functions of the *Department of Public Information* would fall into the following categories: press,

publications, broadcasting, films, graphics and exhibitions, public liaison and reference. . . .

39. The *Conference and General Services* [Department] would occupy a special place in the structure of the Secretariat and would include: . . .

(3) a library with research and reference facilities[73]

This dual mandate will be discussed in greater detail in the next chapter.

chapter 2

Administrative organization

Structure

As noted in chapter 1, the Preparatory Commission in London provided for a reference service in the Department of Public Information and also stipulated that there should be a library in the Department of Conference and General Services. These provisions led to a conflict between the two departments which lasted until 1948. At that time the library in the Department of Conference and General Services was transferred to the Department of Public Information, and the two services were merged.

The Department of Public Information, in carrying out the mandate of the Preparatory Commission, took over the United Nations Information Office Library, which had been under the direction of Miss José Meyer. This office was the executive unit of the United Nations Information Board, a group of information officers or representatives from nineteen different countries. This group had its origin in 1940 when French, British, and Czech information officers met informally to discuss the information activities of their respective countries. Membership increased, and the group was formally constituted as the Inter-Allied Information Center. In 1942 its name was changed to the United Nations Information Board. The reference section, or library, of the board specialized in the acquisition of documentary materials from the United States and foreign countries which were used for the dissemination of information. Miss Meyer, the librarian, was educated in the United States and abroad, and was a graduate of the American Library Association Library School in Paris. She had been stationed in Paris as the European representative of the Library of Congress from 1935 to January 1941. At that time she took a leave of absence from the Library of Congress to administer the United Nations Information Board Library.[1] She later became the first chief of the Reference Center of the Department of Public Information.

The Department of Public Information expanded the Information Board Library at 610 Fifth Avenue, New York, into a Reference Center, and later moved the whole unit, first to Hunter College in the Bronx, and then to Lake Success on Long Island. These were temporary locations of the United Nations organization (see chapter 3 for a discussion of the physical quarters of the United Nations Library).

The Department of Conference and General Services also established a library and a documents service at Hunter College. In London the library had been the responsibility of the documents service. At Hunter College the library was first organized as a subdivision of the documents branch, which later became the Documents Service Division. When the first director of the Bureau of Technical Services was appointed, the library became a division in its own right, reporting directly to him.[2] (See the organizational chart on page 29.)

At this time the assistant secretary-general for the Department of Conference and General Services, the largest of the Secretariat's eight departments, was Adrian Pelt, a journalist from the Netherlands, and a diplomat by training.[3] Mr. Pelt had been director of the Information Section of the League of Nations and, therefore, brought to his new position a wide knowledge of the policies and procedures of the League of Nations. The assistant secretary-general for the Department of Public Information was Benjamin Cohen, former librarian of the National Library in Chile. He was known to be anxious to have the library transferred to his own department.[4] In an undated memorandum Mr. Cohen presented his reasons for recommending the move to the Department of Public Information:

The reasons . . . are: that in theory, the operation of a library is an information operation; that in practice, library work has proved to be an essential part of the work of the Department of Public Information; that for the sake of convenience, the Department of Public Information is the best place for the Library; and that that department has proved it has the ability to render efficient library service.[5]

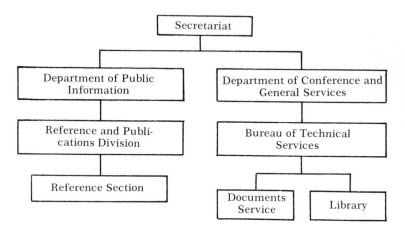

Organization of the Secretariat, Hunter College

Mr. Shaw remarked in his survey of 1947 that formal justification for the transfer of the library to the Department of Public Information appeared to be that it served the public exclusively while the main library served the Secretariat exclusively. He found that this distinction was not correct. The Reference Center actually did serve the Secretariat in addition to the public, and the Permanent Advisory Library Committee had allowed for public use of the main library. The continuance of facilities and staff for two libraries was economically not feasible; therefore, Mr. Shaw recommended the transfer and combination of all library and bibliographical services into a single library in the Department of Public Information.[6]

Objections to this proposed transfer were immediately voiced by the Fifth Committee, one of the seven main committees of the General Assembly, and the Advisory Committee on Administrative and Budgetary Questions,[7] a standing committee whose members are elected by the General Assembly. Both committees were ever watchful of the financial and political implications of library services. The secretary-general, however, decided on the transfer, which became effective 1 January 1948.[8] At the end of 1947, Mr. Cohen announced that he intended to divide the library into two divisions, one handling all administrative and technical services and the other handling reference and the indexing of United Nations documents and of periodicals.[9] In the reorganization under the Department of Public Information, which became effective 17 May 1948, the library was divided into four sections, shown in the organizational chart below: reference and documentation section, processing section, research section, and opinion-survey section.[10] The last two sections had been part of the Department of Public Information prior to this time and actually had little connection with general library functions.

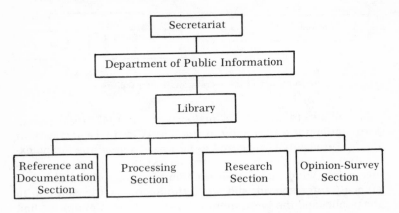

Organization of the library under the Department of Public Information

Although the transfer did indeed effect the amalgamation of library services within the United Nations, the position of the library within the Department of Public Information was not entirely satisfactory. The Advisory Committee on Administrative and Budgetary Questions in its first report of 1948 was

30

under the impression that the reorganization was not a permanent one, but that it had been undertaken as a measure of expediency. The committee stated that "in normal circumstances the Department of Public Information would [not] be the appropriate location. In fact, the library service, in its present form, is not closely allied to the other functions now assigned to any one of the eight departments."[11] In its second report of 1948 the Advisory Committee reported:

> It seems clear that the library is becoming closely identified with the Department of Public Information not only as regards its administrative control but as regards its substantive work. . . . The preparation of public opinion surveys and publicity pamphlets are examples of such work. . . . For its part, the Committee would deprecate any step tending to make the library an organ of the Department of Public Information. The forthcoming meeting of the Committee of Library Experts may discuss the matter, but the Advisory Committee believes that the question to be resolved is not essentially one for library experts; it concerns the extent to which non-library services should be attached to the library and, as such, is an important question of policy to be determined by the General Assembly.[12]

The International Advisory Committee of Library Experts did indeed discuss the matter and made the following recommendations:

> 16. The Committee recommends that the function of the Library be recognized as that of an organization-wide service of a non-administrative character, and that it be given the status and independence appropriate to this function.
> 17. It might be held that in these circumstances the Library has no logical association with any of the existing departments of the Secretariat, and that it might most appropriately be attached to the Executive Office of the Secretary-General. However, having taken all the factors into consideration, the Committee recommends that the present location of the Library in the Department of Public Information be not now disturbed, but that the question be reviewed from time to time with special reference to the public-information services which the Library is now being called upon to perform.[13]

At its 136th meeting the Fifth Committee discussed the transfer of the library to the Department of Public Information in some detail. Several delegates objected strenuously to this transfer, which they felt had been carried out without the specific authorization of the Advisory Committee, but solely on the recommendations of the management survey conducted by Mr. Shaw and with the authorization of the secretary-general.[14] Dr. J. A. W. Burger, a representative of the Netherlands, expressed the point that "By remaining within the framework of the Department of Public Information, the library ran the risk of becoming an instrument of information instead of being a scientific centre"; Mr. Roland Lebeau, an adviser to the Belgium delegation was fearful that the transfer "might prejudice the scientific and objective character of the library and turn it into a propaganda weapon"; Mr. Edouard Bonnefous, an alternate representative of the French delegation, firmly stated that the "library had to be independent" and "should not be mixed up with the information services."[15] At the conclusion of the meeting the Fifth Committee adopted a proposal requesting the secretary-general to make a study of the library services of the United Nations and submit a report at the next session of the General Assembly.[16]

The library, under the direction of Carl H. Milan (about whom more will be said later) remained in the Department of Public Information for two years before the transfer to the Office of the Secretary-General was executed. However, the secretary-general did not particularly want the library under his direct supervision, as Mr. Milam so graphically reported in his diary:

> During the Budget Com. hearing in Paris about 20 Oct. 48, Trygvie Lie came to the top table & sat in the 2d row alongside me. Transfer of Library to DPI . . . [was] being criticized. Proposal was made . . . that library be given a semi-independent status under the S.G. "My God, I don't want it," said the S.G.[17]

Mr. Milam also reported another unrecorded incident in regard to the position of the library in the Secretariat:

> Bryon Price [assistant secretary-general for Administrative and Financial Services] asked me in Paris where in the Secretariat the Library Services should be. I told him pri-

vately that I doubted the appropriateness of being in the DPI, but that, if asked the question publicly I would answer that so far as I can see it makes little difference so long as the Library is permitted & aided to render an organization-wide service without favors to the Dept. in which we are. That DPI has facilitated this kind of service & has asked for no special favors.

Mr. Price later stated to the Budget Com. that he had recommended to the SG that the Library be directly under him but that so far the SG had not seen fit to approve the suggestion.[18]

However, it was not long before the second transfer of the library took place. It was reported to Carl Milam in April 1949 that the library would soon be transferred to the Secretary-General's Office.[19] Mr. Milam's remarks on this move reflected his faith in his own administrative ability:

This sort of puts me on the spot with DPI. My official position is one of neutrality. I have suffered from being in DPI in only one way. That is budget-wise. Adv. Com. & 5th Com. are very hard on Cohen & DPI & while Library is in DPI we must take some of the punishment. But Cohen is helpful & friendly & likes to help the L. He has not interfered in operations. He might if the Director didn't know his own mind.[20]

When transferred to the Executive Office of the Secretary-General on 1 January 1950, the library comprised two sections and five units (organizational chart on the top of page 34).[21] Evidently the combined judgments of the Fifth Committee, the Advisory Committee on Administrative and Budgetary Questions, and the International Advisory Committee of Library Experts outweighed the secretary-general's personal reluctance to have the library directly under his supervision.

Administratively, the library was to undergo one more move. As a result of the secretary-general's survey of the organization of the Secretariat in 1953, the library was transferred, in May 1954, from the Executive Office of the Secretary-General to the newly established Department of Conference Services.[22] This move was made to release the secretary-general from preoccupation with operational procedures so that he could direct his effort to policy matters. The archives unit, although it had been

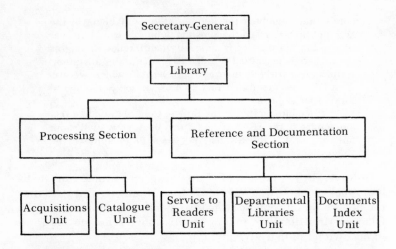

Organization of the library under the Executive Office of the Secretary-General

under the supervision of the library for a short period in 1946, had since that time been under the communications and records service of the Department of Conference and General Services. In 1954, as a result of the general reorganization of the Secretariat, the archives unit was again placed under the supervision of the library.[23]

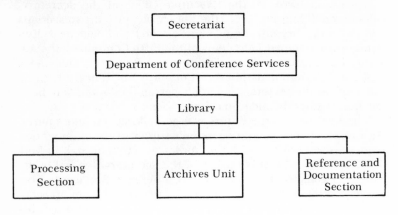

Organization of the library under the Department of Conference Services

Although the library over the years has sustained a series of changes at the upper administrative echelon, in addition to many internal organizational transitions, it has managed to develop and expand under the able administrators who have directed its activities.

Administrators

The library as it was established at Hunter College was hardly deserving of the name since it had neither books nor staff, but Albert C. Gerould was in charge of the services that were

Courtesy of Mr. Gerould

Albert C. Gerould

35

provided. These consisted chiefly of requesting interlibrary loans from other libraries in the New York City area, arranging for the staff of the Secretariat to use the local library facilities, recording requests for publications, and keeping a simple acquisitions record.[24] Mr. Gerould, who had previously been librarian of the College of the Pacific and librarian of the Document Center of the United States Army in Berlin, was a graduate of Columbia University School of Library Service.[25] He was appointed to the United Nations for a fixed term from 18 March 1946 to 15 August 1946, but remained with the library through the end of June 1947.

It was Mr. Gerould who suggested on 7 June 1946, in a memorandum to Mr. Pelt, that several boards and committees be established to advise the Secretariat on the establishment of a library and archives for the United Nations. He suggested that four committees be appointed: (1) a United Nations library committee made up of one representative from ten or twelve member nations to advise the secretary-general on broad aspects of library policy, (2) a secretary-general's library consultants board composed of technical experts chosen on the basis of broad geographical representation, (3) a library executive committee of three or four members available in the immediate geographical area and appointed by the chairman of the previous board to meet several times each year and present recommendations to the secretary-general, and (4) a Secretariat library committee composed of one representative from each of the substantive departments of the Secretariat to meet with the librarian once a month.[26] Only the last of these committees was established, but not until Mr. Rasmussen became librarian.

S. Hartz Rasmussen, who had been in charge of the library of the Economic, Financial and Transit Department of the League of Nations mission at Princeton during the war, and who had previously been head of the Geographical Department of the League of Nations Library in Geneva, assumed the position of librarian on 1 August 1946. Mr. Rasmussen brought to the United Nations the viewpoint of an international civil servant and a wide knowledge of League of Nations practice. He supervised the move of the library from Hunter College to Lake Success. A prolific writer of memoranda and reports, he attempted to develop policies and working procedures for the fledgling library. He worked against gargantuan obstacles, among them lack of sufficient, well-trained staff; lack of shelving and other library equipment; lack of adequate space; budgetary restrictions; and supervisors who were busy with more pressing problems.

While he was in office, the Permanent Advisory Library Committee, composed of representatives of the various departments of the Secretariat, was organized and met almost every

Courtesy of Mr. Rasmussen

S. Hartz Rasmussen

37

week. The number of meetings diminished after the first year, and the last meeting was held on 10 October 1952. The Permanent Advisory Library Committee, which was the name chosen for the Secretariat library committee suggested by Mr. Gerould, had its first meeting in Mr. Pelt's office on 3 March 1947. This committee was established "in order that all interested Departments could express their views on the library, participate in the formulation of its politics [sic] and exchange views with the Librarian on their requirements and the means to meet them."[27] Members of the committee argued again and again for a library equal in stature to the League of Nations Library.

Mr. Rasmussen, with the guidance of the committee, tackled many of the problems inherent in the establishment of any new library. These problems included selection of the classification system, establishment of cataloging procedures, developing a plan of service, recruiting personnel, acquiring the collection and providing adequate space for it, providing a key to the documentation of the United Nations, and arranging for a system of depository libraries all over the world for United Nations documents. Mr. Rasmussen's directorship of the library was too short to solve all of these problems, but his many reports and memoranda indicated that he was aware of them. In 1948, after Carl H. Milam had been employed as director of the library services of the United Nations, Mr. Rasmussen was asked to resign so that Mr. Milam could have a free hand.[28]

Toward the end of 1947, when the library began to receive more attention from the decision-makers of the United Nations, thought was given to the appointment of an eminent librarian to supervise all library services of the United Nations, both in New York and in Geneva. At the 23 December 1947 meeting of the Permanent Advisory Library Committee, Mr. Cohen reported that the United Nations officials were trying to secure the services of a librarian to administer the library services both in Lake Success and in Geneva.[29]

Just before this, however, Dr. T. P. Sevensma, who had been librarian of the League of Nations from 1927 to 1938 and librarian of the University of Leyden from 1938 to 1947, and who was at that time permanent secretary of the International Federation of Library Associations, announced at a meeting of the Association of Research Libraries in New York on 28 November

1947 that he had accepted the post of director of the United Nations Libraries.[30] This was a somewhat premature announcement, as he never assumed the position, although both Mr. Rasmussen and Milton E. Lord, librarian of the Boston Public Library and a member of the International Federation of Library Associations, assumed that he would be the new librarian of the United Nations. Mr. Rasmussen reported that Dr. Sevensma visited him in his office in November and told him "that the position of Director had been offered to him by Mr. Benjamin Cohen," and that he returned later and informed Mr. Rasmussen "that everything had been arranged and that he now had accepted the position."[31] Dr. Sevensma, who had seen Mr. Lord before he left New York at the end of November 1947 had also conveyed to Mr. Lord that the matter of his appointment had been decided in principle by the officials at the United Nations. There only remained the working out of the details of the actual contract.[32] The contract, however, was never offered. Evidently, the offer had been vetoed somewhere in the upper echelon of the United Nations. In the meantime several suitable candidates for the position of director were being suggested to Mr. Cohen by interested individuals. Mr. Ralph Shaw, the librarian of the United States Department of Agriculture and the expert who had conducted the management survey, wrote to Mr. Cohen on 10 November 1947 and brought to his attention the name of Pierre Bourgeois, the director of the Swiss National Library at Berne, a man who had broad experience in both library service and documentation as conceived of in Europe.[33] The New York Public Library suggested the following names for the position: Verner W. Clapp of the Library of Congress, L. Quincy Mumford of the Cleveland Public Library, Charles Gosnell of the State Library at Albany, and Charles Shaw of the H. W. Wilson Company.[34]

It was Luther Evans, the librarian of Congress, who suggested to Arthur Sweetser, who in turn suggested to Mr. Cohen of the United Nations, that Carl Milam work with the Department of Public Information on library reorganization. Dr. Evans remembers his conversation with Mr. Sweetser as:

> Arthur, I have the answer, Carl Milam. He has the competence in library matters, he is a good executive, and what is very important in this post, he is a wonderful diplomat.[35]

Official United Nations photo

Carl H. Milam

Mr. Sweetser was a member of the Information Section of the League of Nations from 1918 to 1932 and participated in the negotiations between the League and John D. Rockefeller, Jr., when the latter donated $2,000,000 to build the library of the League of Nations. Mr. Sweetser later served as chairman of the United Nations Information Board and as director of the United Nations Washington Information Office. He was president of the Woodrow Wilson Foundation from 1943 to 1945. As will be seen in a later chapter, he was one of those responsible for the donation of the Woodrow Wilson Foundation library to the United Nations Library. He served as a wise and devoted counselor to two international libraries.

In his initial letter to Mr. Milam, Mr. Cohen broached to him the subject of being a fulltime consultant to the United Nations Library.[36] Carl H. Milam, a native of Kansas, with an A.B. degree from the University of Oklahoma and a certificate from the New York State Library School at Albany, became executive secretary of the American Library Association in 1920. In this capacity he had been a member of numerous national and international committees, among them the Advisory Committee of the Division of Cultural Relations of the Department of State, the Executive Committee of the American Council on Education, and the National Commission of the United States on Intellectual Cooperation. He had also been elected to several foreign library organizations and academies.[37]

His face was often seen at international meetings: he was an educational consultant for the American Council on Education at the United Nations Conference on International Organization in San Francisco for two weeks in 1945; he was a member of the United States delegation to the UNESCO conference in Paris in November 1946; he attended a regional meeting of UNESCO in April 1947 in Philadelphia; and he was a member of the National Commission for UNESCO when it met in Chicago in September 1947.[38] Along with Ralph Beals, A. C. Breycha-Vauthier, and Luther Evans, he conducted the first survey of the United Nations Library on 22 and 23 April 1947.

Following Mr. Cohen's first letter, an interview was arranged in New York on 5 and 6 February 1948. At that time Mr. Milam talked with United Nations officials, with the staff of the library, with Mr. Beals of the New York Public Library, and with other librarians and friends. He also met with Alger Hiss of the Carnegie Endowment, and noted in his diary:

> It was my first meeting with him. He is constantly in close touch with UN officials. He has discussed library with Price, and could assure me that Price is opposed to building up a great collection. Hiss would guess that he favors good library service. At my request agreed to call Andrew W. Cordier (USA), executive assistant to the Secretary General. Later Hiss telephoned that Cordier says Lie is thoroughly convinced of need for good l. service & of making full use of other library resources.[39]

Byron Price, the assistant secretary-general for Administrative

41

and Financial Services, was a former newspaperman. He had been with the Associated Press from 1912 to 1941 and during World War II had been United States Director of Censorship. Price and Cohen were agreed that

> "we want a reference & research service which is the best in the world & that we don't want to duplicate the NYPL." The secretariat will sympathetically support good 1. service.[40]

Mr. Cohen proposed to Mr. Milam two alternatives, either that he come to the library as a consultant at $50 a day or that he accept a two-year contract at a salary of $10,000. Mr. Milam preferred the latter, and on 19 February 1948 an official letter of appointment was sent to him; on 27 February he accepted the offer.[41]

Although his impression of the library was that it was "a poor thing," he was cognizant of the causes behind the unsatisfactory conditions: the lack of a defined policy; divided resources, personnel, and authority; a general confusion resulting from building a large collection quickly; the necessity to employ persons of many nationalities; relatively weak direction; and the unsettling caused by Shaw's report.[42] He was optimistic, however, and thought that these conditions would respond to such devices as: staff meetings, working committees, meetings with the Permanent Advisory Library Committee and with New York librarians, the advice of specialists, adequate justification of budget requests, and good relations with key people in the Secretariat.[43] In making his decision Mr. Milam noted several cogent reasons for accepting the position: he felt that there was an important job to be done, he thought that it would be a good way to end his career, he had assurances from officials in the United Nations that they wanted good library service, and he hoped that in this position he would be able to do a little to increase the usefulness of the United Nations.[44]

From 9 to 12 March 1948, Mr. Milam, before assuming his permanent duties, served as a consultant to the United Nations Library. At this time he met with the four ranking staff members of the library. In discussing policy it was more or less agreed that the emphasis should be on an aggressive library service to the Secretariat, the development of a legislative reference type of service for Secretariat personnel and delegates, limited research service for outsiders, the acquisition of a currently useful collection, and maximum utilization of the services of the other New York libraries.[45]

Mr. Milam was on the payroll from 1 May 1948 but actually reported to the office on 4 May, and the reorganization of the library became effective on 17 May.[46] His arrival was the beginning of two of the most exciting years in the history of the United Nations Library and two very rewarding years for Mr. Milam. He accomplished much during his short tenure: the International Advisory Library Committee of Experts was convened, an official policy statement was drafted, the internal administrative structure of the library was reorganized, an internship project was begun, a contractual arrangement with the New York Public Library for reference and bibliographical services was put into effect, the index to the United Nations documents was inaugurated, annual reports were initiated, the library was transferred to the Secretary-General's Office, the professional staff was upgraded, preparations were made for moving the library to the Manhattan Building, and the Woodrow Wilson Memorial Library was donated to the United Nations. Each of these accomplishments will be discussed at the appropriate point in this study.

In December 1949, Mr. Milam was asked to stay another year, and by March he had decided that he would probably remain through 31 October 1950.[47] However, due to his wife's ill health, he decided to resign at the end of June 1950.[48]

At the time of Mr. Milam's retirement Mr. Edouard Reitman was named acting director of the library, a position he held for almost four years before another permanent director was appointed. Mr. Reitman, who had been appointed chief of the Reference Center of the Department of Public Information after Miss Meyer left in March 1947, became chief of the reference and documentation section under Mr. Milam's reorganization of 17 May 1948, when the main library of the United Nations and the Reference Center of the Department of Public Information were merged. Mr. Reitman had been educated in Europe and had served with the American Library in Paris. He came to the United States in 1946 as librarian of the French Embassy Cultural Services in New York. After Mr. Milam left,

43

Courtesy of the United Nations

Edouard Reitman

Mr. Reitman was considered for the director's position. He campaigned long and hard for it, but failed to win the post.[49]

It was not until 1954 that a new director of the library was appointed. There is little in the record to indicate why the post was allowed to remain vacant for almost four years. In February 1951, Mr. Reitman reported that Mr. Cordier had discussed with Mr. Lie the post of the director, and both felt that a quick decision should be made. More than a year later, in November 1952, Mr. Reitman again urged Mr. Cordier to speed up his decision on the appointment of a permanent director for the following reasons:

The present provisional situation should not be prolonged because it raises doubts about the Administration's interest in the Library; there is danger that the post will finally be cut, and remarks made by some delegations indicate that such intentions exist; the incumbent of this post must have full authority to administer properly a budget of over a half-million dollars and a staff of 80 to 90 people; the staff is increasingly bewildered about the present situation.[50]

Mr. Cordier replied that he would speak to Mr. Lie again about the situation, and Mr. Reitman mentioned Verner Clapp as a possible director should it be necessary to appoint an outside candidate.[51]

Rubens Borba Alves de Moraes, who became the next director of the United Nations Library, was born in Brazil.[52] He brought to the United Nations varied professional experiences as librarian, historian, editor, author, translator, and bibliographer.

Courtesy of the United Nations

Rubens Borba de Moraes

From 1936 to 1943 he directed the Municipal Public Library of the city of São Paolo, and from 1944 to 1948 he served first as associate director of the National Library of Brazil and then as director.[53] On 1 August 1948 he joined the staff of the United Nations Library to fill the post left vacant when Mr. Rasmussen resigned. He became chief of the processing section and served as Mr. Milam's deputy.[54] He only remained a year in this position and then transferred to the directorship of the United Nations Information Office in Paris.[55] His appointment to the position of director of the United Nations Library was effective 1 February 1954; and Mr. Reitman, who had been serving as acting director for almost four years, since 1950, was named deputy director as of 10 May 1954.[56] Mr. Reitman held this position until his resignation on 1 February 1955.

Three weeks after assuming his position, Dr. Moraes, in writing to Andrew Cordier, reported that he found the library services to be perfectly organized:

> The Library has been excellently administered during these last years. No technical problem demands an urgent solution, the services have been very well streamlined and are functioning with perfect efficiency. Assuming that in the future the aims and means of action of the Library will not change, my task will be to continue along the lines of administration traced by my predecessor, and to introduce only the normal changes that may be called for from year to year.[57]

Dr. Moraes found only one serious problem—the relationship between the headquarters and the Geneva libraries. He felt that his problem was due to the lack of precision in the pertinent clauses of the basic library policy. Library policy in regard to the Geneva library provided only for a "liberal lending policy with other libraries, including the Headquarters Library" and for control "by the Secretary-General administratively through the Director of the European Office, and from a policy point of view, through the Director of the Headquarters Library."[58]

Although Dr. Moraes had served as Mr. Milam's deputy, the responsibilities of the position of deputy director had not been clearly understood. Dr. Moraes, therefore, undertook to define the duties of the director and the deputy director.

The Director will take care of all questions belonging to the administration of the Library—all things done by the Executive Office and details about administration. He will take care of the preparation and discussion of the budget, as well as policies and implications of the budget. The Director will take care of everything connected with personnel—change of assignment, shifts from one place to another, promotions, and so forth. Sometimes these questions are difficult because Directors now have little to do with promotions. There is a Board that takes the final decision; the Director only recommends his choice.

The Deputy Director is in charge of what we can call the routine operations of the Library, with co-ordination between the two Sections, which are supposed to work together. He is also to take the place of the Director when the Director is away.[59]

The main contribution of Dr. Moraes during his five-year administration was to consolidate the gains made by Carl Milam. Dr. Moraes retired at the end of 1958.

The next director of the library was an Austrian, and a compatriot and friend of Dr. A. C. Breycha-Vauthier, the longtime director of the United Nations Library in Geneva. Dr. Josef Leopold Stummvoll, who was born in Vienna, was a well-known national librarian, author, and editor. He had worked in Germany as deputy director of the Berlin Patent Office Library and as director of the reading department at the Deutsche Bücherei in Leipzig, before becoming general director in 1949 of the Austrian National Library, from which he took a leave of absence to serve as director of the United Nations Library.[60]

Dr. Stummvoll's appointment was effective in January 1959, but he was on leave from the United Nations Library from 9 January to 9 October 1961, and again from 26 April to 31 October 1962. In his absences the deputy director served as acting director.[61] The deputy director at this time was Joseph Groesbeck, who received his library training at the University of Michigan. He had served as deputy chief of the Library of Congress mission to Germany in 1946 and had been chief of acquisitions for the United States Armed Forces Medical Library (now the National Library of Medicine) before going to the United Nations Library as chief of the processing section on 15 April

Courtesy of the United Nations

Josef Stummvoll

1951. He later served as acting chief of the reference and documentation section following Mr. Reitman's resignation on 3 February 1955. On 1 January 1956 he was named deputy director of the library.

Dr. Stummvoll resigned upon expiration of his contract in

January 1963, and Mr. Groesbeck again served as acting director until the appointment of Lev Vladimirov as director became
effective in June 1964.[62] This time a university librarian was
selected to be the director of the United Nations Library. Louis

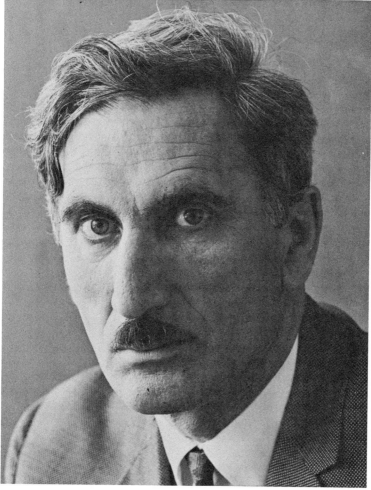

Courtesy of the United Nations

Lev Vladimirov

49

Shores described Dr. Vladimirov as "one of the great librarians of the world."

> His Ph.D. from the University of Vilnius was preceded by graduate studies in German and Slavic languages, German literature, and in Economics at the University of Kaunas, and at Vilnius. His professional degree is from the Institute of Library Science, Leningrad, U.S.S.R., where he subsequently pursued graduate studies in library history. He has served as Director of the University Library at Vilnius since 1948, and as Dean of the Library School there since 1951.[63]

A definite trend seems evident in the past appointments of directors of the United Nations Library. The last three directors have all been noted scholars and librarians with doctoral degrees. Two of them were national librarians, and the present one is a university librarian. The position of deputy director was solidified during the administration of Dr. Moraes. His deputy director was Mr. Reitman, and the present one is Mr. Groesbeck. It would seem that the administration of the United Nations has adopted a policy of appointing a well-known librarian,

Courtesy of the United Nations

Joseph Groesbeck

each time from a different member country, to serve as director for a specified period of time, with a career deputy director providing the necessary continuity in practice and procedure.

Personnel

In the recruitment of personnel the library, as all departments of the Secretariat, is bound by the following sections of the Charter:

> Article 8. The United Nations shall place no restrictions on the eligibility of men and women to participate in any capacity and under conditions of equality in its principal and subsidiary organs.

> Article 101. Section 3. The paramount consideration in the employment of the staff and in the determination of the conditions of service shall be the necessity of securing the highest standards of efficiency, competence, and integrity. Due regard shall be paid to the importance of recruiting the staff on as wide a geographical basis as possible.[64]

Although the first mandate has caused the library no particular difficulty, except that a woman has not yet served in the position of director, the principle of geographical distribution has sometimes taken precedence over the principle of efficiency, competence, and integrity. Evidently, in the appointment of consultants and temporary personnel, geographical distribution has not been of such importance as it has been in the matter of permanent personnel. As has been previously noted, all of the consultants have been American, with the exception of Mr. Breycha-Vauthier from the Geneva library and the members of the International Advisory Committee of Library Experts. Many posts have been filled by Americans on a temporary basis.

When the Secretariat was being organized, the need was to hire personnel quickly, with the result that the initial staff was recruited heavily from the United States, Canada, and Western European countries.[65] In 1947, Mr. Lie defined his conception of the principle of geographic distribution:

> Rightly understood, the cardinal principle of geographical distribution is not that nationals of a particular nation should have a specified number of posts at a particular

51

> grade or grades, or that they should receive in salary as a
> group a particular percentage of the total outlay in salaries,
> but that, in the first place, the administration should be
> satisfied that the Secretariat is enriched by the experience
> and culture which each Member nation can furnish and
> that each Member nation should, in its turn, be satisfied
> that its own culture and philosophy make a full contribu-
> tion to the Secretariat.[66]

Although this was a flexible formula, increasing importance
has been attached to the principle of geographic distribution. In
1963 the concept was made more explicit, when the General
Assembly recommended that the secretary-general "continue
his efforts so that all Member States might be 'represented' at
the Professional level in the Secretariat."[67]

In 1948, Mr. Milam made a count of the professional staff distribution by country for the Department of Public Information:
Australia, 2; Brazil, 2; Canada, 2; Czechoslovakia, 3; Denmark,
1; France, 3; India, 1; Mexico, 1; Norway, 1; Paraguay, 1; Swe-
den, 2; United Kingdom, 6; United States, 18; and Uruguay, 1.
Fourteen countries were represented in the 44 professional
posts, with United States citizens occupying approximately 40
percent of the positions.[68] In the library the principle of geographical distribution lends a particular strength since it
means that the staff is thus able to handle a wide variety of
languages in book selection, cataloging, and reference.

The geographical breakdown for the professional staff in
1969 was: Austria, 1; Canada, 1; Chile, 1; China, 2; Czechoslovakia, 1; Denmark, 2; Dominican Republic, 1; El Salvador, 1; Fin-
land, 2; France, 2; India, 2; Iran, 1; Italy, 1; Jamaica, 1; Japan,
1; Lebanon, 2; Nicaragua, 1; Sudan, 1; USSR, 5; United Arab
Republic, 1; United States, 20; and Yugoslavia, 1.[69] Twenty-two
countries are now represented in the 51 professional positions.
The number of United States citizens in the United Nations
Library has increased from 18 to 20, while the percentage has
decreased slightly to just less than 40 percent of the positions.

Mr. Milam, in recruiting to fill the position of chief of the
processing section after Dr. Moraes left, experienced some frus-
tration in attempting to follow the nebulous principle of geographical distribution. After a long discussion with Byron Price,

the assistant secretary-general for Administrative and Financial Services, he noted in his diary:

> I told him:
> That the position has been vacant since early June except for Osborn's 3 months;
> That I had recruited actively & extensively in S. America, South Africa and Sweden; having been told that they were under-represented countries;
> That I had found no one of the right calibre in Sweden, Immelman, the leading libn. in S.A., & had suggested . . . a few names in Argentina;
> That Immelman was obviously the best; . . .
> That 2 Argentinians had eliminated themselves; . . .
> That this was one of the two top posts under the Director of the Library & and that we could not risk the danger of loss of esprit de corps — which is now excellent — by taking someone in an administrative post who does not work well with his associates;
> That I was not averse to giving national preference in lower positions;
> And probably a good deal more.[70]

Although Mr. Milam had been told to appoint a certain person to the position, he refused to do so. This clash prompted a further diatribe against the Personnel Bureau in his diary:

> The Personnel Bureau is making my life miserable, consuming most of my time, hampering seriously the work of the Library, forcing us to do things which are obviously wrong, promoting inefficiency & extravagance. . . . In my present opinion the Personnel Bureau is in about the same condition as the Library was when I came, namely, chaotic, I could write a book telling why.[71]

In spite of his difficulties with the Personnel Bureau, Mr. Milam was able to employ an excellent staff, although some of the positions were filled by the appointment of United States citizens on a temporary basis. He always insisted on high standards for his professional staff.

Professional librarians at the United Nations must have the equivalent of a professional degree in the United States — the master's degree in library science. This requirement was put into effect during Mr. Milam's administration. He was responsible for establishing the status of librarians at parity with other officers in the Secretariat. In 1950 the single grading scale of the United Nations was changed to the present double scale of general service and professional grades. "At that point Milam defended the professionalism of librarians against those in the administration who thought that librarians' work was clerical, and he did it with such success that about half of the Library's posts were reclassified into the 'Professional' category."[72]

When the library was first organized, the salaries of the librarians in the main library and the salaries of the information officers in the Reference Center were not comparable, with the latter being paid a higher salary. Mr. Rasmussen brought this to the attention of his immediate supervisor, reporting to him that the morale of the library staff was affected by the discrepancy.[73] However, Mr. Shaw in his survey maintained that there was no salary differential because comparable jobs in the Reference Center were actually graded lower than they were in the central library.[74] This discrepancy, if it existed, was eliminated by the merger of the two libraries under the Department of Public Information.

The internship program in the library was initiated during Mr. Milam's administration. In September 1948 he proposed a two-year program of library internship, the purpose being to enable young graduate librarians and research workers with special qualifications, generally from countries other than the United States, to work in the library and thus become acquainted with the United Nations and its problems and gain a fair knowledge of the documentation of the United Nations. He suggested that foreign students in the library schools in the United States and Canada be recruited for internships of from three to twelve months. Mr. Milam further proposed that the program should be directed by someone who had the time and competence to plan the individual schedules, to give lectures, and to hold individual and group conferences. He did not want the program to be a mere excuse to employ cheap labor but to be a genuine program in professional and international education. There were sixty foreign students in accredited library schools during the academic year, 1947/48. A budget of $36,400 was proposed so that the program could be carried on for a two- or two-and-one-half-year period ending 31 December 1950.[75]

54

A proposal for funds was submitted by Benjamin Cohen to Alger Hiss, president of the Carnegie Endowment for International Peace.[76] Although the Carnegie Endowment approved the idea of the proposal, it was unable at that time to approve such a large grant.[77]

This proposal was essentially the same as that suggested in a working paper prepared for the International Advisory Committee of Library Experts.[78] In its final report the committee made the following recommendation:

> 66. The Committee takes cognizance, with approval, of the internship programme already established by the United Nations Secretariat. It recommends that the programme be extended to include the provision of more internships in the United Nations Libraries to enable young graduate librarians and research workers with special qualifications to become acquainted with the United Nations and its problems as they are revealed through the Division of Library Services.[79]

In May 1949 a new proposal was submitted to the Carnegie Endowment for International Peace, requesting a grant of $5,000 for five library interns for the summer of 1949. The proposal was similar to the original one, although in this instance no funds were asked for supervisory personnel. The reason for selecting students in American library schools was to avoid expensive transportation costs. Several foreign students had already filed applications with the United Nations.[80] In June 1949 two internships were granted, one to Miss Rabieb Tantranon from Thailand, a student at the University of Illinois; and the second to Surjit Singh from India, a student at the University of Michigan. The internships began 1 July and continued for four months. The Carnegie Endowment for International Peace provided funds for a monthly stipend of $250.[81]

In 1950 three interns from Korea, India, and France were trained under grants from the Rockefeller Foundation and the Carnegie Endowment, and three other interns under the United Nations program were assigned to the library from Canada, Haiti, and the United States of America.[82]

Although this was a valuable method of training foreign librarians in the use of United Nations documentation, the plan has not been continued, probably because of lack of funds.

Departmental libraries

Because the United Nations could not immediately develop a strong central library, small libraries were begun in many of the substantive departments and divisions of the Secretariat. The establishment of these libraries seemed to be in conflict with the policy outlined in two memoranda of 1946. Actually these memoranda were very confusing and did in effect make some provision for branch libraries in the departments. The memorandum of 16 April 1946 provided:

> After the completion of the move to . . . [Lake Success], there will be only one library. Departments will be entitled to keep a few books of reference, but these will be ordered through the Librarian and kept in the department only on his authority.[83]

In the memorandum of 26 August 1946 the secretary-general envisaged a central library which would "be divided into sections in such a manner that each department requiring special facilities would find in one part of the library such volumes and documents as most immediately affect it."[84] However, he continued in the same memorandum:

> Where the entire Secretariat is housed in one building, the library service will be housed centrally and integrally, but where there is any considerable physical distance between a given department and the central library, then that department section of the library and its staff will be housed with the department while still remaining under the authority of the chief librarian.[85]

This was not, as Mr. Shaw reported, "an excellent and clear-cut statement of policy which everyone should have been able to follow."[86] In his survey Mr. Shaw identified libraries in the following substantive departments: Department of Public Information; the Department of Security Council Affairs; the Department of Trusteeship Affairs; the Department of Social Affairs; the Department of Economic Affairs; the Legal Department; and the Archives Division, the Language Division, the

Editorial Division, and the Document and Sales Division of the Department of Conference and General Services.[87]

In spite of the fact that all of the departmental libraries were unified administratively with the central library, when the library was transferred to the Department of Public Information, both Mr. Milam and the International Advisory Committee of Library Experts recognized the continuing need for limited departmental library service. The International Advisory Library Committee agreed "that the maintenance by the Library of collections within the departments of the Secretariat corresponds to a practical necessity, but recommends that these collections contain only the most needed reference material."[88] This recommendation was later incorporated into the official library policy adopted in 1949.[89] In a discussion of the budget estimates for 1950, Mr. van Asch van Wijck, speaking for the Netherlands delegation, opposed the system of departmental libraries:

> Such a system would entail the virtual disintegration of the Library as an administrative unit; it would lead to an unjustified increase in the number of officials attached to that service and to duplication in the purchase of books and would thus involve unnecessary expense. The Library should be organized in such a way that it could lend books to the Departments, while at the same time retaining complete control over those books.[90]

The justification for departmental libraries rested largely on three factors: each department's need for a specialized and accessible small collection of materials, the need for a librarian trained in the particular subject of the department, and the need for getting materials quickly in order to save the time of the researchers.[91]

When Mr. Milam became director he suggested closer coordination of the departmental libraries and, for economic reasons, the actual consolidation of two of them: the library of the Department of Economic Affairs and the library of the Department of Social Affairs.[92] He was continually asked to justify the existence of the departmental libraries to the Bureau of Finance. In a memorandum prepared by the Division of Library Services, the responsibilities of the departmental librarians were listed as the following: (1) to maintain a working collection of materials on the subjects of main interest to the departments; (2) to offer reference, research, and bibliographical services to the staff members; and (3) to maintain relations between the departments and the central library.[93] Mr. Milam compared the Secretariat to a "great university in its needs for library services," and "the substantive departments . . . to university departments or schools or faculties."[94]

> The research work now carried on in the United Nations is as extensive as that to be found in many great universities, and perhaps even more specialized. While the present and future United Nations buildings may not equal the areas of many large campuses, the desire and need of the departmental workers for immediate access to a small collection of specialized materials and for the services of a librarian devoted exclusively to one department correspond to those which prevail on the campus.
>
> One further similarity is the tendency of special groups, here as in a university, to build up their own libraries—regardless of the regulations—if the Library does not provide adequately for their needs in a location convenient to them. This tendency has appeared in this building in the recent past. Experience seems to show that the only way to avoid this is to provide for a *strong centralized administration* and a somewhat *decentralized service* under firm control.[95]

Plans for the new Secretariat building at the permanent site included the following departmental libraries: the Security Council Affairs branch on the thirty-fifth floor with a capacity of 2,875 volumes; the Legal Department branch on the thirty-fourth floor with a 5,625-volume capacity; the Trusteeship Affairs branch on the thirty-second floor with a 3,000-volume capacity; and the combined Economic Affairs and Social Affairs branch on the thirtieth floor with a capacity of 7,000 volumes.[96]

Although the Advisory Committee on Administrative and Budgetary Questions approved the eleven established posts requested for the branch libraries in the 1951 budget, it made the following comment about the future of these libraries: "Consideration should be given to the possibility of reducing, and ultimately eliminating the branch libraries maintained in certain of the Departments."[97]

Mr. Reitman, who was then acting director of the library, called a meeting of the Permanent Advisory Library Committee to consider the Advisory Committee's report, and to plan a course of action. It was suggested that an official paper be prepared for submission by the secretary-general to the Fifth Committee which would give some background information about the departmental libraries in order to clarify the situation.[98] The final draft of this paper was sent to the members of the Library Committee on 3 October 1950. After justifying the need for departmental libraries, the paper concluded by stating: "The Secretary-General, therefore, recommends retention of the present library system based on the principle of strong central administration and decentralized services under firm supervision."[99]

This paper was never officially adopted. The Advisory Committee in its second report of 1951 again recommended the elimination of the departmental libraries:

> It was contended that the Library requires the continued maintenance of departmental branch units, on the ground that their abolition would entail loss of working time, an increase in the workload of the main Library staff, and a tendency to accumulate reference volumes in individual offices. In the opinion of the Committee, the present location of the Library [in the Manhattan Building] in relation to the main building obviates the necessity for branch offices.[100]

A special meeting of the Permanent Advisory Library Committee was called on 5 October 1951, to reevaluate the situation. It was agreed to prepare another background paper which could be presented to the Fifth Committee.[101] This paper, substantially the same in content as the first one, was approved by the Library Committee and sent to Andrew W. Cordier, executive assistant to the secretary-general.[102] Although the library did not suffer any additional cuts in its budget, the battle of the departmental libraries was still not won, for the Advisory Committee in its first report of 1952, again recommended the elimination or further consolidation of departmental branch units.[103] Earlier, Mr. Reitman and Mr. Cordier had discussed the possibility of reexamining the utilization of the staff in the main library and in the departmental libraries with a view to possible economies, and they both agreed that it would be wise to ask an outside expert to conduct a survey of operations and of staff requirements.[104] This survey (the Clapp survey of 1952) also had the blessings of the Advisory Committee. Mr. Clapp's recommendation in regard to the departmental libraries was as follows:

> It is recommended that no further consolidation take place among the Departmental Libraries, but rather that there be an examination to ascertain whether the present libraries are giving sufficiently good service so as to render unnecessary the development of collections and library services within the Departments.[105]

However, one further consolidation did take place in 1954 when the libraries of the Office of Legal Affairs and the Department of Political and Security Council Affairs were merged.[106] Later the Trusteeship library was disbanded, so that at present only two branch libraries remain, both of them with very special collections. The library in the Office of Legal Affairs contains the law collection, which, even if it were to be transferred to the main library, would require special handling and servicing. The library in the Department of Economic and Social Affairs contains only a statistical collection which has a special classification. As the services and collections of the main library have been strengthened, the need for large departmental libraries has lessened, although at one time they provided a very useful service.

chapter 3

Physical quarters

Hunter College

On 14 February 1946, New York City was selected by the General Assembly as the interim headquarters of the United Nations. On 21 March 1946 temporary quarters were established at Hunter College in the Bronx, where the gymnasium was converted for use by the United Nations. Temporary facilities at Hunter College were also allocated to the library of the Department of Conference and General Services. Library services continued to be given by the former United Nations Information Office Library which became the Reference Center of the Department of Public Information.

Since the installation of the library at Hunter College was only temporary, the secretary-general, in his first report on the work of the organization, stated that it was inadvisable to assemble a large collection of books there, only to move them to Lake Success in August 1946.[1] Initially, therefore, purchases of books were held to the bare minimum of essential reference works.

The library, although small, was in operation on 25 March 1946, when the United Nations held its first sessions in New York City. It was a sad and lonely place. Meyer Berger of *The New York Times* reported:

> Perhaps the saddest place in the UNO main building lies behind the door marked "library." This door opens on empti-

ness, on racks innocent of books of any kind. There are a few brown-wrapped packages on the floor and one or two directories on the tables, and that's all. Albert C. Gerould, formerly of the College of the Pacific in Stockton, Calif., runs the place. . . . There is a chance that maybe some day the old League of Nations library—about 200,000 volumes—may be inherited by the UNO, but so far nothing has been done about that. Before the door closed, Mr. Gerould said wistfully, "There's a library here, in a way: it exists in the mind of God."[2]

Tom O'Hara of the *New York Herald Tribune* reported:

One of the loneliest men in the first floor of the gymnasium was Albert C. Gerould, U.N.O.'s assistant librarian, who started on his job two weeks ago. . . . Mr. Gerould had exactly forty-one volumes for the modest library of U.N.O., and even these were not in the permanent collection. Most of them, he said, were destined for translators and, accordingly, were Russian, Polish, Greek, Spanish, Swiss and German dictionaries. Six copies of the "World Almanac for 1946" were in the collection. The library, Mr. Gerould said, is very much in the formative stage.[3]

This, then, was the beginning of the United Nations Library. It was humble, but no more humble than the beginning of the League of Nations Library in London. Eventually, both of these libraries would occupy magnificent buildings. Albert Gerould, in recalling his tenure with the United Nations Library, described the three different locations which the library occupied while it was at Hunter College.

The first was a large janitor's storage closet on the first floor of the gymnasium building; the second was a corner of what had been the Post Exchange in the adjoining building, and the third, again in the gymnasium building, was the former locker room for girls.[4]

The locker room for girls was amusingly described by Leonard Lyons in his column, "The Lyons Den."

A few days ago the publishers of the Encyclopedia Americana sent a set of books to the United Nations Library. The volumes were delivered to Room 205-C as directed. . . .

62

Then photographers brought their equipment to the building for some publicity photos. But over Room 205-C they
found a sign: "Ladies-Dames". . . . The puzzled photographers waited, and when they saw two men marching into
Room 205-C they decided to recheck. Messengers were sent
to the information desk, and returned with the report that
Room 205-C really is the United Nations Library—that its
quarters are in the women's rest room and that the sign
over the door should have been removed.[5]

When Mr. Rasmussen became the librarian in August 1946,
he had a staff of five; a small, unbound, unclassified, and uncat-
aloged collection of documents on economic and financial subjects; no shelving; no space to house the personnel properly;
and no space to seat readers using the library.[6]

Lake Success

The Secretariat of the United Nations, including the library,
was moved into the wartime buildings of the Sperry Gyroscope
Company at Lake Success on 16–19 August 1946. Up until 14
December 1946, when the General Assembly finally selected
New York as the permanent headquarters, all facilities were
considered temporary. The quarters assigned to the library in
August were in area C. They soon proved to be inadequate.
Because of this, Mr. Pelt, at the 3 May 1947 meeting of the
Permanent Advisory Library Committee, considered proposing
the erection of a separate temporary building at Lake Success,
but he felt that this request would not be granted.[7] He did suc-
ceed in getting the library moved to larger quarters in area B.
The move was made partly in May and partly in October 1947.
The library had grown during this time with the acquisition of
the collections from the Economic and Transit Department of
the League in Princeton and from the United Nations Relief
and Rehabilitation Administration in Washington. In October
1947 the library finally received its bookshelves, designed to
hold 62,000 volumes, and the staff could at last give real library
service. Five branch libraries in the substantive departments of
the United Nations Secretariat were also established at Lake
Success.

United Nations Library, Lake Success: bookstacks [top]
United Nations Library, Lake Success: reading room [bottom]

Later on that year Mr. Pelt reported to the Permanent Advisory Library Committee that the secretary-general had decided, on the advice of Mr. Price, to reduce the amount to be requested for the construction of the new United Nations buildings in New York City from $85,000,000 to $65,000,000. The reduction meant that the separate library building then envisaged on the permanent site had to be sacrificed. The architect of the United Nations complex on the East River had been instructed to provide a library of unknown capacity in the Secretariat building, but Mr. Pelt described the outlook as "fairly black" because he thought it would be extremely difficult to provide satisfactory library space in the remains of the Secretariat building, which had also forfeited a few stories because of the budget cut.[8]

The question of a separate library building was discussed in some detail at a special meeting of the Library Committee on 12 September 1947. The views of the various departments were proffered, and at the conclusion of the meeting Mr. Pelt expressed the consensus of the group:

> With the exception of Mr. Cohen and Mr. Price, the feeling of the Assistant Secretaries General is that the original plan should be adhered to, in principle. If economies must be practised, they should be spread over the entire building project rather than sacrificing the Library. . . . the important thing is that we start with a separate library building especially constructed for that purpose, no matter what its initial capacity, with the possibility of expansion.[9]

The Manhattan Building

The library eventually occupied a separate building; however, it was not an edifice designed for a library, but was a converted office building. When Mr. Milam was interviewed for the position of director, there was some discussion of using an existing office building at the permanent site on the East River for the library. This possibility was also deliberated by the International Advisory Committee of Library Experts: "Clearly, the ideal solution would be to provide a special building, . . . " although it recognized "the practical difficulties of such a solution."[10] "In the circumstances the Committee . . . agreed, with some reluctance, to recommend for the use of the Library the building which now

65

The Manhattan Building

houses the Manhattan office of the United Nations."[11] This building has been popularly called the Manhattan Building.

By 3 September 1948, Mr. Milam knew that the library would be moving into this building, a seven-story structure with two basement levels, at 405 East Forty-second Street.[12] The land on which the building was located was purchased in 1944 by the New York City Housing Authority for a new office building, which it completed and planned to occupy on 1 June 1947. This building cut into the six-block rectangular site presented to the United Nations by John D. Rockefeller, Jr., and New York City.[13] Therefore, the United Nations was permitted to acquire the building. The first offices to occupy it were the temporary offices of the United Nations which had been housed in the Empire State Building and in Rockefeller Center.[14]

In March 1949, Mr. Milam prepared a report on the preparations necessary before the library would be in top condition for moving. His recommendations at that time were: (1) the library should have a complete collection of specialized agency documents, (2) binding of United Nations documents, departmental publications, and periodicals should be completed, (3) the backlog of government documents should be checked in, sorted, marked, and arranged, (4) the departmental library collections should be fully cataloged, (5) the staff for the departmental libraries should be increased so as to meet the expanding research needs of the departments, (6) books out on loan for one or two years should be recalled, (7) the pamphlet file should be brought under control, (8) the map collection should be broadened, (9) cataloging arrears must be cleared up, (10) the huge backlog of gifts must be sorted, discarded, or selected for cataloging, and (11) supplementary catalogs must be prepared for the additional reference rooms planned for the Manhattan Building.[15] Clearly, Mr. Milam wanted to have the library completely organized and up to date before the move to the headquarters site.

The Permanent Advisory Library Committee, in discussing these plans on 16 March, fully endorsed Mr. Milam's memorandum and emphasized two factors: (1) the library must liquidate its backlog of work and organize its collections before moving to Manhattan, and (2) a high level of library service was essential for the entire Secretariat.[16] The memorandum along with

67

the minutes of this meeting was sent to Mr. Cohen on 23 March as a minimum budgetary request.[17]

Mr. Milam hoped to obtain a consultant to help in planning the library in the Manhattan Building and on 7 June 1949 wrote to Joseph Wheeler, a well-known library-building consultant, asking him on what terms he might be able to give the United Nations some help in planning the Manhattan Building for library use.[18] However, on 23 June, Mr. Milam wrote again to Mr. Wheeler withdrawing his request, because he felt that he could not offer him a decent consultation fee for his services.[19]

The building plans for the Manhattan Building were completed in 1950 before Mr. Milam resigned, and the move was scheduled for 1951. The services which had been concentrated on one floor at Lake Success were now spaced over eight, and major reading rooms were provided on three floors. The Military Staff Committee continued to occupy the top floor of the building for the next few years. The subbasement and the basement were devoted to stacks, the former with an eventual capacity of 81,875 volumes, and the latter, the main stack area, with a capacity of 80,875 volumes. The ground floor, with a tunnel corridor to the Secretariat building, had a stack capacity of 14,250 volumes and included the receiving room and the map collection. The second floor housed the loan desk, the main reading room with the periodical and newspaper collection, the reference collection, and bookstacks with a capacity of 16,400 volumes; the third floor housed the documents reading room for United Nations and specialized agency documents and had a stack capacity of 22,200 volumes; the fourth floor contained the documents reading room for the League of Nations publications, and stacks with a capacity of 25,800 volumes (this collection included the Woodrow Wilson Memorial Library of 15,000 volumes); the fifth floor housed the office of the director, other offices, and the acquisition and cataloging units; and the sixth floor sheltered the documents index unit. The plans provided accommodations for approximately 272,000 volumes and for 170 readers. Another 50 readers and 20,000 volumes could be taken care of in the four branch libraries in the Secretariat building.[20]

It was hoped that some remodeling could be done so that the building could function better as a library, but the $500,000 which was requested for the alterations was severely criticized at two meetings of the Fifth Committee.[21] The delegates failed to endorse this amount for remodeling. They approved instead the secretary-general's decision not to appropriate any supplementary funds. It was essential to try to complete the building project within the original provision of $65,000,000.[22]

On 21 August 1950 the first units of the Secretariat were moved from Lake Success into permanent buildings on the East River in New York City. During the late months of 1950 and the early months of 1951, the library completed its move from Lake Success to the Manhattan Building.[23] In a statement to the secretary-general a year later, Mr. Reitman reported: "A year's experience in the new building has proved conclusively its inadequacy for permanent library use."[24]

That a building which was designed for offices could provide adequate facilities for good library service was questioned from the beginning, but it was the only solution possible at the time. The library facilities were inadequate in many ways, as the representative from Peru, Mr. Pareja y Paz Soldan, emphasized in a meeting of the Fifth Committee on 20 February 1957:

> The staff of the United Nations Library provided all delegations with extremely efficient service. They were, however, working under considerable difficulties in their present building; they had to make any [sic] unnecessary journeys from one floor to another; there was no general reading room nor were there any rooms for research and study, such as were found in most libraries. Maintenance costs were on the increase. It was to be hoped that a special report could be submitted to the twelfth session on the question of providing more suitable premises, especially as the addition of so many new Member States made a large increase in the number of volumes inevitable. The possibility of obtaining assistance from United States cultural institutions and foundations to finance that construction might be explored.[25]

The library, however, remained in this building for almost nine years. On 13 November 1959 the library collections began to be withdrawn so that the building could be demolished in preparation for the construction of the new library building on the same site. At this time some 75,000 volumes were relegated to dead storage in the basement of the Secretariat building. The bulk of the circulating collection was moved to shelves on the nineteenth floor made available by temporary storage of the archives in another area. Reading rooms and reference collections were created in the Secretariat building lobby, on the nineteenth floor, and in the fifth-floor staff lounge. The processing sections and other parts of the library were installed in other areas of the Secretariat and Conference buildings. The moving operation was completed on 15 February 1960, with no significant interruption to normal services. Demolition of the Manhattan Building commenced on 15 March 1960.[26]

The events leading up to the building of a permanent headquarters for the United Nations Library and the dedication of that library is the story of a long struggle by the library to provide adequate services and facilities for its clientele.

Dag Hammarskjöld Library

Mr. Price, in replying to a library staff memorandum of 25 September 1950, requesting permission to explore the possibility of obtaining external funds for alterations to the Manhattan Building, replied:

> We have been considering from all angles the problem of converting the Manhattan building for library purposes. In view of everything involved it is not the present inclination of the Secretary-General to expend more money on this project than is absolutely necessary on a temporary basis.
>
> I think it should be recalled that when the Manhattan building was purchased only its temporary use was contemplated. It is not, as you say, ideally fitted for library use and would still have shortcomings after extensive remodeling.
>
> The ideal solution would be, of course, a new library building. I have discussed this matter with the Secretary-General and you are at liberty to explore the possibility of obtaining a grant for the building of a library on the Headquarters site from private sources in a manner similar to the League of Nations.[27]

The League of Nations furnished an excellent precedent for this procedure, since the library at Geneva had been built as a result of a gift of $2,000,000 from John D. Rockefeller, Jr.

As a result of this reply from Mr. Price, a brochure describing the needs of the United Nations Library was drafted to be used to initiate the fund-raising campaign. The brochure described the library in Geneva and the move of the United Nations Library into temporary quarters in the Manhattan Building. From this transient position the library aspired in a few years to "move into a permanent home, a home that should afford it an effectiveness and quiet dignity no less satisfactory that [sic] its sister library in Geneva possessès." [28] Three million dollars was requested for the building plus another $2,000,000 in the form of an endowment to enable the library to function at top speed and efficiency.[29]

In addition to this brochure the library staff worked out a building program, which was revised by Mr. Milam when he came to the library as a consultant on 8 May 1951. This program was sent to Wallace K. Harrison, director of planning in the Headquarters Planning Office. The program covered such items as location of the library, functional plan, reading and book areas,. bookstacks, current periodicals, map collection, space for readers, exhibition room, and staff quarters.[30]

Mr. Milam had previously discussed the matter of fund raising with both Mr. Price and Mr. Cordier on 26 February 1951. Three possibilities for obtaining funds were mentioned: from governments, from American foundations and individuals, and from foundations in many countries. It was agreed that it would be difficult to obtain the money from governments, so the possibility of obtaining funds from American foundations and foundations in other countries was explored. Several foundations were mentioned at this time as prospective donors: Rockefeller Foundation, Carnegie Corporation, Grant Foundation, Ford Foundation, etc.

Regarding the site of the library, proximity to the Secretariat building and ease of access to the library by the Secretariat staff were the two items of paramount importance. Mr. Milam reported, "Unless at least as good a location as we now have can be found, I hope that the decision will be to make the best of the present building."[31] Mr. Milam's final suggestions were the following: (1) reach a decision on the site, (2) if a suitable site is found, have the library director work out detailed specifications of building needs, and have the architects make preliminary sketches, (3) arrange for the secretary-general or his personal representative to interview the presidents of a few large foundations, possibly beginning with the Ford Foundation, and (4) solicit at least token gifts from foundations outside the United States.[32]

A revised edition of the fund-raising pamphlet was issued on 3 May 1951, but Mr. Milam was not convinced that a printed pamphlet was needed. He felt that a better approach would be to try to write individual letters to the presidents of several foundations, and as an example he drafted a letter to the president of the Ford Foundation to be signed by the secretary-general.[33]

Mr. Milam visited New York again from 26 September to 2 October 1951, to discuss the progress of the fund-raising campaign. At this time he redrafted the building-program statement.[34] He also talked with a representative of the Carnegie Corporation about a contribution for the library, but was told very emphatically that the Carnegie Corporation could not participate because its charter limited contributions to the United States and to the British Commonwealth. It was impossible to ease this limitation to include the United Nations, which, although geographically located in the United States, was an international organization.[35]

Mr. Milam returned to New York at the end of November 1951 to continue his fund-raising discussions, but reported to Mr. Cordier, "This trip has been pretty much of a flop."[36] Many people he wished to see were out of town and those he did see were not encouraging. The Rockefeller Foundation through its president indicated that it might participate. The Carnegie Corporation president doubted that the corporation would change its mind. The Ford Foundation had ruled out the granting of funds for buildings, although Mr. Milam felt that in the case of the United Nations, it might make an exception. He concluded his report by saying:

> We still have the possibility of finding an individual angel in this or some other country. Maybe the best way to find one is to let the word get around among the Delegations that the United Nations needs one.
>
> If private funds are not found, then I hope the United Nations will appropriate them. Perhaps it would ease the

burden somewhat if half a million, more or less, of unexpended balances could be set aside each year to accumulate as a Library Building Fund.[37]

In January 1952, Mr. Milam interviewed a representative of the Kresge Foundation in Chicago. Although the foundation could not make a grant for the entire amount of $3,000,000, it indicated a willingness to participate in a joint enterprise with other foundations.[38]

In September 1952, Mr. Cordier wrote to Mr. Milam about the latest developments in the efforts of the United Nations to obtain funds for a new library. He reported as follows:

> Several months ago we presented a brochure . . . to the Ford Foundation. Some of their top officials showed considerable interest but, at the suggestion of their staff, it was felt desirable that some of us should go to Pasadena for direct presentation of the project. As a result, last week-end, Ralph Bunche, Abe Feller, Luther Evans and I appeared in a full dress meeting of the Directors at their headquarters in Pasadena. Milton Katz, whose area this matter covers, presided at the meeting. Paul Hoffman, Chester Davis, Jack McCloy (recently of Germany), Carl Spaeth, John Howard and others were present at the meeting. Bob Hutchins joined us at the luncheon. Their response was uniformly good but the decision remains to be made at the next meeting of the Trustees here in New York in late October. We are keeping our fingers crossed but are very hopeful.[39]

The brochure, which had been completely rewritten and printed, was submitted by Trygve Lie to the Ford Foundation on 29 May 1952. It stated, "Although the need is urgent for an adequate library and its related research and reference services, there is no prospect that under present world conditions the necessary funds could be provided in the official United Nations budget," and it concluded that major funds for the library must be found in private sources providing "an unparalleled opportunity for a profound and enduring contribution to the work and effectiveness of the Organization and to the cause of world peace and stability."[40]

No funds were forthcoming from the Ford Foundation at this time. Two subsequent requests to the Ford Foundation, one in

73

1956 and one in 1958, were also turned down.[41] However, in 1959 the Ford Foundation reversed its previous decisions and voted to award the sum of $6,200,000 to the United Nations for the construction of a new library building.[42] Action to this effect was taken by the Board of Trustees of the Ford Foundation at the meeting of 19 June 1959; and the secretary-general announced the gift to the members of the General Assembly on 29 September 1959.[43] By Resolution 1354 of 3 November 1959 the General Assembly in its fourteenth session accepted the gift of the Ford Foundation, and the dream of a new United Nations Library building was finally a reality.[44] The Ford Foundation, in awarding funds for a library building, adhered to its policy of financing buildings only in exceptional cases. The foundation had finally been persuaded by the smaller delegations of the United Nations and by the Secretariat, both of which strongly supported the project, that the potential contribution of the new library to the effectiveness of the United Nations warranted the grant.

The fund-raising campaign had lasted almost nine years, while the library occupied the inadequate Manhattan Building. During this time, in addition to the problem of raising funds, the problem of designing and planning the new library occupied the time of staff members and consultants alike.

The first building program for the library was included in the plan for the permanent headquarters of the United Nations published in 1947. This plan was based on an anticipated maximum of 1,500,000 volumes, with the total square feet for the library to be 171,000.[45]

The second building program was developed by the library in consultation with Mr. Milam and provided for a capacity of 600,000 volumes in the main stack collection. Again it was hoped that the permanent library building would be as close to the Secretariat building as possible and that it would be an independent structure.[46] In a revision of this program the number of volumes was reduced for some unknown reason to 400,000 volumes.[47] Mr. Milam had several conferences with members of the Headquarters Planning Office in early 1951 when he visited New York, and met with them again in May. The policy decided on at that time was that the library should definitely be limited to 400,000 volumes.[48] A more detailed building program was sent to Mr. Cordier in May 1951, but the number of volumes recommended for the library remained at 400,000.[49]

In October 1951, when Mr. Milam returned to New York, he had the opportunity of examining draft plans drawn up by the architect. At that time he made "the statement that the *draft plans* were not the work of librarians or architects specialized in planning libraries, and strongly urged that a well-known library architect . . . be called in to examine the plans in detail."[50] Although Mr. Milam's suggestion was not acted upon then, it may have influenced the Ford Foundation's decision to select four library consultants to help plan the new building.

The Ford Foundation in presenting its gift attached no conditions. "It asked only that the building to be constructed should be of the highest quality, designed, furnished and equipped in accordance with the most modern library standards."[51] The foundation assumed that the Manhattan Building would be razed and the new building erected in its place.

Preliminary sketches were prepared; the exterior was designed to complement the other buildings on the headquarters site. The plans included six stories in addition to the penthouse, three floors above ground and three below, with a floor area sufficient to house 400,000 volumes and a total of 285 readers. The Ford Foundation, in voting to grant the request of the United Nations for funds, secured the services of four distinguished librarians to assist in evaluating the project and to consult with the Secretariat personnel and the architects in formulating plans: Douglas W. Bryant, associate director, Harvard University Library; Verner W. Clapp, president, Council on Library Resources; Dr. Frank B. Rogers, director, National Library of Medicine; and Frederick Wagman, the librarian of the University of Michigan.[52]

On 3 November 1959 the General Assembly approved the general plan for the construction of the new building.[53] Plans then went ahead for the building of the library: the library staff met with the staff of the architect's office on several occasions; plans were discussed by the library section chiefs; and provisions were made to house the present library staff and facilities elsewhere while the Manhattan Building was demolished. Early in 1960 the plans were mailed to the consultant librarians for study and suggestions.[54]

On 1 July 1960 the secretary-general, Dag Hammarskjöld, held a meeting for a showing of the architect's model of the library building; and he himself made several suggestions, among them, these two: that the pagoda style of the penthouse be modified, and that a balcony proposed for the second floor be eliminated.[55] Construction of the new building began on 21 November 1960.

The architectural firm responsible for the final design was the firm of Harrison, Abramowitz and Harris; the general contractor was George A. Fuller and Company. The completed building has an infrastructure of three floors and a superstructure of three floors and a penthouse. The book capacity is 500,-000 volumes. Special features include an audio study room equipped for individual language study, a 200-seat auditorium, a concourse providing passage from First Avenue to the library and to the Secretariat building, a connecting passage from the library to the Secretariat, ten study rooms for use by individuals engaged in prolonged research, two seminar rooms available for group study, a penthouse lounge for receptions and similar functions, and the Woodrow Wilson Reading Room.[56]

In each of the library's major areas, woods from three continents are used to create different effects. The curved ceiling of the Woodrow Wilson Reading Room, which is two stories high, is of Idaho white pine; the wall-hung catalog, entrance doors, and furniture are in richly grained deep-brown African wenge wood, a strong contrast to the pale color of the pine. All of the furniture, room dividers, and woodwork in the large open area of the main reading room are of German white oak, which has been waxed to resemble ivory. The wood in the penthouse is English sycamore; its pale color and rippled grain make a flattering background for people.[57]

The library also possesses artistic treasures designed expressly for the new building. Two large abstract murals were executed by well-known artists, one Swedish and the other American. The American mural by Fritz Glarner is a series of rectangles of various sizes in bold primary colors and occupies a wall panel facing the marble staircase, which leads from the main lobby to the auditorium level, one floor below.[58] The Swedish work by Bo Beskow covers the concave west wall of the penthouse lounge. Mr. Beskow has described his work as a protest against

Dag Hammarskjöld Library, exterior view

Dag Hammarskjöld Library, Woodrow Wilson Reading Room [top]
Dag Hammarskjöld Library, main reading room [bottom]

Dag Hammarskjöld Library, penthouse lounge. Mural by Bo Beskow modern man's efforts to conquer space. In the composition are large forms reminiscent of the microscopic organisms that make up life on earth.[59]

At the dedication Mr. Michael Harris, of the architectural firm responsible for the plans, spoke about the designing of the new library:

> In the first phase of our planning, we started with basic design principles. A library is a book – a library is books and people – a library is people using books – many books is a stack – rows of stacks with work space between establish an optimum dimension. Repeated, this dimension determines the size of the building – its length, width and height, its structural form, the spacing of its lights and the location of its services.[60]

Dag Hammarskjöld Library, bookstacks

When the original headquarters complex was being designed, Wallace K. Harrison, as director of planning, was asked whether he was designing a palace to arise along the East River, and he replied, "We are not building a palace, we are building a workshop for peace."[61] And Mr. Harris reiterated in 1961, "We have made every effort to maintain this workshop atmosphere in the Library itself—a functional library designed for special purposes and uses."[62]

By late 1961 the construction was far enough advanced to begin planning the dedication ceremonies. Mr. Hammarskjöld himself sent out the invitations to the dedication ceremonies and the library symposium which he had organized for 16–18 November 1961. He wrote to Mr. Milam, "I have felt that the dedication of this Library which has a special role in supporting international programmes and efforts should be marked by the presence and participation of distinguished librarians from all parts of the world."[63] Librarians from all over the world were invited to attend, but Mr. Hammarskjöld did not live to witness the dedication.

After Hammarskjöld's death Henry T. Heald, president of the Ford Foundation, wrote to the president of the General Assembly:

> We hope that the new Library will be considered in some measure an appropriate remembrance of Mr. Hammarskjöld's life. It is in this spirit that the Ford Foundation would consider it an honour if the United Nations would decide to name the new Library "The Dag Hammarskjöld Library." We recognize that the decision is one for the United Nations to make. We believe that his name on the Library would symbolize the hopes we all have for it—that in the years ahead the Library may become a centre for men and women from all parts of the world whose efforts are dedicated, as were Dag Hammarskjöld's, to peace on earth.[64]

The General Assembly looked with favor on this suggestion, and passed a resolution to this effect:

> *The General Assembly,*
> *Mourning* the passing of Mr. Dag Hammarskjöld, Secretary-General of the United Nations,
> *Desiring* to establish an appropriate memorial commemorating his service to the United Nations,

81

> *Noting* with appreciation the hope expressed by the Ford
> Foundation, as donor, that the new United Nations library
> might be considered in some measure an appropriate re-
> membrance of Mr. Hammarskjöld's life,
>
> *Decides* to dedicate the new Library on 16 November
> 1961 as "The Dag Hammarskjöld Library."[65]

The library was so dedicated, and the inscription appears on the
wall at the entrance to the library. The dedication ceremony
took place in the General Assembly hall at 3:00 P.M. on 16
November 1961. The chairs of the delegates were filled with
the official representatives of the United Nations; the visitors'
galleries were crowded with librarians from around the world,
representing thirty-two countries in all, with Luther H. Evans,
former librarian of Congress; Edward G. Freehafer, director of
the New York Public Library; and L. Quincy Mumford, the current librarian of Congress, representing the United States.
Former librarians of the United Nations Library—Rubens Borba
de Moraes, Carl H. Milam, S. Hartz Rasmussen, and Albert
C. Gerould—were also present. The four library building consultants and librarians from the United Nations Library in
Geneva, the library of the Organization of American States, the
library of the Peace Palace, the International Monetary Fund
Library, and the Libraries Division of UNESCO were guests.[66]

The dedication ceremonies and the two-day symposium
which followed, although filled with elaborate language and
ambitious ideas, are described in some detail for they reflect the
somber and official character of the proceedings. U Thant,
the acting secretary-general of the United Nations, dedicated
the library to Dag Hammarskjöld "not as a monument but as a
centre of research and learning inspired by his zest for knowledge and his earnest search for truth."[67]

The dedication was followed by an address by Mongi Slim of
Tunisia, president of the General Assembly, who compared the
United Nations Library to the great library at Alexandria to
which scholars from all over the world flocked to examine the
manuscripts which had been collected there. President Slim
spoke of this as the vision Mr. Hammarskjöld had of the United
Nations Library:

> a storehouse of excellent collections in the fields of its
> specialization acquired through careful selection by its staff

which, together with the pleasant facilities for users, would attract scholars from all over the world to engage in the pure research which gives support to our common search for practical solutions in the cause of peace.[68]

Representing the foundations which had done so much for the United Nations Library were two other people sitting on the rostrum that day, Henry T. Heald, the president of the Ford Foundation, and Ernest A. Gross, the president of the Woodrow Wilson Foundation. Mr. Heald spoke of the basic purpose of the Ford Foundation as being that of advancing human welfare, and he added, "The creation of a new library with the same basic purpose is an appropriate expression of our ideal and fulfilment of our mutual purpose."[69] Mr. Gross perceived "it an honour appropriate to the memory of two of the great navigators of international statecraft that their names should be joined in the meeting place of their common aspirations – the Woodrow Wilson Reading Room in the Dag Hammarskjöld Library."[70]

The dedication was preceded by a luncheon given in honor of the Board of Trustees of the Ford Foundation and was followed by a two-day symposium. At the luncheon there were gracious speeches by U Thant and John J. McCloy, chairman of the board of the Ford Foundation. Then, Andrew W. Cordier, under-secretary for General Assembly and Related Affairs introduced two groups of four persons each who had contributed to the final result. The first group consisted of the library consultants: Douglas W. Bryant, Verner W. Clapp, Dr. Frank B. Rogers, and Frederick H. Wagman. These men had been commissioned by the Ford Foundation in 1959 to advise on the project. The other group of four consisted of Michael Harris, the architect; James Murphy, representative of George A. Fuller and Company; Esme Van Name, the United Nation's own building engineer; and Joseph Groesbeck, deputy director of the United Nations Library, who had supervised a great deal of the library planning.[71] After the dedication there were tours of the library from 4:00 to 7:00 P.M. and a reception in the library's penthouse from 5:00 to 7:30.

The library symposium was held on Friday and Saturday following the dedication. Some thirty leading librarians from as many countries had been personally invited by Mr. Hammarskjöld, and they were joined by approximately eighty other librarians from the United States who had been invited by the United Nations librarian, Dr. Stummvoll. The theme of the morning meeting on Friday was "The Development of the United Nations Library." Mr. Andrew W. Cordier served as chairman. After a tribute to the memory of Dag Hammarskjöld given by Dr. Uno Willers, director of the Kungliga Biblioteket, Stockholm; papers were delivered by Verner W. Clapp, Frederick H. Wagman, Douglas W. Bryant, and Michael Harris. The morning session was followed by a luncheon given by the acting secretary-general in honor of the guest librarians. The theme of the afternoon session was "The Role of the United Nations Library," with Sir Frank Francis, director and principal librarian of the British Museum, acting as chairman. Dr. Frank B. Rogers, Dr. Víctor Belaúnde, Dr. Waldo Chamberlin, and Dr. A. C. Breycha-Vauthier delivered papers. Saturday morning's sessions, chaired by Dr. Abdel Moneim M. Omar, director-general of the Egyptian Library in Cairo, had the theme "The United Nations Library and the Promotion of Research in Its Fields of Specialization." Papers were delivered by Judge Philip C. Jessup, B. S. Kesavan, Kalu Okorie, Harald L. Tveterås, and Dr. J. Lasso de la Vega, representing the International Court of Justice, the National Library in Calcutta, the Regional Central Library at Enugu, Nigeria, the Universitetsbiblioteket of Oslo, and the University of Madrid respectively.[72]

In the concluding discussion accolades were generously distributed. Mr. Milam, in speaking for the past directors, remarked:

> In whatever may be said about the success of the United Nations Library in its few years of history, we ex-librarians may be inclined to think that we deserve some credit, but I am sure we would be the first to acknowledge that dozens of persons have participated in the progress of the United Nations Library, not the least of whom were the consultants, the Mr. Clapps, the various other people, the Advisory Committee that met in 1948, and the dedicated and devoted, sympathetic attention that we have had from the officers of the United Nations.[73]

Mr. Clapp concluded by giving a tribute to Andrew W. Cordier:

84

I have been in and out of the United Nations Library now for some fifteen or more years. I find borne in on me in this experience what I have had borne in on me in other experiences, namely, when you seek to trace administrative management, you usually come across the trail of a man. And so it is here in the case of the United Nations and its Library.

In my remarks yesterday I attempted to describe the contribution that Mr. Carl Milam had made to the organization, functioning and continuing direction of the Library. We have during the past days heard a great deal, and it is not too much, of the great contribution which Mr. Hammarskjöld himself has made to the planning, the design, the preparation, and the *élan* with which the Dag Hammarskjöld Library is now launched.

Nevertheless, there is another trail here, and I would like to emphasize it in our closing minutes. Ever since my first introduction through my ex-chief, Dr. Evans, into the affairs of the United Nations Library, I have seen that trail, and I have seen a shadow cast: in the original decisions regarding the Library and its place in the Organization, in the employment of Mr. Milam, in the successful effort to get a library policy through the Assembly, in the decisions regarding the abandonment of the plans proposed by the librarians for a library building of the United Nations to be associated with the Secretariat Building in 1947, and in the deferment of it until a later time when the Plaza could be completed.

I have seen that shadow over the preparation of plans way back in 1951 when beautiful plans were drawn up —not quite as beautiful as those which have since been adopted in 1961—over the continuous pressure to complete the site, to obtain the funds for it, to put everything in order. And finally—though I am being very brief and I am not trying to give an administrative history of the Organization—over the plans and preparations for the present symposium.

I find the shadow of one man cast across all these trails. It is the shadow of Andrew Cordier. I think when the Library is opened for business his shadow will be found lying on the portico! And I hope it may lie there forever in association with the name of his revered chief, Dag Hammarskjöld.[74]

Mr. Cordier graciously accepted these remarks and declared

with great reluctance that the symposium had been completed.

That the symposium was a success was attested to not only by the excellent press coverage but also by the many letters of appreciation which were received by the library after the symposium was over. Arthur E. Gropp, librarian of the Columbus Memorial Library of the Pan American Union, wrote expressing his immense pleasure and satisfaction in being privileged to participate in the dedication. He added, "I believe the Dag Hammarskjöld Library should be more than a service agency within its own organization; it should become a stimulant, a catalyst as it were, to promote not only the development of libraries along international levels but also to lead in the formation of thinking internationally, through its services to other libraries and organizations."[75]

Dr. C. Wormann, director of the Jewish National and University Library, was also deeply impressed by the dedication ceremonies and the symposium. He expressed his readiness to give the United Nations Library his full help and cooperation.[76]

But Mr. Sweetser's letter was perhaps the most touching since he had been closely involved not only with the United Nations Library but also with the League of Nations Library in Geneva. After expressing his deepest appreciation for being included in the dedication ceremonies, he continued,

> let me congratulate you again on a masterful job of planning and organization.
>
> The first flush of this came over me as a [sic] realized that the regular work of the UN was being put aside for the moment in order that the opening ceremony could be held in greatest dignity in General Assembly's own meeting-room. . . .
>
> The Library building itself surpassed all my anticipations for beauty, grace, calm and, I should imagine, efficiency. Mr. Hammarskjöld had written in his original letter that it was to contain a "Woodrow Wilson Reading Room," which again was a most delicate touch, and that, in his judgment, that room was the most beautiful in the building. Careful though I knew he always was as to the precision of his language, the room surpassed greatly anything that I had imagined; it is, in fact, a jewel and by far the most effective memorial that I know to the man who more than any other laid the foundations of the United Nations as they stand

today. . . . I was even more struck by the Catalogue running the length of the opposite wall. Here is illustrated without words or fanfare the continuity of the League and the UN which is so often forgotten. The long line of drawers begins with the League documents, which, with their 26 years of records, occupy a good part of it; where they end the UN documents begin—with 16 years so far and all posterity ahead. How many times, by how many people, did I hear the composite expression: "This collection of League of Nations and United Nations Documents." This is as it should be; history is being gently righted. . . .

To me this whole event spells the welding together of a number of kindred activities which at times have seemed strangely isolated from each other and even antagonistic. I like to see the New York Library of the UN as a companion to the Geneva Library of the League, now also the UN; to see the central catalogue room in it dedicated to Woodrow Wilson who largely founded the League and laid the groundwork for Hammarskjöld's great extension of the United Nations; to feel, in effect together in the continuing flow of history, as they should be . . . and that, too, very largely through American foresight and generosity. And if that has been done, it is you who have the great credit, first in fighting ceaselessly to inspire the Ford Foundation to its most generous action, and second, in organizing the Dedication ceremonies in what I repeat from above seems to me to have been a truly masterful way. A thousand thanks to you again for inviting me to be present and to see what had to be seen to be fully appreciated.[77]

This was an appropriate tribute to an event which was a fitting denouement to years of tremendous efforts by many people, and a symbolic prologue to a new era in the library's history. The growth of the United Nations Library from its conception in a humble janitor's closet to its renaissance in the marble and glass edifice it now occupies is a significant chapter in the annals of international librarianship. A library, however, is not only building and people, but events. The events of the years preceding the dedication shaped the library's development and its future. The next chapters will describe some of those events.

chapter 4

Development of policy

General policies

Prior to the move from Hunter College to Lake Success, the librarian was guided solely by a few principles and instructions drawn up by David Vaughan, the director of the Department of Conference and General Services. The most important of the five guidelines were numbers three and four:

3. After the completion of the move to the Sperry Building [at Lake Success], there will be only one library. Departments will be entitled to keep a few books of reference, but these will be ordered through the Librarian and kept in the department only on his authority.
4. Until the move has been completed, there will be no bulk buying of books whatsoever. Departments which are in need of a particular work of reference will order it through the Librarian but will limit these orders to a strict minimum.[1]

It was not until François Stefanini became the first director of the Bureau of Technical Services with the library a division reporting directly to him; and not until Arkady Sobolev, the assistant secretary-general for Security Council Affairs, brought Trygve Lie, the secretary-general, into the library, that more definite policies were outlined and conditions began to improve.[2]

After this visit, on 26 August 1946, the secretary-general sent to Mr. Pelt, the assistant secretary-general for Conference and General Services, a two-page, six-point memorandum outlining the library policy. The gist of the memorandum was that there was to be a centralized library facility in the Department of Conference and General Services, but that departmental libraries could be established if there was any considerable physical distance between a department and the central library.[3] This document is notable not for its commissions but for its omissions. There is no statement on the desirable size of the collection, no policy on types of materials to be acquired, no statement about which groups of patrons should be served, and no statement about interlibrary cooperation. And these were the very policy problems which became the bane of the library's existence during its early years. The memorandum was passed on to Mr. Stefanini with a handwritten note that these guidelines should be used in the establishment of the library.[4]

As a result of these memoranda, Mr. Rasmussen drew up a plan for the development of the library. This plan, after passing through several drafts, finally became the "General Plan for the United Nations Library Service." The first six points are identical with the guidelines outlined by the secretary-general, but the remainder of the twelve-page document is devoted to such items as: collections, personnel, budget, relations with governmental agencies, exchange relations with nongovernmental agencies, a library committee, the problem of physical quarters, relations with the Geneva library, and an organization chart.[5] This document reflected Mr. Rasmussen's experience with the League of Nations. He assumed that the library in New York would provide service to the same extent as the library in Geneva. At this time he estimated that the number of volumes by 1951 would be 150,000.[6]

The prediction of the optimum size of the library in terms of volumes was a matter of a great deal of deliberation during the early years of the library. Three alternatives were posed: (1) Was the library to consist of a small reference collection and depend, through interlibrary loan and contracted services, on the vast resources of the great libraries along the eastern seaboard of the United States? (2) Was the library to consist of a specialized but substantial collection of materials designed to serve the delegates and the staff of the Secretariat? (3) Was the library to become a large research library rivaling that of the New York Public Library and serving the field of international scholarship?

In the discussions relating to the size of the library, this study will refer to these three types of collections as a small reference collection, a specialized but substantial collection, and a large research collection. For ease of analysis the small reference collection will be considered as one of less than 100,000 volumes; the specialized but substantial collection will be one of less than 1,000,000 volumes; and the large research collection will be one of more than 1,000,000 volumes.

During this time the New York Public Library, one of the great research libraries in the United States, was carefully observing the development of the library of the United Nations. On 26 December 1946 the president of the New York Public Library, Morris Hadley, wrote to the secretary-general:

> What I wish to discuss with you is the possibility of working out joint plans for the future. You will presumably require certain library facilities on the East River to meet routine needs, but I feel when it comes to the great reference collection which the United Nations must have available, you will find it advantageous to build on the foundation of our extensive collections, many of which it would be impossible to duplicate, and plan to have your library center at 42nd Street and Fifth Avenue. We already had been working on plans to obtain additional space for our constantly growing collections. If those plans should now be revised to provide for the United Nations as well, this is an ideal time to do so.[7]

The first alternative, that of a small reference collection, was hereby presented to the United Nations. Mr. Rasmussen, in commenting on Mr. Hadley's letter, "recommended accepting the fullest possible use of the New York Public Library's facilities, but warned against planning the main reference center of the United Nations in that Library."[8]

The New York Public Library, although it may have been overzealous in guarding its own reputation, did extend to the United Nations Library the unique privilege of borrowing books from its Reference Department.[9] The Reference Department of the New York Public Library is administered by a private corporation and is financed almost entirely from private gifts and an endowment fund. It is public, however, in the sense that its collections may be consulted by anyone over high school age. Since the collections are designated as reference materials, they are not allowed to leave the building. It was a generous gesture on the part of the Board of Trustees of the New York Public Library to exempt the United Nations Library from this rule. Mr. Hadley's plan, however, was not accepted; because the Secretariat, as well as the librarian, favored the second alternative, that of developing a specialized but substantial collection.

On 27 January 1947, Mr. Rasmussen drew up a "Report on the United Nations Library Service" in response to a request from his supervisor, Mr. Stefanini. In this report he spoke about the "General Plan" of 1946, stating that it was elaborated under instructions regarding size of staff and collections based on the assumption that only a small working reference library of 40,000 volumes was needed. However, at the request of the substantive departments of the Secretariat, the advisory group of experts granted, and the General Assembly approved, an increase in the library's book budget. This threw the plan entirely out of focus. In the new report Mr. Rasmussen estimated, "In order to satisfy the requirements of the Secretariat a fully classified and catalogued collection of some 500,000 volumes is necessary."[10]

On 5 February 1947, Mr. Stefanini wrote an expanded version of this report and a supplement to it. He agreed with Mr. Rasmussen that the Secretariat needed a library of some 500,000 volumes.[11] In the supplementary report Mr. Stefanini referred again to the exchange of letters between Mr. Hadley and the acting secretary-general. He also referred to a conference with Ralph Beals, the director of the New York Public Library. Mr. Beals offered to the United Nations the complete cooperation of the New York Public Library. He wished, however, to avoid overlapping and duplication of resources in both the New York Public Library and the future permanent library of the United Nations. Mr. Beals was worried about the possibility that the United Nations would establish a large research library rivaling the public library. "Mr. Beals made it clear that by large he did not mean a library like the League Library in Geneva, which has been built for 1,000,000 volumes, but a library of several million volumes approaching the size and conception of their own library."[12] Mr. Stefanini replied that his department had requested a library of 1,000,000 volumes, equal in size to the optimum capacity of the Geneva library, but he went on to report that "the choice would lie between two extremes: i.e., between a limited working library and an all-comprehensive worldwide conception."[13] After much discussion about the one extreme of 40,000 volumes and the other extreme of several million volumes, the middle course was finally adopted by the United Nations.

Library policy was also discussed by the Permanent Advisory Library Committee at several of its meetings in 1947. At its first meeting on 3 March 1947, Mr. Pelt discussed the necessity of establishing a permanent library policy. He mentioned two alternatives corresponding to alternatives one and three mentioned previously which should be considered:

1. that the United Nations Library be conceived as a working library for the Secretariat and the Delegations, or
2. that the Library be considered as one of the general libraries of the world on the lines of that of the Library of Congress.[14]

He again referred to the building of a library to hold 1,000,000 volumes, which was the optimum size of the United Nations Library in Geneva (although the library in Geneva had not yet reached that capacity) and which represented an intermediate solution between the two alternatives suggested by the library committee.

Mr. Shaw in his survey of the library incorrectly concluded:

Since there was no discussion of this policy decision at this meeting, it is apparent that the alternative accepted, in default of discussion or any decision to the contrary, was that the United Nations attempt to build up one of the great general libraries of the world.[15]

Mr. Rasmussen, however, in discussing the events of this meeting at a later time said:

While it is correct that this statement was made in the

Committee [the statement made by Mr. Pelt on 3 March 1947], I want to say that I never heard a single individual, inside or outside the United Nations, argue for the latter alternative. When that type of library was mentioned in the discussions, it was to hold up a contrast to the type of library the Secretariat wanted. As you will see from the records, it was never seriously considered by anybody in the Secretariat.[16]

What the officials of the United Nations wanted was a library similar to the one in Geneva; it would be beneath the dignity of the United Nations to accept anything less. Before the United Nations Library could achieve its present level of service, many surveys, both internal and external, were conducted by various experts.

The first survey was requested as a result of the discussions at the 17 March and 31 March 1947 meetings of the Permanent Advisory Library Committee. The question of size was being debated again. Was the library to be a mere reference library, or was it to be a library of worldwide scope? The figure one million volumes was again mentioned. At the 17 March meeting Mr. Gerould reported that Carl Milam of the American Library Association had offered his assistance to the United Nations Library in the capacity of a consultant.[17] At the 31 March meeting a decision became imperative because of Mr. Pelt's impending meeting with the planning staff for the new headquarters building.

The planning staff had in mind a highly technical, small reference library and nothing more; they had not envisaged a large library consisting of one million volumes. The planning director had thought mainly of the needs of the delegations and not of the Secretariat. Because of the need for determining at this time the approximate size of the library for the planning staff, Mr. Pelt decided to cable Mr. Breycha-Vauthier of the United Nations Library in Geneva, asking him to come to New York to assist in settling the matter.[18] He also invited three American librarians to join Mr. Breycha-Vauthier: Ralph A. Beals, director of the New York Public Library; Luther H. Evans, librarian of Congress; and Carl H. Milam, executive secretary of the American Library Association. It might be suggested that Mr. Beals had some conflict of interests in serving with this group, since he did not wish to see the United Nations Library become a large research library. The inclusion of librarians from other countries would have been a welcome addition to this first survey group.

The four men conducted their survey at Lake Success on 22 and 23 April 1947 and met with the library committee on 22 April at 3:00 P.M., with Mr. Pelt presiding. Two members of the Planning Committee for the permanent site of the headquarters of the United Nations were also present. The purpose of the meeting was to give the departmental representatives an opportunity to present a statement on each of the department's views, and to give the consultants an opportunity to present their recommendations. Each member of the library committee made a statement, but the consensus of the group as expressed by the representative of the Security Council Department was that a substantial library was envisioned with a collection covering all the subjects referred to by the Charter as well as "the local literature of a country, including all the political literature, much historical literature and many books (such as memoirs) which would be regarded perhaps as purely literary books."[19] Abraham Feller, the representative from the Legal Department, commented, "We are not in a position to build a great world library, but should have as good a library covering our fields of endeavor as you would find in a first-class university —in the million-volume class."[20]

The consultants immediately pointed out the impossibility of realizing in a short time a library meeting the ideals expressed by the departmental representatives. Mr. Beals argued that, in order to fulfill all of the conditions presented by the representatives, a library of five to seven million volumes would be needed; but Mr. Breycha-Vauthier replied that the library in Geneva operated with only one-third of a million volumes, although the capacity of the Geneva library was one million volumes.[21] The League of Nations Library in Geneva was constantly brought up in these and other discussions as the library to emulate.

Mr. Milam reiterated what Mr. Evans had said earlier in the meeting, "that the latest conception of a library is that of a service agency; however, the conception of collection and preservation hangs on. The U.N. Library, it would seem, should be an effective working service agency."[22] Later, in a letter to

John E. Burchard, director of libraries at the Massachusetts Institute of Technology, he said, "Apparently we are all going to be needed to keep U.N. from trying to develop a huge research library."[23] However, after he had become director of the United Nations Library, he had a change of mind and reported that "it will be obvious to anyone who thinks about the matter that the needs of the Secretariat, Delegations and Commissions cannot be met except by a fairly substantial collection."[24] There seemed to be no agreement on whether this substantial collection was to be 100,000, 500,000, or 1,000,000 volumes.

At the 22 April meeting the librarian, Mr. Rasmussen, pointed out that the dimension of time must be included in any estimate of the size of the library. He said, "The Secretariat can probably be satisfied at the present time with a collection of half a million volumes"; with a "total of one million volumes at the end of twenty years."[25] Although Mr. Milam did not disagree with the United Nations librarian on his figures, he felt that numbers could not just be fabricated and suggested another survey to determine a more realistic figure. Mr. Pelt also was of the opinion that a calculated figure could be more easily justified to the budget committee.

An official report of the first survey was submitted by the four consultants — Breycha-Vauthier, Beals, Evans, and Milam. They made twelve recommendations, the most important of which were the following:

> I. The Library Consultants believe that the United Nations must have a library service of the most advanced type, specially developed to meet the particular needs of the Secretariat, organs of the United Nations, the Delegations and the Specialized Agencies.
> II. They believe that the emphasis should be on reference, bibliographical and documentation services, including detailed analysis of many important publications, rather than on accumulation and preservation of great stocks of books.[26]

They did not specify a certain number of volumes for the library, but recommended that "a competent librarian be engaged to make a quick estimate of the quantities of materials which will probably be needed" and that "a competent library expert be engaged immediately to translate the requirements of the library into a building program and a list of space requirements."[27]

Four surveys followed this original survey before an official library policy was finally drawn up. All of the surveys of the United Nations Library were conducted by Americans with the exception of the first one, in which Mr. Breycha-Vauthier participated, and the fifth one, which was the meeting of the International Advisory Committee of Library Experts in which librarians from many parts of the world participated.

Verner W. Clapp, perhaps on the recommendation of Mr. Evans, was asked to conduct the second survey of the United Nations Library—to make an estimate of the quantities of materials required by the library. Mr. Clapp at this time was the chief assistant librarian of Congress. He began his library career with a summer job at the Library of Congress in 1922, immediately after his graduation from Trinity College, and returned there in the summer of 1923 for a permanent position. He was with the Library of Congress for thirty-three years, where he served in several positions: as a member of the reference staff, as supervisor of the work of the division for the blind, and as director of the Acquisitions Department. In 1956 he resigned to become the first president of the Council on Library Resources. It was while he was at the Library of Congress that he was appointed to organize the conference library at San Francisco and was requested to direct his many surveys of the United Nations Library. Because of his interest in and consultative work for the library, he has become known as the unofficial adviser to the United Nations Library.

Mr. Clapp visited the library on 29–30 April and 1 May 1947 and conducted a series of interviews with a representative group of users of the library and with members of the Secretariat staff. The results of his survey were sent to Mr. Pelt on 3 May 1947.[28] He referred to the report submitted by the previous consultants and assumed that the group charged with the responsibility for planning the library had accepted the recommendations of that report. That assumption was essentially correct. The purpose of Mr. Clapp's survey was to make a quick estimate of the amount of material needed in each important subject field and geographical area.

96

Mr. Clapp's report comprised eighteen statements, of which the following were the most important: (1) The library of the League of Nations at Geneva was held up as a prototype of the type of library desired by those members of the Secretariat who had served in Geneva and by the members of the Secretariat responsible for the development of the library in New York; (2) although the experience of the League Library should be drawn upon in planning the new library, other considerations must be taken into account: the more favorable location in New York City in the midst of large research collections, a considerably larger Secretariat staff, expanded interests of the United Nations, and the proliferation of publications bearing on the work of the United Nations; (3) the United Nations Library should explore the possibilities of a union list or catalog of the holdings of libraries in the New York area of materials relating to the interests of the United Nations, thus facilitating interlibrary borrowing for books in little demand; and (4) a general reference collection should be acquired with the number of volumes to reach 300,000 in from six to twelve years, 500,000 volumes in from ten to twenty years, and 1,000,000 volumes in from nineteen to thirty-eight years, or 1,500,000 volumes (if the collections of the specialized agencies were added to the United Nations Library).[29]

The third survey of the United Nations Library was conducted by John E. Burchard, director of libraries of the Massachusetts Institute of Technology. He was charged with the problem of converting the general space requirements into specific terms by allocating staff and space on a square-foot basis for each of the functions of the library, i.e., order work, processing, storage, reference services, study rooms, and special rooms. He submitted his report to Mr. Pelt in a letter, and because he questioned the premise that the United Nations Library would ultimately reach 1,500,000 volumes, he drew up two plans: proposal A—for the ultimate storage of 1,500,000 volumes, and proposal B—for the ultimate storage of 500,000 volumes, which is the plan that he recommended.[30]

The two reports by Clapp and Burchard were studied by members of the Permanent Advisory Library Committee and were discussed by them at their 19 May meeting. The committee was disturbed because it felt that the reports as they were submitted contrasted with statements made by these gentle-men when they were in New York.[31] Mr. Clapp had expressed the opinion originally that a 1,500,000-volume collection ap-peared a reasonable estimate. Actually, as can be seen from his recommendation, he did propose this figure, but he argued that it would not be reached for nineteen to thirty-eight years. The initial figure that he recommended was much lower. There was quite a bit of discussion about the reports by the various mem-bers of the committee, and all members present agreed that the initial figure of 300,000 expressed by Mr. Clapp and the figure of 500,000 expressed by Mr. Burchard were far too low. Mr. Pelt suggested that the committee agree to a figure of 1,000,000 volumes, provided expansion was possible.[32] Mr. Rasmussen was requested to draft a statement which would

> explain briefly the extent of the procedure which the Committee has followed; the fact that the Secretariat's figure of one and one-half million volumes had first been considered reasonable by the two experts; that later the written reports had given a lower figure to which the Com-mittee did not agree because of (1) the difficulties involved in borrowing books, (2) the lack of space for the libraries of the specialized agencies and gifts, and (3) by relying on other libraries the United Nations Library will never be a free agency. It is not proposed to build a universal library but one that is complete in the fields of our work.[33]

It seems evident that the library committee was not fully aware of the time and money it would take to build up a collec-tion of one million volumes and the staff that would be neces-sary to select and arrange all this material. Even with an unlim-ited budget, it would take all of the twenty years envisioned by Mr. Clapp before the United Nations could possibly have such a collection. But the committee members were concerned with the status of the library, and they were in complete agreement that it should be no less than the League of Nations Library had been. At the next meeting it was reported that the commit-tee's recommendations had been sent to the Planning Commit-tee and Mr. Price.[34]

But the question of size was still not to be settled. In July 1947 the Bureau of Administrative Management and Budget was commissioned to "undertake a management survey of all activities of the Secretariat for the purpose of submitting to the Secretary-General recommendations designed to achieve the maximum efficiency."[35] The assistant secretary-general for Administrative and Financial Services (Byron Price) was appointed to review the survey recommendations before presenting them to the secretary-general. Ralph R. Shaw was asked to conduct that part of the survey dealing with library services. Mr. Shaw received his initial library education at Columbia University School of Library Service and received a Ph.D. in library science from the University of Chicago in 1950. At the time of the survey he was director of the United States Department of Agriculture Library.

In his 107-page report, released on 12 September 1947, Mr. Shaw described the library as inefficient. There were, however, excuses for the lack of good library service, and these were mentioned in the survey: the newness of the organization, frequent changes in physical quarters, a confusion of function between the library and the Reference Center in the Department of Public Information, need for time to build up a large collection, lack of definite policies, and difficulties in recruiting personnel. Mr. Shaw concluded, however, that

> even after liberal allowance is made for these factors, it appears that the present library operation is a model of inefficiency, waste, and blundering; that time and more money will not cure all its ills; and that fundamental recasting of the operation and its reorientation to sound management and a philosophy of dynamic service are essential.[36]

The accuracy of his allegations of inefficiency was contested by the librarian, Mr. Rasmussen, and questioned by others. Mr. Shaw did, however, make some proposals and recommendations which are worth considering. He listed the minimum requirements for library and bibliographical services as the following: (1) the United Nations must have adequate library service to meet its daily needs, (2) the United Nations Library should be responsible for the collection, organization, and indexing of the publications of the United Nations and its affiliated international organizations, and (3) the fundamental philosophy in the operation of the library must be that it is to be a service agency rather than an end in itself and that it should, therefore, stress documentation services and use of available resources rather than building up a large library just for the sake of a large library.[37] The Shaw survey reiterated many of the points brought out in the previous surveys, although two new ideas were presented—the transfer of the library to the Department of Public Information and the dissolution of the Geneva library.

Mr. Shaw divided his recommendations into two phases: what should be done immediately, and what should be done in the future when the library was permanently situated. He recommended that the immediate needs of the library be met by these steps: (1) the transfer and combination of all library and bibliographical services into a single library in the Department of Public Information, (2) the reduction of the budget for 1948 from $919,656 to $300,000 with approximately $100,000 available for contractual services (including both reference and technical services) with the New York Public Library, (3) the employment of the most competent head librarian in the world, (4) the transfer from Geneva to New York of the publications of the various international organizations, and (5) the transfer of the remainder of the Geneva library to UNESCO or to some other organization.[38]

For the future he recommended: (1) the establishment of a branch of the New York Public Library in a suitable location in the United Nations building, and (2) the continuation of the above arrangements.[39] The idea of housing a branch of the New York Public Library in the United Nations building complex was in direct opposition to the Hadley proposal which recommended that the United Nations Library be housed in the New York Public Library. Neither plan came to fruition.

In terms of the size of the collection, Mr. Shaw made three varying statements:

> If we assume that the library should keep publications used as much as four times a year, a maximum book collection of 125,000 would meet all the conceivable requirements of the Secretariat. . . .[40]

> If allowance is made for the large number of books which will be used ten, twenty, or even fifty times a year, it be-

comes obvious that instead of 125,000 volumes, a collection of not more than 50,000 to 75,000 volumes, with the books carefully selected in terms of actually current needs, would satisfy the day-to-day requirements of the Secretariat.[41]

It appears further that if books no longer needed constantly . . . be discarded from the collection . . . then the United Nations will never need a general bookstock of more than 100,000 to 150,000 volumes in order to meet the ninety percent of its working needs which can feasibly be met from its own collections.[42]

These figures were, of course, at odds with the one million volumes recommended by the Permanent Advisory Library Committee.

Mr. Rasmussen sent two memoranda to his supervisor containing detailed comments on the management survey, one dated 10 October and one dated 13 October 1947. Because he was allowed to keep the report for one night only, Mr. Rasmussen's first memorandum was "therefore concerned only with a few of the numerous absurdities, unfounded accusations, distorted statements, and glaring omissions with which the report abounds."[43] He was then allowed to keep the survey over the weekend and submitted the second memorandum which he did not have time to finish because he had to return the report.[44] His two memoranda are well documented and include appendices from other library staff members refuting many of Mr. Shaw's statements and statistics.

Although Mr. Milam, who was at that time serving as a consultant to the library, stated that the management survey report had not been approved as a whole,[45] the United Nations Fifth Committee on Administrative and Budgetary Questions did take cognizance of Mr. Shaw's recommendations. The *Report on the Management Survey on United Nations Headquarters* presented the most outstanding recommendations of the entire survey. Those relating to the library were as follows:

In addition to the recommendation that the Library be transferred to the Department of Public Information, operating policies are suggested covering the following aspects:

1. Major use be made of the New York Public Library as the central reference source under a contractual arrangement.
2. The Library be divided into sections, each under an Assistant Librarian who will be an expert in a particular range of subject matter.
3. Intensive indexing of the publications of the United Nations, Specialized Agencies and other research bodies be initiated so that the Library will constitute a basic research service.
4. Purchase of books be centralized.[46]

Mr. Milam, in commenting on the survey, reported that he found no evidence of gross inefficiency in the library. He did find a lack of coordination and team work; but he felt that this was due to understandable factors, such as the fact that the library policy had been undetermined, that authority had been divided and uncertain, that there had been no assurance of security, and that the physical arrangements for the library had been continually upset.[47] In his diary Mr. Milam noted: "I have finished reading Shaw's management study of UN L. services. It is full of useful information and suggestion. But I must and will be on my guard, knowing how unreliable [it might be]."[48]

Only three recommendations of the survey were executed. The library was transferred to the Department of Public Information in January 1948. In May 1948, Mr. Milam became the director of the United Nations Libraries. On 16 December 1948 a contract was signed by the United Nations and the New York Public Library. The New York Public Library agreed to provide the following services: "requests for specific information, the preparation of bibliographies, searching for bibliographical information, preparation of reports, and abstracts on specific subjects or other similar undertakings."[49] The term of the contract was for one year from 1 January to 31 December 1949; and $2,500 was advanced to the New York Public Library for the payment of these services. The contract did not include any provisions for the performance of technical services. Although this contract did not come up to the expectations of Mr. Shaw, either in the type of service or in the amount of the fees, it has provided a valuable service for the United Nations Library. It has been renewed annually since that time. A similar contract with the Library of Congress was executed, but it has not been continued.

Another factor of more pragmatic importance in September 1947 was the budget cut that went into effect. The amount of money appropriated for the new buildings on the headquarters site had been slashed from $85,000,000 to $65,000,000. This, perhaps more than the recommendations of the surveys, meant that the dream of a separate library building with a substantial collection of materials had to be postponed for the time being.

The Permanent Advisory Library Committee, upon hearing that the separate library building was to be sacrificed in the new headquarters plan, made an effort, after solemn deliberations on 9 September and 12 September 1947, to save the library by adhering to its original conception of a collection of one million volumes. At the meeting of September 12 the departmental representatives explicated the viewpoints of their respective assistant secretaries-general. With the exception of Mr. Cohen and Mr. Price, the feeling of the assistant secretaries-general was that the original prospectus, the library of one million volumes, should continue to be advocated.[50] Since Mr. Cohen, the assistant secretary-general of the Department of Public Information, was soon to be in charge of library services, his dissenting opinion is important:

> Mr. Cohen's opinion is that the solution of the library problem should be the establishment in the Secretariat area of a documentation service with a reduced working library, the collection of which would not exceed about 200,000 volumes. This collection would be periodically renewed and dead material weeded out.
>
> Standing arrangements with American libraries, general and special, would provide, by the most rapid means, for documentation needed for current research purposes.
>
> A union catalogue of all the resources of the main American libraries in the field of politics, international law, economics, etc., would be progressively established in the library.
>
> This solution would relieve the library of a heavy budgetary burden for purchase of books and for the staff, and would enable the library to concentrate its main effort on the development of its bibliographical, documentary, and reference activities.[51]

103

The views of the library committee were sent to the secretary-general in a memorandum written by Mr. Pelt, and a copy was also sent to Mr. Cohen. Mr. Cohen's reply seems to have settled the matter for some time to come:

> I am afraid that to maintain the primitive policy [a library of one million volumes] on the library would mean no library at all for some time to come.
>
> Besides, a documentation and reference center, which is what the Organization really needs would meet every requirement. Once it has operated well, over a period of let us say five years, it would be time to consider any actual increases in books and staff, and the consequent need for additional space.[52]

Four surveys had been completed, and a new librarian, known to be in agreement with Mr. Cohen's views, had been employed. Before Mr. Milam assumed his duties on a permanent basis, he came to the United Nations in March 1948 as a consultant; and one of the items discussed at that time was general library policy.

In a written report to the members of the library staff, he outlined a preliminary policy statement in which emphasis was to be on service, not on accumulation of a large stock of books; service was to be primarily for the official family, but the needs of the press and scholars were to be recognized; and materials most relevant and urgent were to be obtained and processed first.[53] In his report to Mr. Cohen, Mr. Milam noted that he had been impressed by three things in the library after his two-day visit: (1) the friendly, thoughtful and intelligent helpfulness of everyone in the Department of Public Information, (2) the widespread interest in the library throughout the Secretariat, and (3) the deplorable inadequacy of the library.[54] However, he was optimistic and felt that a good library service could be developed. He discussed this matter with many of the top officials of the Secretariat, and the result of his inquiries was epitomized by one assistant secretary-general in these words: "We want the best reference and documentation service in the world, but we don't want to duplicate the New York Public Library."[55]

Before the final library policy was adopted, advice was sought once more from outside the United Nations family. This time a conference was called, and seven librarians of worldwide renown were invited to convene in Lake Success on 2 August for a series of meetings. The committee was composed of the following members: Verner W. Clapp (chief assistant librarian of Congress, United States of America) substituting for Luther H. Evans, librarian of Congress, who was unable to attend because of illness; Frank C. Francis (keeper of the Department of Printed Books, British Museum, United Kingdom); Miss Yvonne Oddon (Musée de l'Homme, France) representing Julien Cain, director of the Bibliothèque Nationale; Abdel Moneim M. Omar (deputy-general of the Egyptian National Library, Egypt); S. R. Ranganathan (professor of library science, Delhi University, India); Jorge Ugarte Vial (director of the Bibliotéca del Congreso Nacional, Chile), substituting for Jorge Basadre, director of the Department of Cultural Affairs, Pan American Union, who was unable to attend because of illness; and Kwang Tsing Wu (formerly of the National Library of Peiping, China, but at the time of this conference, chief cataloger of the Chinese Section of the Division of Orientalia of the Library of Congress).[56]

Frank C. Francis was elected chairman and Verner W. Clapp, the vice-chairman. Three subcommittees were formed: one on general library policy, one on the distribution and use of United Nations documents and departmental publications, and one on the relationship of the United Nations Library to the Geneva library and the libraries of the specialized agencies. The last subcommittee was also charged with the responsibility of considering internships, fellowships, and exchanges. Seven plenary sessions were held on 2–5 August 1948. Subcommittee meetings were held on 6–7 August and two final plenary sessions were held on 9 August. Working papers were prepared for each of these subcommittees which summarized the recommendations of the previous surveys, the views of the Permanent Advisory Library Committee, and other important letters and memoranda. In the preamble to the report of the committee, the purpose of the meetings was set forth:

> The Committee considered at length the kinds of library service required by the United Nations, and the methods by which such service can be most effectively provided. The Committee is strongly of the opinion that the provision

105

of an adequate library service is essential to the proper functioning of the Secretariat and of the other organs of the United Nations, and thus to the effectiveness of the Organization as a whole. Without such service the Organization would lack effective means for securing the benefits of work already done and of information already assembled.[57]

The committee made fifty-seven recommendations, many of which were later to be incorporated into the official library policy. Some of these recommendations will be discussed in other sections of this study. The following recommendations are most germane to the development of general library policy:

12. The primary function of the United Nations Library is to enable the Secretariat, delegations, and other official groups to obtain with the greatest possible efficiency, speed and convenience, the library materials and information needed in the execution of their responsibilities.

14. These services should be based on a compact collection of library materials systematically selected, organized and administered. They should be effected in the following ways; through direct access, reading-room service, reference and informational services, services through departmental collections, bibliographical services including accession lists, subject lists, abstracts and the preparation of background material.

19. In the formation of the collections, the emphasis should be on service, not on accumulation and preservation; on immediate not ultimately potential usefulness. No attempt should be made to assemble comprehensive collections, and the Library must continuously discard material which is no longer useful to it. The Library must expect to be balanced only in terms of United Nations interests.

20. In one field the Library should be complete, namely, in the publications of the United Nations and of its antecedent and related organizations. The Library should also possess all important publications concerning these organizations. In all other fields, the selection of material to be acquired should be guided (1) by its usefulness

to the United Nations, and (2) by the extent to which it is satisfactorily available elsewhere.[58]

Mr. Ranganathan, the noted librarian from India, was particularly concerned about the recommendation dealing with contract services, because he felt that it impinged on his second law of library science, "Every Reader His Book." He was so moved as to make a speech at the time of the discussion on this point:

> The consideration for the contractual service will have to be monetary. But it is essential that no occasion should be created for any library to give its service to any individual — personal or corporate — on the basis of "so much money for so much service." The Anglo-American world for example has succeeded after a century's arduous thinking and living in this matter in setting up the principle that service of a library should be free. This, I regard as the Library Magna Carta, for which the world is indebted to Anglo-American countries. . . . This Committee must be extremely on the alert to see that no element in the policy it recommends puts the unique UN Library in a position that may be interpreted as helping perpetuation of that gravitation [the old tradition of inserting a money sieve between the resources of a library and its potential customers], directly or obliquely, and knowingly or unknowingly. . . . I would appeal to this Committee of Library Experts to resist outright whenever the "service for payment" spirit begins to appear among libraries in an apparently innocent form.[59]

Although the committee met in August 1948, the basic document of library policy for the United Nations Library was not adopted until 21 September 1949. The Fifth Committee of the General Assembly of the United Nations, which deals with administrative and budgetary questions, at its 136th meeting requested the secretary-general to submit a special report on library policy for consideration by the General Assembly.[60] A draft of this policy, prepared by Mr. Milam in April 1949, consisted of two parts: the first part devoted to library policy and the second part devoted to library organization. Not only were the recommendations of the International Advisory Committee of Library Experts taken into consideration in writing this draft, but two reports of the Advisory Committee on Administrative and Budgetary Questions were also consulted.[61] The same theme of a compact collection of library materials was reiterated in this draft, but was not to be incorporated into the final policy which was issued as a document of the Fifth Committee. This document omitted the word *compact*, so that the sentence regarding library collections read as follows: "These services will be based on a collection of library materials, systematically selected from all countries, organized and administered for easy use."[62] In other respects the policy as adopted followed the recommendations of the International Advisory Committee of Library Experts, including the statement that the emphasis in building up the library collections should be on service and on immediate usefulness rather than on accumulation and preservation.

Although the library policy was issued as an official document of the Fifth Committee, it was never officially approved by the committee at any of its meetings nor was it presented to the General Assembly for approval.

This should have been the final word on the subject and a positive guideline for the library to follow in developing its programs and procedures during the succeeding years, but many other consultants were called in to survey the library, some on general policy and some on specific functions of library services. In fact, there have been so many surveys of the library that Mr. Clapp commented, "Indeed, the United Nations Library is undoubtedly the most 'surveyed' library in the world."[63] Most of these surveys deal with the specific operations of the library, such as acquisitions, cataloging, and documents indexing; and they will be discussed in the chapters covering these subjects. But there was one more general survey of the library in 1952, again directed by Verner Clapp. According to his count of surveys, this was the twenty-first survey of the library.

The Advisory Committee on Administrative and Budgetary Questions in commenting on the budget estimate of the library for 1952 had urged that "a further review should in any case be made of the utilization of staff, both in the main Library and in the departmental branches."[64] Mr. Clapp was employed to conduct this review. He visited the library from 28 April to 3 May

1952 and compiled an 82-page report of his recommendations. The recommendations numbered eighteen, the most pertinent one of which was:

> iv. It is recommended that the statements of Library policy and practice be collected and given the necessary authority.[65]

The report is elaborate, detailed, and extremely favorable. Mr. Reitman, the acting librarian, likened the report to that of a surgeon called in on a case of an acute and severe illness, who after the necessary examination, came to the conclusion that the patient was in perfect health.[66]

Acquisitions policy

The acquisitions policy is linked in many ways to the general policies described in the preceding section, as the size of a collection is an important factor in determining the composition of a library.

In determining the extent of the scope of the collection, Dr. Frank B. Rogers, director of the United States National Library of Medicine, said, "Scope may be defined as the range in breadth of a subject field; in considering matters of scope proper, only subject content is pertinent."[67] To provide books in all subjects subsumed by the Charter plus a representative selection of the world's literature would be impossible if the collection was to be kept compact. In one of the working papers prepared for the International Advisory Committee of Library Experts, the acquisitions policy was outlined in some detail.[68] The gist of this policy is that only those materials of immediate and/or continuing use are to be selected. This policy, still in effect today, means that the library does not generally buy material for historical research, it does not purchase large collections, it screens requests from the Secretariat staff, and it also screens gifts and materials received on exchange. Certain materials of continuing use constitute a core collection. Two acquisitions processes are actually going on at the same time: the selection of the core collection, with the aim of completeness in some subject fields, and selection on the basis of need and permanency of usefulness in other fields. The core collection can be defined as: basic reference books, a complete collection of the publications of the United Nations and the specialized agencies, extensive holdings of the publications of other international organizations in fields of interest to the United Nations, works about the United Nations, official publications and unofficial standard works in the field of international affairs, compilations of national and international law, and governmental and commercially subsidized compilations of statistical materials. In all other categories it is the practice to select carefully rather than to collect exhaustively.

In the fall of 1948, Mr. Milam asked Helen Wessells, on leave from the United States Information Service of the Department of State and acting temporarily as director of the International Relations Office of the American Library Association, to spend five weeks making a survey of all the active and potential programs underway at the United Nations. This survey was designed to serve three purposes: as a guide for evaluating holdings and services, as the basis for the establishment of official library acquisition policies, and as an aid to the planning of future library developments. Her research, which was done on a contractual basis, was conducted at the New York Public Library and at Lake Success.

After examining all of the published United Nations documents, she compiled a list of research projects under way or soon to be started by the United Nations, a list of other special projects, and a list of tasks performed by members of the Secretariat.[69] The compilation was arranged by the names of the various departments of the Secretariat. Each section included a brief summary of the department's responsibilities, a list of its functions and areas of interest, member states and potential members of concern to the department, and bibliographies and publications completed and in preparation. After covering the departments of the Secretariat, she included a list of the United Nations staff by types of occupations, a list of equipment to be serviced, a list of centers for training and proposed training schemes, a list of conferences scheduled, and a list of new commissions and agencies to be established.

This compilation was used by a staff committee of the library in the development of a list of *Subjects of Interest to the United Nations Library.*[70] Prepared only in a preliminary draft for

110

criticism, this list of about 250 subject headings was arranged by broad subject categories, such as: history, political science, international and national law, armaments, atomic energy, trusteeship and non-self-governing territories, economics, transport and communications, social problems, science and technology, geography, and general works. Each broad subject area was divided into smaller categories; for instance, the section on social problems was further divided into these areas of study: demography, human rights, the status of women, social welfare and standards of living, relief and rehabilitation and refugees, housing and town and country planning, education, narcotic drugs, and administration. In developing the list of subject headings, each of the subcategories was further refined by the staff committee, so that the section on human rights included such subjects as: the preparation of an international bill of human rights, freedom of information and of the press, the prevention of discrimination and the protection of minorities, the functions of information groups and local human rights committees, genocide, slavery, the right of asylum, and the protection of stateless persons. The Wessells report was valuable in that it provided a means for the library staff to evaluate the various projects and tasks being carried on by the United Nations in terms of the support needed from library services. The list of subjects of interest to the United Nations provided a means to survey library holdings in specific subject areas and to plan future acquisition policies.

In determining the coverage of the library collection, Mr. Rogers' definition is again the most succinct: "Coverage . . . may be defined as depth of penetration into a subject field; in matters of coverage, language, form, imprint date, or any other such qualification may be introduced."[71]

The United Nations Library, unlike some public libraries, cannot limit its collection by language or by geographic area since it is a library serving people of all nations. Language dictionaries and national bibliographies are examples of two types of reference books in which the library has to specialize and which it collects in depth. Almost every language is represented in the library for it receives the white papers, official gazettes, ministerial decrees, and many other publications of all the governments of the world. This means that the document is

the most prominent form of publication in the library (table 1).
Exhaustive coverage of the League of Nations documents, the
United Nations documents, and the documents of the special-

TABLE 1

DOCUMENTS AND SERIALS ADDED TO THE UNITED NATIONS LIBRARY, 1952–1967

Year	Documents[a]	Serials[b]	Total
1952	223,956	53,520	277,476
1953	167,706	61,773	229,479
1954	172,838	61,389	234,227
1955	173,239	69,246	242,485
1956	168,979	70,693	239,672
1957	171,967	73,739	245,706
1958	172,588	81,157	253,745
1959	182,321	83,124	265,445
1960	173,422	86,022	259,444
1961	174,596	103,659	278,255
1962	194,538	110,192	304,730
1963	242,450	109,241	351,691
1964	193,434	114,890	308,324
1965	208,341	111,066	319,407
1966	221,363	110,804	332,167
1967	264,762	115,304	380,066

All figures are taken from the *Annual Reports* of the United Nations Library.
Comparable statistics did not appear in the *Reports* until 1952.

[a]Figures for documents include government documents, United Nations documents, specialized agency documents, and League of Nations documents. Official documents are seldom discarded, although many individual documents may be bound together in one volume.

[b]Figures for serials include newspapers and periodicals. For the years 1953 to 1966 they also include yearbooks and continuations, which had previously been counted as new books. Many serials are retained only for specified periods of time, after which they are discarded.

ized agencies is the goal of the library. An analysis of the acquisitions at the United Nations Library in New York (table 2) indicates that only 3.2 percent of the number of pieces or volumes acquired during 1965 consisted of monographs. It is in this area of monographic publications that the library is most

TABLE 2

ANALYSIS OF ACQUISITIONS AT THE
UNITED NATIONS LIBRARY, 1965

Item	Volumes	Pieces	Percentage
Books and pamphlets	10,746		3.2
Periodicals and newspapers		111,066	33.3
Documents		79,975	24.0
Maps		3,101	.9
United Nations documents		97,166	29.2
Specialized agencies publications		31,200	9.4
Total	333,254		100.0

selective (tables 3 and 4). "Thus at a conservative estimate, it may be said that the Library selects annually less than one third of the books known to have been published in the legal, political, economic and social sciences."[72]

The library staff carries on the work of book selection by a systematic examination of current issues of national and trade bibliographies and subject periodicals (the book selection procedure will be discussed in greater detail in the next chapter). They also consult with experts in the Secretariat to determine the library implications of research projects and the desirable scope and nature of subject and area coverage. Of the total number of books acquired each year, the library chooses about 80 to 85 percent, and the remaining 15 to 20 percent are selected by the delegations and Secretariat staff.[73]

Another criterion useful in controlling the degree of coverage

113

TABLE 3

MONOGRAPHS ADDED TO AND WITHDRAWN FROM
THE UNITED NATIONS LIBRARY, 1952–1967

Year	Additions[a]	Withdrawals[b]	Cumulative Total
Prior to 1952			150,600[c]
1952	8,503	3,000	156,103
1953	11,146	7,000	160,249
1954	7,274	1,351	166,172
1955	9,026	1,790	173,408[d]
1956	10,750	1,775	182,383
1957	9,015	1,803	189,595
1958	7,143	2,480	194,258
1959	8,259	5,426	197,091
1960	7,693	10,493	194,291
1961	7,502	1,560	200,233
1962	9,810	2,616	207,427
1963	10,388	3,375	214,440
1964	9,927	3,590	220,777
1965	10,746	4,048	227,475
1966	9,877	2,889	234,463
1967	9,136	4,970	238,629

All figures are taken from the *Annual Reports* of the United Nations Library, which are the only statistics publicly available. Comparable statistics did not appear in the *Reports* until 1952. Mr. Groesbeck, although questioning this approach in compiling the data, states that these figures are as close as any the library could supply using other approaches (Joseph Groesbeck to the author, 28 Oct. 1969).

[a]Figures for additions from 1952 to 1969 represent number of titles (books and pamphlets) added to the collection each year by purchase, gift, and exchange. It is not known if the figure for 1964 represents titles or volumes. Figures for 1965 and 1966 represent volumes added. Yearbooks and continuations were counted as books in 1952 but thereafter were counted as serials.

[b]Figures for withdrawals include only volumes or pieces withdrawn from the cataloged collection.

[c]As of 31 December 1951, the holdings of the library were estimated at 150,600 items (1951 *Annual Report*, p.9).

[d]This figure is at variance with the approximately 200,000 volumes reported in the collection in 1955 (1955 *Annual Report*, p.3), but the figure in the *Report* probably includes bound volumes of documents as well as monographs.

TABLE 4

NET GROWTH OF UNITED NATIONS LIBRARY
IN TERMS OF VOLUMES SHELFLISTED, 1959–1967

Year	Volumes Shelflisted	Volumes Withdrawn	Cumulative Total
1959			200,000[a]
1960	15,908	10,493	205,415
1961	13,791	1,560	217,646
1962	11,343	2,616	226,373
1963	17,441	3,375	240,439
1964	13,741	3,590	250,590
1965	19,247	4,048	265,789
1966	18,264	2,889	281,164
1967	18,969	4,970	295,163[b]

The data for this table were supplied by the United Nations Library, as an alternate to the data presented in table 3.

[a] Based on the count of the shelflist.

[b] This figure of 295,163 for 1967 may be compared with the figure of 238,629 for 1967 from table 3. The monographs counted in table 3 include books and pamphlets. Material shelflisted may include, in addition, bound serial publications not included in the monographic count.

is quality. Because the library must be selective, quality has to be considered; but the library also needs to be impartial.

By far the most fascinating aspect of the policy of coverage in the library is the "time dimension," as it is called by Dr. Rogers. In the working paper prepared for the International Advisory Committee of Library Experts, the policy in regard to discarding as well as selecting materials was discussed. Two factors strongly motivated the formulation of this policy in 1948; limited stack space and the proximity of the library to large research libraries in the New York area.[74] The library policy adopted in 1949 contains a specific statement on discarding materials:

> In most fields no attempt will be made to assemble comprehensive collections or to build up collections for purposes of general historical research and the Library must continuously discard material which is no longer useful to it.[75]

115

The library has made some attempts to implement the policy on discarding. The *Annual Reports* of the library indicate that some discarding has been done (table 3), but staff and time have not always been available to do this task properly. Mr. Clapp in his 1952 survey stated that the continuous execution of the discarding policy must be regarded as one of the fixed costs of the library, and he recommended that the necessary staff be provided for routine discarding operations.[76]

As a result of his survey, particular attention was paid in 1953 to a systematic reduction of the collections.[77] This was achieved by two principal methods: the withdrawing of titles no longer of immediate usefulness and the discarding of periodicals and newspapers, particularly those duplicated in one of the departmental libraries.

In addition to its regular acquisitions program, the library collections have been augmented by the receipt of many gifts both large and small. Two of the most significant gifts were the collection of League of Nations documents and other materials which had been held at Princeton during the war, and the Woodrow Wilson Memorial Library.

The Economic, Financial and Transit Department of the League of Nations had been housed in the Institute for Advanced Study at Princeton University during the war, and 350 boxes of publications were stored there, containing some 14,000 volumes of government documents, books, periodicals, and pamphlets. In 1946 this collection was transferred to the United Nations.

Although this material was valuable, the new United Nations Library was still in need of a complete set of the League of Nations documentation. Some of the documents were sent from the Geneva library, but the most complete collection of the League of Nations documents in the United States was held by the Woodrow Wilson Memorial Library at 45 East Sixty-fifth Street in New York City.

It took almost two years of negotiations with the foundation before the gift was received; Mr. Milam played an important part in these proceedings. Although it was not published in its official report, the International Advisory Committee of Library Experts made a special recommendation to the secretary-general concerning this library:

The International Advisory Committee of Library Experts has been informed that the Woodrow Wilson Foundation is considering whether the Foundation should continue to support its library or whether it should make other arrangements. The collection of the documents of the League of Nations, the Permanent Court of International Justice, and the International Institute of Intellectual Cooperation in this library is unique in the western hemisphere both because of its completeness and because of the admirable way in which it has been classified and catalogued. The Woodrow Wilson Memorial Library also contains much other material of great interest to the United Nations.

The Committee recommends that the United Nations endeavor to obtain this collection as a gift for its Library. The Committee further recommends that in the event of such a gift the Director of Library Services be authorized to insert in the volumes so given a suitable bookplate designating them as the gift of the Woodrow Wilson Foundation.

The Committee requests the Secretary-General to transmit this recommendation to the Directors of the Woodrow Wilson Foundation and to take other appropriate steps toward obtaining this collection for the United Nations.[78]

This recommendation was sent to the secretary-general on 8 September 1948. In a draft memorandum written sometime after this, Mr. Milam outlined the following reasons for requesting the transfer of the collection: (1) the United Nations was devoted to carrying out the ideals of Woodrow Wilson and the League of Nations, (2) the United Nations delegates and Secretariat staff needed a complete collection of the League of Nations documents, (3) the Geneva library was not going to be moved to New York, (4) the United Nations Library collection of League documents was incomplete, (5) microfilm or microprint copies, even if they should become available, would not be a satisfactory substitute for the printed documents because consultation would be more difficult and time consuming, (6) the memorial feature of the library in honor of Woodrow Wilson would be perpetuated in the United Nations Library and the collection would be appropriately housed, and (7) the collections would be available to any scholar or writer needing the complete documentation of the League.[79]

The secretary-general's letter of 20 October 1948, proposing that the Woodrow Wilson Memorial Library be placed in the United Nations Library, was submitted to the Executive Committee of the Woodrow Wilson Foundation, which in turn requested additional information.[80] This was provided in two letters sent to Mrs. Julie d'Estournelles, executive director of the foundation, by Mr. Cohen; the second letter contained a brief (Mr. Milam's draft) in support of the proposal.[81] The proposal was not accepted at this time; Mr. Milam reported in his diary, "We have apparently failed to get the Woodrow Wilson Library."[82]

Negotiations, however, were reopened in February 1950, after Mr. Milam wrote to Cleveland E. Dodge (president of the foundation). He also met with some of the directors of the Woodrow Wilson Foundation on 9 March.[83] This time the fight was won, as Mr. Milam later reported so enthusiastically in his diary:

> The W. W. Library comes to the U.N. The final vote was 11 to 8. Hail to
> > Arthur Sweetser
> > Clyde Eagleton
> > Raymond Fosdick
> > Louise Wright
>
> But especially & emphatically Arthur Sweetser. I thought this fight was lost. It was my one big defeat. But, thanks largely to A W [*sic* — this should be *A. S.* for Arthur Sweetser], we finally came out on top.[84]

The formal transfer of the Woodrow Wilson Memorial Library to the United Nations took place on 12 June 1950, when Secretary-General Trygve Lie accepted the foundation's 16,000-volume library at a ceremony in the headquarters of the foundation, during which Dr. Harry D. Gideonse, president of the foundation at that time, signed a contract with Mr. Lie. Other participants in the ceremony were Raymond Fosdick, a board member; Arthur Sweetser, chairman of the foundation's Library Committee; Carl H. Milam; Cleveland E. Dodge, former president of the foundation; Mrs. Eleanor Wilson McAdoo, a witness to the contract; and Miss Harriet Van Wyck, the librarian of the Woodrow Wilson Memorial Library.[85]

The library was not actually moved to the United Nations until 1951, when it was transferred to the fourth floor of the

Manhattan Building on the corner of Forty-second Street and the East River, with Miss Marie J. Carroll in charge.[86]

Other small but significant gifts included the Jackson H. Ralston collection of books and original documents on international law and arbitration, the bequest of Abraham H. Feller, and a gift from the United States of an atomic energy library.[87]

The library of the United Nations Relief and Rehabilitation Administration was also transferred to the United Nations Library early in 1947. This was an extensive collection and much of it had to be stored until the library moved into larger quarters. Although this was a welcome addition, the library had to expend $15,000 out of its budget for this collection.[88]

Besides purchase and gift, another method of acquiring material is by exchange, and in order to facilitate this procedure, a system of depository libraries was established. The library was responsible for the arrangement of exchanges of all unrestricted United Nations publications in return for publications issued by any organization. The library was also authorized to arrange exchanges with recognized centers for the study of international affairs, even though the return of publications might be disproportionate.[89]

As early as December 1946, Mr. Rasmussen suggested that a policy be established regarding depository libraries which would receive complete sets of United Nations documents. He had been familiar with the designated depository libraries for League of Nations materials whereby League publications were made available free of charge to the public, and he suggested that a similar policy be followed in regard to United Nations documents.[90]

The American Library Association was also interested in this idea and in the spring of 1947 made arrangements with the United States delegation to the United Nations for twenty-five leading American libraries to function as depositories for United Nations documents.[91] They were to receive the mimeographed documents of the United Nations and of the American delegation, as well as to receive on subscription the complete printed documentation of the United Nations.

The establishment of the United Nations Library network of depository libraries was announced by Mr. Rasmussen in 1947. The plan, as he outlined it, called for the eventual establish-

119

ment of some 215 depositories in national and university libraries.[92] Each library would receive all of the printed publications in one of the appropriate official languages. The plan started with the twenty-eight libraries in the United States that had already put the system into partial operation.

The depository system was tentatively approved by the Publications Board of the United Nations on 23 March 1948. At present the designation of depositories is the responsibility of the board, acting on the advice of the director of the library.[93] "All designated depository libraries . . . [must] undertake to keep the material received in good order and under adequate control, and to make it accessible to the public, free of charge, at reasonable hours."[94] A national library has been designated wherever possible. A few of the depositories are parliamentary libraries and others are research institutions specializing in international studies. Mr. Milam hoped that every nation in the world would have within its borders at least one depository of United Nations documents.[95]

The number of depository libraries increased from 184 at the end of 1950, to 241 at the end of 1960, and 280 at the end of 1967. Despite the increase, there were thirty-four member states without depository libraries at the end of December 1967.[96]

The United Nations may inquire into the observance of the conditions of the depository libraries by questionnaire or by visits. The first questionnaire was sent in 1952 and the most recent one was distributed in 1966. Replies to the 1966 questionnaire revealed that most depositories maintained their United Nations publications in special collections, and statistics of use indicated that consultation of United Nations material was increasing. Some parliamentary libraries have been removed from the list of depositories since they reported that they were not open to the public. However, the results of the questionnaire indicated that United Nations publications are valued in most libraries, and depository status is considered a privilege.[97]

chapter 5

Implementation of policy

Technical services

During the first year of the existence of the United Nations Library, the collection remained unorganized for the obvious reasons that both the number of volumes in the library and the number of staff were very small. Mr. Rasmussen described the collection very vividly:

> On August 1, 1946 there was no library in the sense of the word in which we use it. I do not only mean that there was no library shelving and library equipment, but there was no library collection. My notes on the contents of the library, when it was packed on August 8, 1946 (one week after I took over) for transfer to Lake Success from Hunter College, read: Property consists of Encyclopedias Britannica and Americana, Cumulative Book Index, one Who's Who, a handful of odd publications and pamphlets issued by ILO, Pan American Union, World Peace Foundation, Carnegie Endowment.[1]

After the move of the library to Lake Success, Mr. Pelt, who was responsible for the library, suggested that the collection be classified according to the Universal Decimal Classification (UDC) system, arguing that it was the system used by the Geneva library, and that it would be easier to merge the two collections if the same classification system was used by both libraries.[2] At this time there was still some speculation that the Geneva library might be transferred to New York.

121

In December, Mr. Rasmussen submitted his recommendations concerning the adoption of a classification system to Mr. Stefanini, his immediate supervisor, for a decision. In this memorandum Mr. Rasmussen argued against the use of the Universal Decimal Classification at the headquarters library at Lake Success. The Geneva library was still using the 1905 edition of UDC, an edition that had been out of print for several years. The 1928 edition was the only one available, and in order to use UDC in New York, a great deal of coordination of the two editions would be necessary. Even if the Geneva library was transferred to New York, classification numbers would have to be reviewed. Mr. Rasmussen studied the various classification systems and, although he had misgivings about using the Universal Decimal Classification system, recommended:

> After much thought and hesitation, I have come to the conclusion that since our collection of government documents will be separate from our collection of non-official publications and each type of documentation will be handled by separate units in the Catalogue Section, it would be advisable to use the 1928 edition of the Brussels [UDC] classification . . . for our official publications and the Library of Congress system for the classification of our nonofficial publications.[3]

This dual system was adopted in spite of a memorandum from Mr. Cohen of the Department of Public Information (the library at this time was still under the Department of Conference and General Services) to the secretary-general in which he advocated the use of the UDC exclusively and expressed his opinion that the Library of Congress Classification system was inadequate for two reasons:

> 1. It is incomplete and as yet does not include any definite printed scheme for classifying books and documents on law. . . . 2. It is less convenient and less known, even to American librarians and readers, than the Brussels [UDC] scheme, which is based on the internationally used Dewey decimal classification.[4]

As soon as Mr. Milam became director, it was decided to unify the classification system. He reported to the Permanent Advi-

122

sory Library Committee that as of 17 May 1948 the collections would be classified according to the Universal Decimal Classification (the Brussels classification).[5] This, of course, necessitated the reclassification of the books which had previously been classified by the Library of Congress system, and the task was accomplished over the next few years.

The development of the document series symbols for the United Nations publications was much more complicated.[6] Although a classification system was developed for the League of Nations documents, it could not be applied to the United Nations documents because there were a greater number of principal and subsidiary offices in the United Nations, the membership was much more extensive, and the documentation was more voluminous.[7]

The preliminary meetings of the United Nations at San Francisco and London provided a period for experimentation in notation symbols before the present system was put into effect. Two numbers were assigned to each document issued by the United Nations Conference on International Organization (UNCIO) held in San Francisco in 1945.[8] The documents were numbered consecutively as they were received and registered by the documents officer, Waldo Chamberlin; and in addition to this serial number, each document was assigned a symbol classification and a paper number indicating the organ of the conference from which the document originated and that particular paper's relation to previous documents issued by that organ. The published set of the UNCIO documents is arranged roughly by subject following neither the document numbering nor the series symbol notation. Since there is a detailed index to the collected published documents of this conference, both notation schemes are actually unnecessary for retrieval purposes.

The notation system for the documents of the Preparatory Commission, which was convened for the purpose of making provisional arrangements for the first sessions of the United Nations, was based on the experience with the UNCIO documentation. Each UNCIO document had carried both a document serial number and a committee symbol and number. Because of the confusion of having two numbers, the Preparatory Commission documents bore only one designation, based on a system of committee symbols and numbers. The development

123

of the new classification system was largely under the supervision of Harry N. M. Winton, the index officer.[9]

While the documentation of the Preparatory Commission is now primarily of historical value,

> an understanding of the documents system is useful not only to those performing research in the United Nations Archives on the machinery by which the United Nations as an organization was brought into being but also to those wishing a full appreciation of the documents system of the present organs of the United Nations. This is true because the documents system now used by the United Nations Secretariat is to a considerable extent based upon that of the Preparatory Commission, with modifications drawn from the system used by the League of Nations.[10]

The first outline of the present scheme for classifying United Nations documents was published on 3 January 1946 as the first document of the General Assembly.[11] Symbols representing the issuing agency are used, such as: "A" for the documents of the General Assembly, "A/C.1" for the documents of the First Committee, and "S" for the documents of the Security Council.

The scheme has been revised often as the organization of the United Nations has expanded. Subsequent editions were issued separately for each organ: the General Assembly, the Economic and Social Council, the Trusteeship Council, the Secretariat, the Security Council, and the Atomic Energy Commission. In September 1952 a consolidated list was issued in a preliminary edition which superseded all previous editions.[12] The latest edition of the classification scheme appeared in 1965.[13]

For a detailed description of the symbol series system, the reader is referred to an excellent handbook entitled *A Guide to the Use of United Nations Documents*.[14]

The establishment of efficient cataloging procedures in the United Nations Library was a long, tedious process. The library, at first understaffed, was unable to keep pace with the incoming materials, especially when acquisitions of complete libraries amounting to thousands of volumes, such as the League of Nations collection at Princeton, were received. It was a long time before the core collection was cataloged, and the arrears soon became disproportionately large.

For the solution to this problem, the United Nations Library is largely indebted to two members of the Harvard University Library staff who served in temporary capacities in the library. In 1949, largely through the efforts of Mr. Milam, Andrew D. Osborn, the assistant librarian at Harvard, came on loan to serve as acting chief of the Processing Section of the United Nations Library for three months. After his return to Harvard, Miss Susan Haskins, also from Harvard, served as acting chief of the Catalogue Department for nine months, with Mr. Osborn returning at frequent intervals as consultant. All new decisions were made at staff conferences which were attended by catalogers and by representatives of all library units. A few of the far-reaching decisions arrived at included: (1) the United Nations Library was recognized as a special library; that is, a library serving a special, limited clientele with well-defined informational needs; (2) subject headings had to be in the terminology used by the United Nations, such as "Human Rights" instead of "Civil Rights"; (3) the usefulness of every item, whether purchased or received as a gift, had to be challenged; (4) there had to be no unnecessary duplication of records available elsewhere in the library; and (5) the card catalog was divided into two parts, author and subject.[15]

On 11 July 1949 the Catalogue Department began issuing a bulletin periodically, and at least eighteen numbers were edited by Mr. Osborn, covering such topics as: organization of the Catalogue Department, the shelflist, searching instructions, filing, typing of preliminary entries, transcription of the title page, collation, added copies, serial records, cataloging statistics, publications of the specialized agencies, classification policies, subject headings, and added entries.[16] In April 1950 these bulletins were codified into a *Manual of the Cataloguing Unit*, which was compiled by Mr. Osborn and issued in a preliminary edition for criticism by members of the unit as well as by staff members of the library.[17]

In a chapter devoted to "General Cataloguing Policies," the statement that the library has been defined as a special library is reiterated: "Its catalogue records must therefore follow the principles and practices of a special library, and must conform closely to what are considered to be the needs of the Library, as of the United Nations in general."[18] The objectives of a special

125

library are threefold: (1) to acquire a collection of materials relating to the work of the parent organization, (2) to provide information upon request, and (3) to arrange the collection and the catalog so that they can be most effectively used by the staff and library clientele. In the United Nations Library the importance of the catalog is played down. The catalog has been planned as a finding list rather than as a definitive bibliographical tool. It exists primarily to enable the users to find a particular item in the catalog easily and to locate that item in the library's collections.

Among the consequences of establishing the library catalog according to the principles of a special library are the following: (1) emphasis is placed on the acquisition of needed material and speed in processing that material, (2) self-cataloging methods (such as arranging periodicals in alphabetical order) are used whenever they are applicable, (3) serial publications are especially important and methods are provided for processing them expeditiously, (4) the entries made are direct and concise so that readers can readily find them in the catalog, (5) the principle of no-conflict cataloging (accepting the author's name as it appears on the title page) is followed for personal-name entries, (6) general references and added entries are held to a minimum, and (7) a simplified alphabetical sequence is used for filing so that cards are easily filed and located.[19]

In outlining subject heading policies the *Manual* stated that the subject headings were to follow as closely as possible the terminology used in the *United Nations Documents Index* so that readers and staff would find it easy to transfer from entries in the catalog to entries in the *Index* and vice versa.[20]

The policies drawn up by Mr. Osborn and Miss Haskins proved to be effective, for Mr. Milam reported on 30 June 1950 that current acquisitions were being handled promptly, and much of the backlog had been eliminated.[21]

In the summer of 1951, Miss Laura C. Colvin, a member of the Simmons College (Boston) School of Library Science faculty, spent two months on a special assignment to study the policies and operations of the serials cataloging of the United Nations Library. She was commissioned to draft a blueprint for the reorganization of the serials file to conform to the policy decisions and recommendations contained in the *Manual*.

Because the card catalog provided only brief information for serials, it was necessary that the serial checklist be a completely reliable union list of all serial publications received in the central library and in the departmental libraries. To achieve this goal, Miss Colvin outlined a complete reorganization of the serial checklist with the changes effected comprising the definition of fields of responsibility, the style of checklist equipment, the establishment of entries for serials, and the arrangement of the files.[22] To create a concrete basis for the general policies and procedures which she advocated, a pilot study was made on the Netherlands documents so that these could thus be taken as a model for the reorganization of the serial checklist.

Two studies were made of the acquisitions unit of the library: the first, a survey conducted by Mr. Osborn, and, the second, a review of the Osborn survey by Mr. Groesbeck, who was at that time chief of the Processing Section.

Mr. Osborn's report, consisting of a series of twenty-three case studies, is based on data accumulated by direct observations during 1949 and 1950. Each of the case studies presented concludes with a recommended course of action. Some of the procedural recommendations made included the following: (1) the library should use air freight for basic bibliographies, publications from distant countries, and newspapers in urgent demand; (2) adequate library discount should be sought in all countries; (3) book and periodical purchasing and gift and exchange work should be centralized; (4) at least one member of the staff should be recruited from the organized book trade, and one should be recruited from the Soviet Union or one of the other Soviet bloc countries; (5) a roster of reliable book dealers in various countries should be established; (6) a regular weeding program should be initiated, and if it is to be successful, additional staff should be added to the manning table; (7) more material should be bound; (8) a sound program of document procurement from each member country should be instituted; (9) a policy for the library's map collection should be established; and (10) searching routines should be simplified.[23]

Mr. Osborn devoted a complete chapter to the problem of book selection, pointing out that this was a problem of paramount importance to research libraries:

> There is no easy way of handling the problem. Locally the realities must be faced squarely if the United Nations Library is to operate successfully; for all the Library's work performance is dependent on a prompt, thorough, and effective programme of book selection.[24]

> Since the Library aims at being a current-information centre, rather than an historical research institution, it follows that material must be selected and acquired while it still is of current interest.[25]

A book selection committee was established early in 1950, under Mr. Milam's administration, but the move to Manhattan disrupted the work of the committee and prevented the program of book selection from taking hold. Mr. Osborn recommended that such a committee should be reinstated and that it should meet daily, its selection work being given the highest priority. Only in this way would book selection be given the attention it deserved and would current books be ordered on a regular basis.

> The plain fact of the matter is that the United Nations Library must bring itself to do a hard and systematic job of book selection if it is to lift itself above mediocrity. A few people on the Library staff must face the daily grind of it so the right publications may be secured on a world-wide basis.
> The job to be successful must not be everybody's responsibility and none. It must be the responsibility of a determined few, who nevertheless can and should seek help and advice on occasion from the many.[26]

It was on the matter of book selection that the library personnel seriously disagreed with Mr. Osborn's recommendations. They believed that his method would be too time-consuming and favored instead continuation of the method of distributing lists to competent individual staff members, qualified by educational background and language skill to make intelligent selection. However, this method also had serious disadvantages, and Mr. Groesbeck. in his review, suggested a compromise embodying the best features of both book selection devices. He proposed that: (1) initial selection be made by the chief of the acquisitions unit and/or the chief of the Processing Section from publishers' catalogs and from basic national bibliographies of the

United States and major Western European countries; (2) initial selection be made by designated assistants with the necessary language and subject facility from the national bibliographies of Latin America, the Scandinavian, East European, Near Eastern, and Far Eastern countries; (3) after initial selection is made, lists be forwarded to the chief of the service to readers unit, or to the director, for review; and (4) after this review, lists be returned to the acquisitions unit for processing.[27] This procedure has been adopted and today approximately twenty professional staff members participate in book selection.

Mr. Groesbeck also suggested that a book selection committee, serving a different function, be appointed to develop from the 1949 library policy a "fuller and more precise statement of the criteria of selection which should govern the Library's acquisition program"; a statement which would "recognize the two dimensions of book collecting, horizontal subject coverage, and vertical penetration into a subject"; a statement which would also serve "to keep attention focused on the Library's goals and would provide a measure of success or failure in their attainment."[28] This committee has not been appointed, but policies are frequently discussed at the regular meetings of the section chiefs. In the meantime, the principles established by the 1949 library policy are followed. Since acquisition of materials according to these guidelines has resulted in an effective library collection, perhaps a more precise book selection statement is unnecessary.

The development of expeditious book selection procedures is to a great extent dependent upon the development of both general library policy and, especially, policies covering the acquisition of materials, for whether the selection is done by a small committee or a large group of individuals, an adequate book sellection policy in writing will help to ensure that the right books are purchased.

Public services

The library collection at Hunter College was so small that very little in the way of reference services could be provided for the delegates and Secretariat staff. There was a strict order forbidding all bulk buying of books and limiting purchase to what

129

was immediately needed and requested. The librarian's main duties consisted of helping the Secretariat staff use the local library facilities in New York City and in keeping a simple acquisitions record. After the library was moved to Lake Success, the League of Nations collection which was received from Princeton augmented the small collection of reference books which had been collected at Hunter College, and it was possible to provide reference service for the second part of the first session of the General Assembly, which met in October 1946. Library service was provided in the Assembly building, in the central library of the Secretariat, and in the library of the Department of Information. While the library service at the Assembly building was open to the delegates, the Secretariat staff, and the general public, the services of the main library were available only to the delegates and Secretariat staff.[29]

The library collection had increased by this time, chiefly through gifts and generous loans of material, so that it consisted of: that part of the library at the San Francisco Conference which the Library of Congress had provided and which it now lent to the library at Lake Success, an additional collection of reference works lent by the Carnegie Endowment for International Peace, a collection of League of Nations documents lent by New York University Library, the collection of League of Nations documents which had been stored in Princeton and which were transferred to the library, the material acquired by the United Nations Library during the few months it had been in existence, and a complete set of United Nations documents.[30]

To provide efficient reference service for this session of the United Nations, even the reference librarians were on loan from other libraries. The reference work was under the supervision of Miss Helen Lawrence Scanlon, librarian of the Carnegie Endowment for International Peace; and the staff consisted of Miss Elly van Aalten, on loan from the Library of Congress; Miss Nona Doherty, again lent by the Department of State (she had also been lent to the conference library in San Francisco); Miss Margaret Hall, lent by the Law Library of Columbia University; and Miss Marie Carroll, librarian of the United Nations Trusteeship Department branch library.[31]

The type of service provided, based as it was on both the loan of materials and the loan of librarians, was similar to the service provided at the conference library in San Francisco. To give efficient service on a long-range basis, a much more permanent type of organization was needed.

In Mr. Rasmussen's comments on the experience of the library during this session, he remarked that it was largely due to the competence of the librarians that reference services were performed in a satisfactory manner, since the library lacked documentation, proper physical facilities, and sufficient staff.[32] However, at least thirty-two delegations were supplied with books and information on a wide array of subjects, and some selective bibliographies were compiled. The services of other libraries in the New York area were also used.

This, then, was the nucleus of a reference service which was to grow in magnitude until approximately 100,000 inquiries were to be answered each year (table 5). Inquiries for materials,

TABLE 5

REFERENCE INQUIRIES ANSWERED BY THE
UNITED NATIONS LIBRARY, 1954–1967

Year	Main Library	Departmental Branches	Total
1954	47,331	15,003	62,334
1955	48,206	10,531	58,737
1956	49,898	15,966	65,864
1957	57,799	25,859	83,658
1958	66,620	34,732	101,352
1959	69,746	34,793	104,539
1960	70,130	30,764	100,894
1961	73,364	23,674	97,038
1962	82,712	18,614	101,326
1963	80,244	19,325	99,569
1964	71,846	19,339	91,185
1965	67,502	18,275	85,777
1966	83,980	17,250	101,230
1967	94,908	15,935	110,843

Figures are taken from the *Annual Reports* of the library. Comparable statistical tables were not included until the 1954 *Report*. Number of inquiries reported for 1952 and 1953 were listed by each room or unit in the library, and it was impossible to equate them with the new categories begun in 1954.

information, and bibliographies follow a well-defined pattern, a pattern governed by the agenda of the General Assembly, and by political, social, and economic developments throughout the world.

Reference service was also evaluated in some detail by the International Advisory Committee of Library Experts when it convened in August 1948. A working paper prepared for this group described the library in its daily contact with users as acting in three capacities: as a service agency of the United Nations, as an observation station surveying current international issues, and as an information center concerned with the activities, problems, and documents of the United Nations. These three functions entail the performance of the following types of service: general reference service to readers, specialized reference service on the United Nations and the specialized agencies including service of the United Nations documents, and circulation of materials and the borrowing of materials which the library does not own.[33]

To fulfill the demands made upon it, it is necessary for the reference staff to keep informed of all research projects, current or pending, in the Secretariat; to be aware of the interests of all working units; and to solicit advice from field specialists engaged in research. They must also be aware of current trends in international affairs so as to anticipate new subjects of interest. The Wessells study, previously mentioned, was a compilation of subjects of interest to the United Nations.

In 1948 the staff in the main reading room answered an average of 375 reference inquiries a week, about one-third of which were major inquiries involving research, collation of material, checking of bibliographies, and compilation of data. The other two-thirds represented current demands for information of a legal, historical, economic, or other character, which required checking of texts and statements, verifying translation, finding dates of events, and securing bibliographies and documents.[34]

When the Assembly chose to meet in Paris in 1948, the library operated a special reference service for the delegates. Books and documents were borrowed from headquarters, the Geneva library, and the libraries of Paris; and some books were purchased in Paris. The staff consisted of Mrs. Denise Ravage from the headquarters library, Miss Scanlon from the Carnegie Endowment Library in Washington, Miss Phyllis Molesworth from the Royal Institute of International Affairs in London, plus three other assistants.[35]

In the autumn of 1949 the library published a small leaflet inviting delegations and the staff of the Secretariat to use the library.[36] Issued in English, French, and Spanish and widely distributed, it helped to inform the United Nations personnel that the library's services were available to all of them. In fact, from *You Are Invited to Use Your Library*, some staff members learned about the library for the first time.[37]

The library as it was originally planned was designed only for the use of the delegates and Secretariat staff, although the Reference Center of the Department of Public Information, before its transfer to the central library, did provide reference service to members of the mass media and the public. The policy which was adopted in 1949 reiterated this principle, but also added:

> The services of the Library will also be made available, as far as feasible, to the specialized agencies, accredited representatives of mass media of information, international governmental organizations, affiliated non-governmental organizations, educational institutions, scholars and writers. No one needing to use full sets of the documents and publications of the League of Nations, the United Nations or the specialized agencies will be denied access to the Library. Service to the public, however, must necessarily be subordinated to the service needed by the United Nations.[38]

The acting director of the library, Edouard Reitman, in 1951 prepared two papers which represented a tentative interpretation of the basic library policy in this matter. These were sent to Mr. Cordier, executive assistant to the secretary-general, with the intention of clarifying the meaning and implications of the basic library policy. The first paper was devoted to the policy toward visitors. Although the library was not to be considered a stopping place for the regularly conducted tours, group visits could be arranged for persons professionally related to library work, such as librarians, archivists, and documentation specialists.[39] The second paper dealt with the use of the library by the public, and was intended to serve as an outline of the nature and extent of services to be given to university and college teachers, students, correspondents, and representatives of the nongovernmental organizations.[40]

The secretary-general reported in 1967 that the use of the library by outside scholars was expanding (table 6), probably due in part to an increased interest in the United Nations as a subject for research and in part to the uniqueness of the collection.[41]

TABLE 6

EXTERNAL READERS PASSES ISSUED BY
THE UNITED NATIONS LIBRARY, 1952–1967

Year	Number of Passes
1952	368
1953	396
1954	497
1955–62[a]	–
1963	740
1964	547
1965	624
1966	709
1967	956

Figures are taken from the *Annual Reports* of the library. They are not included in the annual statistical tables but are extracted from the text of the *Reports*.

[a]Numbers of readers passes issued were not included in the *Annual Reports* from 1955 to 1962.

Indexing and bibliographic services

The indexing of the documents issued by the United Nations soon became an essential part of the responsibilities of the United Nations Library. The conference library at San Francisco assumed the responsibility for collecting and collating the documents of the United Nations Conference on International Organization. In London the documents index unit was established with the library actually subordinate to it. This arrangement persisted when the library was first established at Hunter College. The unit then became a part of the Documents and Sales Division of the Department of Conference and General Services, where it remained until 1 January 1948, when it was transferred to the Division of Library Services in the Department of Public Information. Early in 1947 a Publications Board was established in the United Nations to coordinate all printing and publishing activities of the United Nations including sales and distribution of documents.[42]

Before the United Nations started to publish adequate indexes to its own publications, libraries and international organizations had to do their own indexing of these publications. Several conferences and meetings were held on the problem of international documentation; some were called by private organizations, and some were held under the auspices of the United Nations. In the spring of 1947 the first of two Conferences on the Distribution of Documentary Materials, convened by the World Peace Foundation, noted two main trends: the issuance in printed or processed form of the most important documents of the major international organizations, and the issuance in mimeographed form of preliminary or more ephemeral material.[43] At the second meeting, 19 June 1947, the reports of four committees appointed at the first conference in March were discussed. These reports dealt with: every library's need for adequate indexing of international documents, and bibliographical servicing of the documents on international relations.[44] The conference adopted two specific recommendations, only the first one of which concerned United Nations publications:

> First, it agreed that in lieu of official indices of United Nations and specialized agency documentation, a quarterly selected bibliography covering both printed and processed documentation should be issued as at least a partial guide. With the assistance of the Carnegie Endowment, the Carnegie Corporation, and the Rockefeller Foundation, the World Peace Foundation has undertaken this assignment, and the first issue of *Documents of International Organizations: A Selected Bibliography* appeared in November under the guidance of an advisory committee composed of Philip C. Jessup, Verner Clapp, Walter R. Sharp, Ruth Savord, and Harry N. M. Winton.[45]

This bibliography was published from November 1947 until September 1950, and at that time was discontinued because the *United Nations Documents Index* supplanted it.

An Advisory Committee of Information Experts meeting at the United Nations in the spring of 1948 recommended that an index of all UN documents be compiled.[46] In the fall of 1948 the International Advisory Committee of Library Experts tackled the problem of document indexing along with all the other problems it was considering. One of its working papers was devoted completely to *Distribution and Use of United Nations Documents and Departmental Publications.*[47]

This paper listed the principal functions of the documents index unit as: "(1) Answering inquiries from the Delegations and the Secretariat concerning documents and speeches during sessions at Headquarters; (2) publishing indexes and check lists of United Nations documents; and (3) advising the Bureau of Documents on the creation of document series symbols."[48] Although the library tried, through a series of cards, indexes, and other devices, to establish clues to all of the United Nations publications, it had little time for the publication of up-to-the-minute checklists or of detailed subject indexes.[49] The first index proposed by the working paper was a checklist of all the documents published during the first two years of the United Nations, to be issued in several parts, one for each of the main organs, commissions, and conferences, and to be kept up to date by annual supplements.[50]

The most important recommendations of the International Advisory Committee of Library Experts on documents were:

> 49. The Committee endorses the plan to publish the United Nations Check List, and expresses the hope that it be brought up to date as quickly as possible and maintained on a current basis. . . .
>
> 50. The Committee recommends the publication of a brief weekly subject index. . . .
>
> 52. The Committee strongly urges that a consolidated check list of the documents and publications of all United Nations organizations be published as soon as possible.[51]

On 21 and 22 November 1948 the Conference on United Nations and Specialized Agencies Documentation, under the auspices of the Carnegie Endowment for International Peace, was convened in Paris. Sixty-four representatives of libraries and other institutions from eleven countries met to discuss the documentation of the United Nations and the specialized agencies. The following resolutions were passed: (1) the United Nations should publish French editions of all bibliographical tools; (2) complete bibliographical information should be given on each document, whether printed or mimeographed; (3) indexes should provide access by subject, delegation interested, person interested, and organization interested; (4) the proposed index should be initiated immediately; (5) the documents classification system adopted should be published in detail; (6) all documents should have a subject classification; and (7) there should be one center to prepare, print, and distribute documents.[52]

Clearly the time had come for something positive and constructive to be done, and again Mr. Milam was to be the catalyst. He had felt for some time that the publication of the checklists was not moving rapidly enough. Upon the recommendation of the Publications Board, to whom the matter had been referred, the library produced three experimental weekly issues of a subject index covering all documents including those published by the specialized agencies.[53] A preliminary report in January 1949, prepared by the Division of Library Services for the Publications Board, summarized comments on the experimental issues of the weekly list.[54] The lists were well received by both the Secretariat staff and outside librarians to whom they had been sent, although there were several suggestions that they be issued monthly and cumulated on an annual basis. No action was taken by the Publications Board at this time because a more detailed survey was then underway by the Inspection Service of the United Nations. A preliminary report of that survey was presented to the library in March by K. P. R. Menon of the Inspection Service, and this report was the basis for considerable discussion by two outside experts who had been requested by Mr. Milam to review and study the programs of the documents index unit.[55]

R. B. Eastin, assistant superintendent of documents of the United States Government Printing Office, spent one day in March reviewing the plans which had been prepared by the library staff and the representatives of the Inspection Service, and pronounced them "technically sound and quite practical."[56] It was agreed that a suitable program of card indexing would be desirable so that it could satisfy two functions: to answer reference questions and to provide data for the publication of subject indexes and checklists of documents.

Mr. Eastin expressed the opinion in his report that the success of any documents indexing program would be contingent upon the following management decisions: (1) the organization of the indexing staff into a unit free from all other duties; (2) the commencement of indexing of current publications, with provision made to liquidate the backlogs by contract or by employing a special staff; (3) the organization of page indexing of individual documents independently of this unit, the most satisfactory arrangement being to have page indexing the responsibility of the editors of the various publications of the United Nations; (4) the provision of reference service by a staff other than those engaged in producing the basic index cards; (5) the establishment of priorities for the operations of the unit so that if the staff was inadequate at any time, it would be understood which programs were to be continued and which were to be sacrificed; and (6) the provision of adequate financial resources.[57] In concluding his report, Mr. Eastin said:

> The Documents Index Unit under Mr. Winton has produced checklists of the highest technical excellence. The experimental issues of the Weekly Subject Index have been of the same calibre. The staff of the Documents Index Unit deserves nothing but the greatest commendation for the quality of the programs which they have been attempting to discharge in the face of an overwhelming flood of publications far beyond their resources to meet.[58]

Mr. Jerome K. Wilcox, librarian of the City College of New York, and chairman of the Public Documents Committee of the American Library Association, participated in the discussions with Mr. Eastin. In a letter to Mr. Reitman he reported that he completely concurred in Mr. Eastin's statements.[59]

Mr. Milam then called a meeting of the Permanent Advisory Library Committee for 27 April 1949 to consider the problem of documents indexing. Periodicity of issue was discussed first, and it was agreed that a monthly index would be adequate and that more frequent issuance could be considered later if the need was felt. It was planned to make the index as inclusive as possible for all the documents and publications of the United Nations and the specialized agencies, although the committee agreed that press releases, posters, radio scripts, filmstrips, reprints from the *United Nations Bulletin*, and domestic papers of the Secretariat should be excluded.[60]

Format and arrangement were then discussed. Entries in the experimental issues of the weekly index had been arranged by subject, but the arrangement proposed for the monthly index was an author list by issuing body, with the use of entry numbers in the index (as is the case with the *Monthly Catalog of Government Publications* covering United States documents), and a monthly subject index to be cumulated annually. Most members of the committee preferred that the index be printed, although it was agreed that it might have to be started by internal production if the budget would not permit printing. Page indexing of individual documents was also discussed at this meeting. The final decision of the committee was to propose that the Publications Board be asked for two policy decisions, the first on the issuance of a current index, and the second on page indexing.[61]

Mr. Menon's final report was issued on 19 May 1949, and his recommendations were essentially in agreement with the preliminary draft report of the survey, the communications from the two outside experts (Mr. Eastin and Mr. Wilcox), and the discussions of the library committee.[62] The Menon report did not, however, separate the functions of the documents index unit. The report described the primary functions of the unit as a combination of three duties: to publish checklists and indexes which would assist users of the United Nations documents to locate the material they needed (a monthly index with annual cumulations was recommended); to provide reference service on the United Nations documents; and to produce other special indexes requested by the Secretariat and to page index publications and official records insofar as special funds and personnel were available.[63]

A report issued simultaneously with the Menon study and compiled by the library listed three principal recommendations: (1) "An indexed *Monthly List* of documents and publications of the United Nations and the specialized agencies should be issued for wide distribution beginning as soon as feasible"; (2) "A separate temporary [staff] is recommended to complete for publication the parts of the definitive, indexed *Check List* covering the 27,300 documents issued in these three years [1946, 1947, and 1948]"; and (3) "Page-indexing of departmental monographs should be done on contract."[64]

The first monthly *United Nations Documents Index*, dated January 1950, finally appeared on 15 February and covered the United Nations and specialized agency documents received by the documents index unit during January. The first issue of the *Index* listed all of the documents under the name of each individual agency or organ of the United Nations. The index to the documents was arranged principally by subject, but included some titles. It was a monthly index, with annual cumulations planned. References were given to the documents by means of entry numbers rather than page numbers. The first issue included a general introduction and a list of abbreviations used. Part 1 listed all of the documents and publications, with those of the organs of the United Nations first, followed by those of the specialized agencies arranged in alphabetical order according to the English abbreviation of the name of the agency. This part included complete bibliographical data for each publication. Part 2 listed revisions, addenda, corrigenda, and non-English language editions. Part 3 listed publications reprinted. This is essentially the arrangement of the *Index* today except that references in the subject index are now to the document series symbols rather than to entry numbers and that both the monthly listings of the documents and the monthly indexes are cumulated on an annual basis.

Although Mr. Milam noted in his diary that the index had been well received but had caused no sensation, the reviews were uniformly good.[65] One reviewer reported: "The new index is in every respect the equal of the best national documents indexes."[66] A note in the *Library of Congress Information Bulletin* reported: "It represents the growing appreciation that one of the important steps towards making a global international organization work is not only to publish its documents fully but to publish as complete a current catalog as possible."[67] At a meeting of the Association of Research Libraries in July 1950,

"Mr. Clapp moved that the executive secretary be instructed to communicate to the U.S. Secretary of State the approbation felt by this association regarding the *United Nations Index* [sic] and to request the Secretary of State to make this approbation known to the United States delegate to the United Nations."[68] The motion was passed. The need for such an index was succinctly stated in another review:

> The need for such an index must have been acutely felt by librarians and secretaries of organizations who have endeavoured to keep abreast of the spate of documentation issuing from the different sections of the United Nations, and who have been goaded to superhuman efforts by the knowledge that buried in the mass were items of burning interest and information which could not be neglected and which might at some unforeseen juncture be highly relevant to the needs of inquirers or research workers.[69]

From the beginning, the documents of the specialized agencies were included in the index. This was done on a cooperative arrangement with the individual agencies. The Library Coordinating Committee, which had been in existence since 1948, had given special attention to the problem of cooperative indexing.[70] This committee was composed of members of the Secretariat in New York and representatives of the following specialized agencies:[71] International Labour Organisation; Food and Agriculture Organization; United Nations Educational, Scientific and Cultural Organization; International Civil Aviation Organization; International Bank for Reconstruction and Development; International Monetary Fund; and the World Health Organization.[72] The rules of procedure adopted at the first meeting stated: "The purpose of the Library Co-ordinating Committees of the United Nations Organizations is to facilitate co-operation between the United Nations and the Specialized Agencies in library and kindred matters."[73]

The Library Co-ordinating Committee at its meetings in Geneva and Paris in 1949 and 1951 discussed various aspects of the documentation of international organizations, library implications of the technical-assistance programs, interlibrary cooperation, and such technical matters as cooperative indexing and cataloging, exchange of official publications and bibliogra-

141

phies, disposal of duplicates, and coordination of translations of legal texts.[74] The *Index* was not perfect, however, and changes and improvements have been made in it since its first appearance. A sudden increase in the quantity of documents published precipitated the first major change in the *Index*. In 1962 it was reported that "The sheer volume of documentation was startlingly greater than in any previous year, an increase which appears not in the number of documents indexed but in the bulk of the individual documents and the many more index entries required properly to record the interventions of a Membership which has doubled over the last decade."[75]

Mr. Groesbeck, in writing about the accessibility of the United Nations documents, said:

> From the start, the effort [of cooperative indexing] was less than completely successful, not for want of good will, but by reason of the extreme variance . . . [in the publications]. It was apparent quite soon that the consolidated UNDI was neither comprehensive nor truly cooperative, because some agencies were without the means or the incentive to carry their share of the responsibility to make it so.[76]

Therefore, it was decided that beginning with the January 1963 issue of the *Index*, the documents and publications issued by the specialized agencies were to be excluded from the *Index*. Although this seemed to be a step backwards in the long-range attempt to provide complete bibliographical control of the documentation of the United Nations family, the curtailment was necessary if improvements were to be made in the *Index* and if the projected French version of the *Index* was ever to be a reality.[77] Since many of the agencies produced and published their own indexes, and since most of them issued sales catalogs, it was decided that it would be better if the headquarters library should cease "trying to bag together oranges and apples, a few figs and many thistles," and instead try to coordinate the indexing activities of the various agencies.[78]

To achieve this goal the Inter-Agency Working Party on Indexing was established for:

1. Reviewing current indexing activities;
2. Establishing and developing common standards for the organization, indexing, storage and dissemination of the

documents produced by the United Nations, the specialized agencies and IAEA [International Atomic Energy
Agency];

3. Considering ways and means to achieve and maintain
   compatibility between existing and planned systems of
   indexing and retrieval of documents;

4. Formulating recommendations to the ACC [Advisory
   Committee on Coordination] on these matters, taking
   into account the various needs and practices of each individual agency and other users.[79]

The interagency committee is confident that, through its efforts,
a measure of compatibility among the indexing systems of the
participating agencies may be achieved and maintained, and
that this will expiate the lack of complete indexing of all of the
publications of the specialized agencies in the *United Nations
Documents Index*.

Still the demand persists for a single index which would be a
current and comprehensive bibliographical record of all of the
publications of the members of the United Nations family, and
it has recently been proposed to the newly organized Association of International Libraries that a counterpart to the *United
Nations Documents Index* be established which would cover
not only the specialized agencies of the United Nations but also
other international organizations.[80]

However, "The sheer bulk of the material which *should* be
analyzed and the *limited* manpower available to the task have
forced policies of selection, both of documents to be indexed
and of details of their content to be brought out in the indexes,
whereas *comprehensive* cover [sic] and *maximum* depth of
indexing are the ideals."[81] There are three major shortcomings
of the *United Nations Documents Index*: (1) it is limited to the
indexing of publications in the English language, (2) it does not
reveal the position of a country on a particular question, and (3)
the delay in its publication means that documents issued in one
month are uncontrolled bibliographically until the end of the
next month.

In the summer of 1966 the library began considering the possibility of mechanizing some aspects of its operations. To ascer-
tain more accurately the documentation needs of the delegations, missions, and Secretariat staff, a questionnaire was sent

to 442 members of the United Nations. Besides including questions regarding the types and nature of documentation used, the questionnaire included items relating to the use made of library services, the use made of indexes and bibliographies prepared by the library, the form of documentation preferred, sources of dissatisfaction with present library services, and willingness to cooperate with the library. Questions were graded according to three categories of use: primarily or frequently, occasionally, and rarely or never. Space for comments and remarks was provided at the end of each group of questions.[82]

Exactly 50 percent of the forms were returned, which the library considered sufficient to indicate trends in use and need.

> The statistical summary turned into hard facts some of the things which hitherto could only be surmised, e.g. an overwhelming demand for increased indexing and bibliographical services, the necessity to issue the indexes in languages other than English, the need for timely publication and for expanded coverage of materials indexed at present. It revealed the differences in approaches and requirements between the Missions and the Secretariat which will have to be given due consideration when new techniques are introduced.[83]

One of the new techniques which the library has been exploring is the possibility of computer manipulation of indexing information. The library is satisfied that the application of certain computer-assisted techniques would yield these results: the library could publish some sort of an index in two or more language versions without the enormous increase in personnel which the conventional approach would require; details of the content of the documents could be analyzed in greater depth than are now described in the *United Nations Documents Index*; and indexes could be published at any desirable frequency and cumulated when necessary.[84]

In addition to studying the possibilities of improving the indexes of the United Nations documents, the library is also exploring the feasibility of the miniaturization of documents for the purposes of preservation, reduction of storage space, ease of retrieval, and facility of reproduction.

Both of these projects, although still in the incubation stage, indicate that the United Nations Library is awake to the possibilities of computer technology. They also indicate that the library, in implementing the policies developed over the years, has been aware of its responsibilities not only to its own clientele but also to researchers and scholars in the professional and academic communities.

chapter 6

Conclusions

This historical study of the United Nations Library from its birth in 1945 to its maturity in 1961 has attempted to answer nine questions which relate to the basic problems and decisions of the library.

Within the United Nations, who were the decision-makers of library policy? Delegates, Secretariat staff, and librarians all played a role in the development of the library. The first policy which served as a guideline for the development of library services was drawn up by David Vaughan, the director of the Department of Conference and General Services, the department in which the library was originally located. Arkady Sobolev, the assistant secretary-general for Security Council Affairs, took an interest in the library and brought Secretary-General Trygve Lie in for a visit. The secretary-general then conferred with Adrian Pelt, the assistant secretary-general for Conference and General Services, and sent him a memorandum on library policy in 1946. Although the decision-makers were far too busy establishing the fledgling United Nations to give very much attention to the library, it was taken for granted that a library was needed. On the opening day of the General Assembly, a modest library, hardly a harbinger of the magnificent Dag Hammarskjöld Library, was in operation at Hunter College; and although the library had few books and no bookshelves, the librarian was able to refer delegates and Secretariat staff to the peerless library facilities in the New York area. Dr. Víctor

Belaúnde of the Peruvian delegation, who had attended the United Nations Conference on International Organization in San Francisco and had used the excellent library facilities there, was a staunch advocate of good library service for the new United Nations. The Netherlands delegation was also intensely interested in good library service.

What factors were to be decisive in determining the ultimate size of the library? This was the most controversial policy question deliberated in the infancy of the library. The interaction of both internal and external forces (such as the many surveys conducted at the library) was most intensive respecting this question. The Permanent Advisory Library Committee, consisting of representatives from each of the substantive departments of the United Nations, repeatedly advocated a research library of moderate but substantial proportions, which the departments felt was necessary to meet their needs. It need not be a universal library of record, but the committee was adamant in insisting that it be larger than a minuscule reference library of useful titles. The fact that the League of Nations had developed a substantial research library was raised constantly in meetings and discussions, and this type of library was especially championed by delegates and staff who had previously been closely allied with the League. Although the force of internal consensus favored a research library similar to the League Library, it was the reduction in capital budget that forced the library planners to abjure immediate plans for a separate building and to concentrate on perfecting library service to delegates and staff.

It was partially because of these forces that the library evolved into a very special research library devoted to serving the needs of a very special clientele. Although this specialization meant that the size of the collection would be smaller than originally envisaged, it did not denote a diminution of the significance of the library, for in the library's selectiveness it became unique and as such it possessed some materials that no other library owned. In terms of the documents of the League of Nations, the United Nations, and the specialized agencies attached to the United Nations, the library knows no equal.

How did the precedent of the League of Nations Library interact with other forces influencing the development of the new

147

library? Although Mr. Rasmussen suggested that the library in Geneva be transferred to Lake Success for two very cogent reasons – to provide an adequate library service for the new Secretariat, and for very practical reasons of economy – the secretary-general indicated that he would not consider this suggestion. The International Advisory Committee of Library Experts reaffirmed the judgment of the secretary-general. It recommended that since the library served a useful purpose in Geneva by providing service to the specialized agencies located there, it should continue to be maintained in Geneva. The Geneva library was constantly brought up as an example of the size and type of library needed for the new United Nations. Many of the publications of the Geneva library were also copied or continued by the United Nations Library in New York; the classification scheme in use at Geneva was finally adopted by the United Nations Library in New York; and the composition of the International Advisory Committee of Library Experts reflected the composition of the Library Planning Committee which advised the League Library on operational and building policies.

What force did the administrative structure of the United Nations have on the development of the library? First located in the Department of Conference and General Services, the library suffered neglect because this was the largest of the departments, and there was little time to take cognizance of the library's multitudinous problems. The early years were difficult ones for the United Nations as administrators sought to find suitable places in the administrative structure both for services and personnel. The library was transferred in 1948 to the Department of Public Information largely through the efforts of its dynamic assistant secretary-general, Benjamin Cohen, who was himself at one time librarian of the National Library in Chile. This transfer had the effect of bringing the Department of Public Information's Reference Center into the library. Mr. Cohen's reasons for recommending the transfer were four: the operation of a library was an information operation, library services were essential to the work of the Department of Public Information, the library belonged in his department for the sake of convenience, and the Reference Center had demonstrated the ability to render efficient library service.

Although the transfer resulted in the centralization of library services and in the employment of Mr. Milam, who shared Mr. Cohen's views that the library should be an information service, the Advisory Committee on Administrative and Budgetary Questions did not comprehend why the library should be attached to the Department of Public Information. The functions of the library were not closely allied to functions assigned to any one of the eight departments of the United Nations Secretariat. The committee was apprehensive that the library would become a propaganda instrument of the Department of Public Information. The library was eventually transferred to the Executive Office of the Secretary-General, where it remained until, as a result of the secretary-general's survey of the Secretariat in 1953, it was transferred in May 1954 to the Department of Conference Services, where it has remained up until the present.

What was the role of the departmental library in the flow of information from central library to reader? The research staff of the Secretariat insisted on departmental libraries, which were established in spite of repeated statements about the need for centralizing library services. These small departmental libraries were initiated mainly because the central library could not immediately acquire a strong collection. The policy statements were at times confusing. The secretary-general himself envisaged a central library divided into subject sections corresponding to the needs of each department. In a 1946 memorandum he hoped that when the Secretariat was housed in one building, the library services could be housed centrally and integrally; but he also perceived that if a considerable physical distance existed between a given department and the central library, then that departmental section of the library should be housed in the department even though still under the administrative authority of the central library. The Advisory Committee on Administrative and Budgetary Questions periodically recommended reducing and ultimately eliminating the branch libraries. As the services and collections of the central library increased, the need for departmental libraries decreased, and today only two remain. These two libraries provide a vertical means of communication in the flow of information, for the branch libraries may in turn obtain services from the central library. If the central library cannot supply the information or materials from its own collection, it has available on interlibrary loan not only the resources of the libraries of New York City but also the resources of the libraries of the world.

What was Carl Milam's contribution to the library? It was Carl Milam's administration, although lasting only two years, that set the library on a firm course. He was responsible for internal administrative reorganization and the recruitment of an excellent staff which he used to good advantage. He was a member of the first survey group of the library and commissioned many other surveys, the most important one of which was the International Advisory Committee of Library Experts. This was an example of an internal agent commissioning an external group, the combined deliberations of which led to a series of recommendations and eventually to a written library policy. Mr. Milam was also responsible for bringing the Woodrow Wilson Memorial Library to the United Nations. Even after he resigned from the directorship he continued to be of service to the United Nations by aiding in the fund-raising campaign for a new building and by drawing up building programs. The librarians who followed in his footsteps continued his policies and practices, a course which was in itself a strong vote of confidence for his administration.

Were the recommendations of the external surveys adopted by the library? The first three surveys of the library (the Evans, Beals, Milam, Breycha-Vauthier study; the Clapp survey; and the Burchard survey) were mainly concerned with questions of quantities of materials required by the United Nations Library and with space requirements. All of the surveyors felt that 1,000,000-volume library recommended by the Permanent Advisory Library Committee, which represented the views of the Secretariat, was too large; and they advocated instead a more modest ultimate goal of 300,000 to 500,000 volumes with a much smaller collection initially. Because of the difficulties of acquiring such a large library rapidly, this goal is just now being approached by the library.[1] These consultants felt that the United Nations should have a library service of the most advanced type, specifically developed to meet the needs of the Secretariat, the delegations, and the specialized agencies. They felt that emphasis should be placed on reference, bibliographical, and documentation services rather than on the accumulation of books. The slow growth of the monographic collection of the library in contrast to the rapid growth of primary source materials reflects the farsightedness of these first consultants.

Mr. Shaw in his survey, which was part of a larger management survey of the complete Secretariat, made seven major recommendations, only three of which were adopted either in whole or in part. He recommended that the library be transferred to the Department of Public Information, and this transfer was effected soon thereafter. And he also recommended the employment of the most competent head librarian in the world. This recommendation was satisfied in the employment of Carl H. Milam. The proposed contractual arrangement with the New York Public Library was accepted only insofar as bibliographical and reference services were concerned.

The most important advice given to the United Nations Library was the result of the meetings of the International Advisory Committee of Library Experts. Commissioned by Mr. Milam in August 1948, this was the only consultation group to include members from countries all over the world. The International Advisory Committee prescribed that emphasis should be on service and not on accumulation and preservation of materials, although it did recommend that in one field the library acquisitions should be exhaustive, namely, in the publications of the United Nations and its antecedent and related organizations. Many of the fifty-seven recommendations made by this committee were included in the basic document of library policy which was adopted on 21 September 1949 and which remains in force to this day.

Most of the other surveys of the library dealt with practical matters of operation rather than with policies. Because many of the surveyors were temporary employees of the library or were of such expert practical qualifications, their recommendations were usually put into effect. These surveys had to do with such diverse matters as documents indexing, cataloging, acquisition procedures, and serial checklist procedures.

What were the relations of the United Nations Library with other libraries? The answer to this question may be divided into two parts: first, the library's relations with other libraries in the New York area, especially the New York Public Library; and second, its relations with other international libraries.

151

The libraries of New York were quick to extend to the United Nations Library the privilege of interlibrary loan, a privilege which is generally extended by all libraries to all other libraries. The New York Public Library went beyond its usual practice, however, in extending to the United Nations Library the rare privilege of borrowing from its noncirculating reference collection. It extended this privilege not only to be of service, but also because it felt that the United Nations should not develop a large research library when there was one already in the same geographical area. Such a collection would have been a duplication of both effort and materials. In 1948 the United Nations Library negotiated contracts with both the New York Public Library and the Library of Congress, not only for assistance in facilitating interlibrary loans, but also for the preparation of bibliographies and the performance of specific research assignments. That with the New York Public Library is still in effect.

The relations of the United Nations Library with other international libraries, such as the Food and Agriculture Organization, UNESCO, the World Health Organization, and the libraries of the economic commissions have been especially cordial. From the outset the United Nations Library in Geneva has served the specialized agencies located there, and in fact this was one of the major reasons for maintaining the Geneva library. In 1948 the Library Co-ordinating Committee, composed of members representing each of the specialized agencies, was established. Through this committee the United Nations Library has been able to keep open the horizontal flow of information between international libraries. One of the major accomplishments of the committee was to initiate the cooperative indexing of the specialized agency publications for the *United Nations Documents Index*, although this project was discontinued in 1963.

Because indexing of the publications of both the United Nations and its specialized agencies is of paramount importance to the scholarly community, means are continually being sought to improve indexing services. A newly established committee, the Inter-Agency Working Party on Indexing, with Mr. Groesbeck as the chairman, is studying methods whereby compatibility may be achieved and maintained among the indexing systems of the participating agencies.

In addition to publishing *The Libraries of the United Nations: A Descriptive Guide,* which contains short descriptions of all of the libraries in the United Nations family, the United Nations Library has also initiated a newsletter entitled *United Nations Libraries Information Bulletin.* This newsletter is intended to keep each library informed of programs and activities of each of the other libraries. Since 1954 the annual reports of the United Nations Library have included the reports of the Geneva library, and since 1965 the reports of the libraries of the economic commissions have also been included.

What contribution did the Ford Foundation make to the United Nations? Although the Ford Foundation has left a lasting imprint on the United Nations which is visible in the beautiful library building, it studied the matter of the gift very carefully for several years before deciding to finance the project. A separate library building was one of the early dreams of the library planners. It was discussed in detail at a 1947 meeting of the Permanent Advisory Library Committee, and the consensus reached was that the library should start with a separate building especially constructed for that purpose. Fourteen years elapsed before the dream was a reality. In the meantime, the library occupied a separate building, one not specifically constructed for library use but a converted office building. Because the structure was unsatisfactory, the library planners still hoped to have a new building and soon received permission from the secretary-general to explore the possibility of obtaining funds from external private sources. The League of Nations again presented a precedent, for the library at Geneva had been built as a result of a gift of $2,000,000 from John D. Rockefeller, Jr. The first fund-raising brochure was drafted in 1950, but it was 1952 before it was printed and formally presented by the secretary-general to the Ford Foundation.

Although overtures were made to several foundations, it was decided to concentrate the fund-raising efforts on the Ford Foundation. Several attempts were made to convince the Ford Foundation that a library building would be a lasting contribution to the work and effectiveness of the United Nations and to the cause of world peace and stability. But it was not until 1959 that the foundation decided to give the munificent sum of $6,200,000 to the United Nations for the construction of a new library building. At the fourteenth session of the General Assembly the gift was formally and graciously accepted. The fact that the gift of the Ford Foundation for a new library building came later in the library's history than the gift of Mr. Rockefeller to the League of Nations was very beneficial, as by then the policies of the library had been firmly established and a building could be designed to fulfill those policies most efficiently. The secretary-general took a keen interest in the designs for the library building and made several suggestions regarding architectural embellishments. After his death, and on the suggestion of the president of the Ford Foundation, the General Assembly passed a resolution dedicating the new library as the Dag Hammarskjöld Library. It was dedicated on 16 November 1961, a little more than fifteen years after the first library was established in Hunter College.

In the years since the dedication the collections have grown and have become even more specialized, with particular emphasis being placed on the acquisition of primary documents. Although the *United Nations Documents Index* is now limited solely to the publications of the United Nations and excludes those of the specialized agencies, it appears in a new, easier-to-use format. Studies previously had been undertaken in an attempt to determine the feasibility of publishing the *Index* in French. With the adoption of computer techniques, this may soon become an eventuality: two exploratory projects were begun in 1968. The library has considered the possibility of computer manipulation of indexing information. If the application of computer-assisted techniques proved feasible, the library could publish an index to its publications in two or more language versions; the index could also analyze details of the content of the documentation not now described in the *United Nations Documents Index*; and indexes could be published at any desirable frequency. The second of the library's exploratory projects was the miniaturization of documents for the purposes of preservation, reduction of storage space, ease of retrieval, and facility of reproduction.

Without adequate physical quarters, staff, and budget, experimentation and progress are made much more difficult. The new building has provided an impetus to the improvement of techniques and services. Early in its history the United Nations Library was planned in such a way that it would become a special library serving a limited clientele. This trend has continued and has been intensified. By concentrating on being the elite in its field, it has become a library of great value not only to the United Nations researcher, but also to the outside scholar seeking the documentation which the library has so assiduously collected and indexed.

The United Nations Library developed in response to the needs of the United Nations, just as the League Library developed in response to the needs of the League of Nations. The library in New York was not limited as the library in Geneva was by a gift which specified that the library be open to the public as an agency of international research. All of the surveyors of the library advocated, and the officials of the United Nations finally agreed, that a special collection designed for a special clientele would provide the best type of library service. That the library has been so successful is due in no small measure to this principle. It is evident that the library will continue to develop as a special library, molding its collections and services to fit its own needs, but by so doing the library will also provide an invaluable service to international scholarship.

Notes

Preface

[1]United Nations, Library, *The Libraries of the United Nations: A Descriptive Guide* (ST/LIB/17: 1966). All United Nations documents, once cited, will thereafter be cited by document number, if there is one.

[2]Verner W. Clapp, "The Development of the United Nations Library since Its Beginning," in United Nations, Library, *The Dag Hammarskjöld Library: Gift of the Ford Foundation*, p.56–62; idem, "The United Nations Library: 1945–1961," *Libri* 12:111–21 (1962).

[3]Verner W. Clapp, "The Library of the United Nations Conference on International Organization: San Francisco, 1945," *Library Journal* 70: 871–78 (1 Oct. 1945).

[4]S. Hartz Rasmussen, [Notes for a History], n.d. (in the files of Mr. Rasmussen).

[5]Carl H. Milam, "Diary on U.N." (in the files of Mr. Milam), hereafter to be cited as Milam Diary: idem, "The United Nations Library," *Library Quarterly* 23:267–80 (Oct. 1953).

[6]Josef Stummvoll, "Als Bibliotheksdirektor bei den Vereinten Nationen: Tagebuchnotizen, 1. Teil," *Biblos* 8:53–59 (1959); "Als Bibliotheksdirektor bei den Vereinten Nationen: Tagebuchnotizen, 2. Teil," *Biblos* 8:124–45 (1959); "Als Bibliotheksdirektor bei den Vereinten Nationen: Tagebuchnotizen, 3. Teil," *Biblos* 9:57–76 (1960); and "Als Bibliotheksdirektor bei den Vereinten Nationen, 4. Teil, Die 'Dag Hammarskjöld Bibliothek' in New York," *Biblos* 12:87–96 (1963).

[7]Doris Cruger Dale, "The Origin and Development of the United Nations Library" (D.L.S. dissertation, Columbia University, 1968).

Chapter 1

[1]William Penn, *An Essay towards the Present and Future Peace of Europe*, p.6, 9–10, 13–19.

[2]League of Nations, Covenant, articles 2, 6, and 7; United Nations, Charter, articles 7, 97, 98, 99, 100, 101, and 105.

[3]United Nations, Charter, article 1.

[4]Ibid., article 99.

[5]Víctor Belaúnde, "The United Nations Library As Seen by a User," in United Nations, Library, *The Dag Hammarskjöld Library: Gift of the Ford Foundation*, p.84.

[6]United Nations, General Assembly, *Staff Regulations of the United Nations*, Res. 590 (VI), 2 Feb. 1952 (A/2119: United Nations, General Assembly, Official Records, 6th sess., Suppl. no.20), p.76. Official Records will hereafter be cited as UNGAOR.

[7]Marguerite E. Day, "The Library of the League of Nations," *Library Assistant* 15:212–15 (Nov. 1921).

[8]*Who's Who in America*, v.21 (Chicago: The A. N. Marquis Co., 1940), p.2789.

[9]A thorough search of the United Nations documents and archives has failed to uncover this document. Mr. Norman S. Field, Associate Chief Librarian of the United Nations Library, Geneva, was unable to trace this report in the Geneva collection; Miss Wilson, who now lives in Switzerland, does not possess a copy. See letter from Mr. Field to the author, dated 20 October 1969.

[10]Florence Wilson, "The Library of the League of Nations," *Library Journal* 47:1060 (15 Dec. 1922).

[11]Muriel Hoppes, "The Library of the League of Nations at Geneva," *Library Quarterly* 31:265 (July 1961).

[12]Florence Wilson, "The Library of the League of Nations: A Description of Its Functions, Scope and Work," p.16–17.

[13]League of Nations, *Rules of Procedure of the Assembly* (C.144.M.92.1937: Apr. 1937), rule 16.

[14]United Nations, Office of Public Information, *Everyman's United Nations:* A Complete Handbook of the Activities and Evolution of the United Nations during Its First Twenty Years, 1945–1965, p.13.

[15]Letter from Miss Mary Florence Wilson to the author, dated 11 Nov. 1969.

[16]"Offer by a Group of American Citizens for the Construction and Endowment of the League of Nations Library," *League of Nations Official Journal* 8:1132–33 (Oct. 1927).

[17]"Gift of $2,000,000 to League of Nations," *New York Times*, 11 Sept. 1927. All references to *The New York Times* refer to the late city edition unless otherwise specified.

[18]"Topics of the Times: Another Unofficial Adviser," *New York Times*, 13 Sept. 1927.

[19]Hoppes, "The Library of the League," p.257.

[20]League of Nations, Library Planning Committee, "Preliminary Report to the Secretary-General," p.1.

[21]Ibid., p.4.

[22]League of Nations, Library Planning Committee, "Second Report to the Secretary-General," p.1.

[23]"Text of the Agreement Regarding the Ariana Site," *League of Nations Official Journal*, Special Suppl. no.75:491–92 (1929).

[24]League of Nations, Library Planning Committee, "Third Session Minutes."

[25]League of Nations, Library Planning Committee, "Fourth Session Report to the Secretary-General."

[26]Letter from William Warner Bishop, Librarian, University of Michigan to Mr. Sweetser, dated Geneva, 8 June 1932, ibid., attachment.

[27]League of Nations, Library Planning Committee, "Fifth Session."

[28]William Warner Bishop, "International Relations: Fragments of Autobiography," *Library Quarterly* 19:283 (Oct. 1949).

[29]The crowning of the roof tree with flowers is probably "a reference to the custom in some European countries of tying a small branch of a tree to the roofs of buildings at such time as they are completed." See letter from Norman S. Field, Associate Chief Librarian, United Nations Library, Geneva, to the author, dated 20 Oct. 1969.

[30]League of Nations, *Report on the Work of the League 1936/37* (A.6.1937 or Gen.1937.3), p.239.

[31]Vernie H. Wolfsberg, "Three International Libraries," *Minnesota Libraries* 19:107 (Dec. 1958).

[32]Rudolph Gjelsness, "William Warner Bishop Dies," *Library Journal* 80:622 (15 Mar. 1955).

[33]S. Hartz Rasmussen, "The League of Nations Library during the War," *College and Research Libraries* 5:195–99 (June 1944).

[34]Ibid., p.202.

[35]UNGAOR, 1st sess., 1st pt., League of Nations Committee, Summary Record of Meetings, 30 Jan.–1 Feb. 1946, p.8, 15, 17.

[36]United Nations, General Assembly, *Transfer of Certain Functions, Activities and Assets of the League of Nations: Report of the League of Nations Committee to the General Assembly*, 12 Feb. 1946 (A/28: UNGAOR, 1st sess., 1st pt., Annex 16 to 29th Plenary Meeting), p.600.

[37]Memorandum from A. C. Breycha-Vauthier to Adrian Pelt, dated 27 Aug. 1946 (United Nations Archives: Record Group 19, A/369, box 1). Record groups will hereafter be cited as UNA: RG.

[38]Memorandum from S. Hartz Rasmussen to Adrian Pelt, dated 7 Jan. 1947 (UNA: RG 18, A/363, box 1), p.4–5.

[39]Memorandum to Benjamin Cohen, Andrew W. Cordier, Antoine Goldet, Martin Hill, Byron Price, and David Vaughan, dated 14 July 1948 (UNA: RG 18, A/193, box 4).

[40]United Nations, International Advisory Committee of Library Experts, "Working Paper 3: Special Considerations," 23 July 1948 (UNA: RG 18, A/193, box 4), p.3, 5.

[41]United Nations, Library, Permanent Advisory Library Committee, Summary of Meeting, 7 July 1948 (UNA: RG 15, A/122, box 26), p.2. Committee will hereafter be cited as PALC.

[42]United Nations, International Advisory Committee of Library Experts, *Report of the Session Held at Lake Success, New York, 2 to 9 August 1948*, 30 Aug. 1948 (A/C.5/222 and Corr. 1:UNGAOR, 3d sess., 1st pt., Fifth Committee, Annexes, Agenda item 33 [c]), p.12–13.

[43][Ralph Shaw], *Library and Documentation Services of the United Nations*, p.48.

[44]United Nations, Library, *The Division of Library Services as of 1 January 1949*, p.6.

[45]United Nations, Economic and Social Council, *Use of the Central Library at Geneva by the United Nations and the Specialized Agencies*, Res. 260 (IX), 6 July 1949 (E/1553: UNESCOR, 9th sess., Suppl. no.1), p.76.

[46]UNGAOR, 4th sess., Fifth Committee, 207th Meeting, 25 Oct. 1949, p.137.

[47]"The Conference Library," *The United Nations Conference on International Organization Journal*, no.1:4 (25 Apr. 1945).

[48]Clapp, "The Library of the United Nations Conference on International Organization," p.871–78; idem, "Report on Activities of the Conference Library," 10 July 1945 (in the files of Mr. Clapp).

[49]Jerrold Orne, "Super-Library Service for an International Conference," unpublished paper, n.d. (in the files of Mrs. Wessells); Paul Kruse, "A Special Library at the Conference," *Special Libraries* 36: 431–35 (Nov. 1945).

[50]Letter from Luther H. Evans to Archibald MacLeish, dated 11 Aug. 1945 (in the correspondence files of the Library of Congress).

[51]Letter from Luther H. Evans to the secretary of state, dated 17 Mar. 1945; and letter from Archibald MacLeish to Luther Evans, dated 26 Mar. 1945 (in the correspondence files of the Library of Congress).

[52]Clapp, "Report on Activities of the Conference Library," p.2.

[53]United Nations Conference on International Organization, Conference Library, *Short Title Classified Catalog*.

[54]Clapp, "Report on Activities of the Conference Library," p.5.

[55]Rose C. Suttey, "San Francisco Public Library Makes Twofold Contribution to Conference," *Library Journal* 70:625 (July 1945).

[56]Lawrence E. Davies, "Delegates' Leisure a Parley Problem," *New York Times*, 25 Mar. 1945.

[57]Joseph Henry Jackson, "Library of 3000 Reference Books for Delegates," *San Francisco Chronicle: The World of Books*, 22 Apr. 1945, p.3.

[58]Jerrold Orne and Verner W. Clapp, "Conference Library," 21 May 1945 (in the correspondence files of the Library of Congress), p.4.

[59]Clapp, "The Library of the United Nations Conference on International Organization," p.877.

[60]Orne and Clapp, "Conference Library," p.5–6.

[61]In the correspondence files of the Library of Congress.

[62]Letter from Verner W. Clapp to James B. Childs, dated 11 June 1944 [sic—this should be 1945 as it is in response to a letter dated 4 June 1945](in the correspondence files of the Library of Congress).

[63]Kruse, "A Special Library," p.434.

[64]Letter from A. F. Anders, Personnel Officer, U.S. Naval Training Center, San Diego, to Yeoman 3/c Jerrold Orne, dated 19 Apr. 1945 (in the files of Mr. Orne).

⁶⁵Orne, "Super-Library Service" p.5.

⁶⁶*Who's Who in Library Service*, 4th ed. ([Hamden, Conn.]: The Shoe String Press, Inc., 1966), p.384.

⁶⁷Ibid., p.520.

⁶⁸Kruse, "A Special Library," p.434.

⁶⁹Richardson Dougall, "The Archives and Documents of the Preparatory Commission of the United Nations," *American Archivist* 10:26 (Jan. 1947).

⁷⁰United Nations, Preparatory Commission, *Memorandum from the Executive Secretary on the Provision of a Library* (PC/EX/18: 28 Aug. 1945).

⁷¹United Nations, Preparatory Commission, *Library Arrangements* (PC/EX/AD/7: 11 Sept. 1945).

⁷²United Nations, General Assembly, *Handbook, First Session of the General Assembly*, rev. ed., p.9.

⁷³United Nations, Preparatory Commission, *Report of the Preparatory Commission of the United Nations* (PC/20: 23 Dec. 1945), p.89.

Chapter 2

¹José Meyer, "United Nations Information Board and Its Library," *Library Journal* 69:7–10 (1 Jan. 1944).

²Letter from Albert C. Gerould to the author, dated 18 Mar. 1968.

³"U.N. Names in the News: Adrian Pelt," *United Nations Newsletter* 3:6 (Jan. 1950).

⁴Milam Diary, entry dated 11 Feb. 1948.

⁵Memorandum from Benjamin Cohen, undated, but written after the issuance of the management survey (UNA: RG 18, A/193, box 4), p.1.

⁶[Shaw], *Library and Documentation Services*, p.94–95, 105.

⁷UNGAOR, 2d sess., Fifth Committee, 94th Meeting, 10 Nov. 1947, p.406.

⁸United Nations, *Annual Report of the Secretary-General on the Work of the Organization, 1 July 1947–30 June 1948* (A/565: UNGAOR, 3d sess., Suppl. no.1), p.123.

⁹PALC, Summary of Meeting, 23 Dec. 1947 (UNA: RG 15, A/122, box 26), p.1.

¹⁰Memorandum from Carl H. Milam to Members of the Permanent Advisory Library Committee, dated 17 May 1948 (UNA: RG 15, A/122, box 26), p.1.

¹¹United Nations, General Assembly, Advisory Committee on Administrative and Budgetary Questions, *First Report of 1948 to the General Assembly*, Apr. 1948 (A/534: UNGAOR, 3d sess., Suppl. no.7), p.4.

¹²United Nations, General Assembly, Advisory Committee on Administrative and Budgetary Questions, *Second Report of 1948 to the General Assembly*, Aug. 1948 (A/598: UNGAOR, 3d sess., Suppl. no.7A), p.27.

¹³A/C.5/222, p.7.

[14]UNGAOR, 3d sess., Fifth Committee, 136th Meeting, 20 Oct. 1948, p.396.

[15]Ibid., p.394, 397, and 398.

[16]Ibid., p.402.

[17]Milam Diary, entry dated 28 Nov. 1948.

[18]Ibid.

[19]Ibid., entry dated 21 Apr. 1949.

[20]Ibid.

[21]United Nations, *Annual Report of the Secretary-General on the Work of the Organization, 1 July 1949 – 30 June 1950* (A/1287: UN-GAOR, 5th sess., Suppl. no.1), p.141.

[22]United Nations, *Organization of the Secretariat: Report of the Secretary-General's Survey Group*, p.180, 187.

[23]Marjan Stopar-Babsek, "Establishment and Organization of United Nations Archives," Prepared as a Working Paper for the 6th Round Table Conference on Archives, Warsaw, May 1961, p.3, 9.

[24]Letter from S. Hartz Rasmussen to Josef Stummvoll, dated 8 Jan. 1962 (in the files of Mr. Rasmussen).

[25]*Who's Who in Library Service*, 4th ed. ([Hamden, Conn.]: The Shoe String Press, 1966), p.236.

[26]Memorandum from Albert C. Gerould to Adrian Pelt, dated 7 June 1946 (UNA: RG 15, A/122, box 26).

[27]PALC, Summary of the 1st Meeting, 3 Mar. 1947 (UNA: RG 15, A/122, box 26), p.1.

[28]S. Hartz Rasmussen, "Factual Information Related to My Resignation from the Post of Librarian of the United Nations Library," ca. May 1948 (in the files of Mr. Rasmussen), p.4.

[29]PALC, Summary of Meeting, 23 Dec. 1947 (UNA: RG 15, A/122, box 26), p.2.

[30]"Former League of Nations Librarian Assumes Same Post at U.N.," *Library Journal* 72:1740 (15 Dec. 1947).

[31]Rasmussen, "Factual Information," p.2.

[32]Letter from Milton E. Lord to T. P. Sevensma, dated 1 Mar. 1948 (in Mr. Milam's diary).

[33]Letter from Ralph R. Shaw to Benjamin Cohen, dated 10 Nov. 1947 (UNA: RG 18, A/193, box 4).

[34]V. J. G. Stavridi, Note on Conversation with New York Public Library, 30 Dec. 1947 (UNA: RG 1, box 509).

[35]Letter from Luther H. Evans to Jack Dalton, dated 20 Nov. 1968 (in the author's files).

[36]Letter from Benjamin Cohen to Carl H. Milam, dated 22 Jan. 1948 (in Mr. Milam's diary).

[37]"The Contributors to This Issue: Carl H. Milam," *Library Quarterly* 23:297 (Oct. 1953).

[38]Milam Diary, entry dated 7 Feb. 1948.

[39]Ibid., entry dated 6 Feb. 1948.

[40]Ibid.

[41]Letter from Mary G. Smieton, Director of Personnel, to Carl H. Mil-

am, dated 19 Feb. 1948; and letter from Carl H. Milam to Mary G. Smieton, dated 27 Feb. 1948 (in Mr. Milam's diary).

[42]Milam Diary, entry dated 9 Feb. 1948.

[43]Ibid.

[44]Ibid.

[45]Ibid., entry dated 9 Mar. 1948.

[46]Ibid., entry dated 16 May 1948.

[47]Ibid., entry dated 8 Mar. 1948.

[48]Ibid., entry dated 28 June 1950.

[49]Letter from Joseph Groesbeck to the author, dated 28 Oct. 1969.

[50]Memorandum for File from Edouard Reitman, dated 24 Nov. 1952 (UNA: RG 21, A/428, box 1).

[51]Ibid.

[52]Rubens Borba Alves de Moraes was called Dr. Moraes in the United Nations. Outside the United Nations he was generally called Dr. Borba, which, in the Portuguese style, is the more usual – Borba being his father's name. See letter from Joseph Groesbeck to the author, dated 28 Oct. 1969.

[53]Arthur E. Gropp, "Personnel: Dr. Rubens Borba Alves de Moraes," *College and Research Libraries* 16:98 (Jan. 1955).

[54]Memorandum from Carl H. Milam to Members of the Permanent Advisory Library Committee, dated 6 July 1948 (UNA: RG 15, A/122, box 26), p.5.

[55]"Borba de Moraes, Rubens," in *Who's Who in the United Nations*, p.58.

[56]United Nations, Library, *Report of the Headquarters Library and of the Geneva Library, 1954* (ST/LIB/1: 6 Apr. 1955), p.3.

[57]Memorandum from R. Borba de Moraes to Andrew W. Cordier, dated 5 Apr. 1954 (UNA: RG 21, A/428, box 1).

[58]United Nations, General Assembly, Fifth Committee, *Budget Estimates for the Financial Year 1950*, 21 Sept. 1949 (A/C.5/298: UNGAOR, 4th sess., Annex, v.1, Agenda item 39[a]), p.43, 44.

[59]United Nations, Library, Minutes of Meeting with Section and Unit Chiefs, 6 Oct. 1954 (UNA: RG 21, A/428, box 2).

[60]"Stummvoll, Josef (Leopold)," in *Current Biography 1960*, p.410.

[61]United Nations, Library, *Report of the Headquarters Library and the Geneva Library, 1961* (ST/LIB/9: 4 Dec. 1962), p.2; ibid., 1962 (ST/LIB/11: 30 Dec. 1963). p.1.

[62]Ibid., 1963 (ST/LIB/14: 28 May 1964), p.2; ibid., 1964 (ST/LIB/16: 1 June 1965), p.2.

[63]Louis Shores, "Epitome," *Journal of Library History* 1:206–207 (Oct. 1966).

[64]United Nations, Charter, article 8 and article 101, section 3.

[65]Leland M. Goodrich, "Geographical Distribution of the Staff of the UN Secretariat," *International Organization* 16:467 (Summer 1962).

[66]United Nations, General Assembly, *Composition of the Secretariat and the Principle of Geographic Distribution*, 2 Sept. 1948 (A/652: UNGAOR, 3d sess., pt. 1, Annexes, Agenda item 40), p.157.

[67]United Nations, General Assembly, *Geographical Distribution of the Staff of the Secretariat*, Res. 1928 (XVIII), 11 Dec. 1963 (A/5515: UNGAOR, 18th sess., Suppl. no.15), p.60.

[68]Memorandum from Carl H. Milam to George Janecek, dated 4 Aug. 1948 (UNA: RG 1, box 509).

[69]Letter from Joseph Groesbeck to the author, dated 28 Oct. 1969.

[70]Milam Diary, entry dated 15 Dec. 1949.

[71]Ibid., entry dated 29 Dec. 1949.

[72]Letter from Joseph Groesbeck to the author, dated 28 Oct. 1969.

[73]Memorandum from S. Hartz Rasmussen to François Stefanini, dated 30 July 1947 (UNA: RG 18, A/363, box 1).

[74][Shaw], *Library and Documentation Services*, p.95.

[75]Carl H. Milam, "Internships, United Nations Library," 7 Sept. 1948 (UNA: RG 1, box 509).

[76]Letter from Benjamin Cohen to Alger Hiss, dated Sept. 1948 (UNA: RG 1, box 509).

[77]Memorandum from Carl H. Milam on conversation with Alger Hiss, dated 26 Oct. 1948 (UNA: RG 1, box 509).

[78]United Nations, International Advisory Committee of Library Experts, "Working Paper 3," p.14–16.

[79]A/C.5/222, p.14.

[80]United Nations, Library, "Interns in the United Nations Headquarters Library," 11 May 1949 (UNA: RG 1, box 509).

[81]Letter from Carl H. Milam to Rabieb Tantranon, dated 8 June 1949; and letter from Carl H. Milam to Surjit Singh, dated 8 June 1949 (UNA: RG 1, box 509).

[82]United Nations, Library, *The United Nations Headquarters Library, January, 1950*, p.16.

[83]Memorandum from David Vaughan to Waldo Chamberlin, Albert Gerould, et al., dated 16 Apr. 1946 (UNA: RG 18, A/193, box 4).

[84]Memorandum from the Secretary-General to Adrian Pelt, dated 26 Aug. 1946 (UNA: RG 19, A/369, box 1).

[85]Ibid.

[86][Shaw], *Library and Documentation Services*, p.22.

[87]Ibid., p.91.

[88]A/C.5/222, p.8.

[89]United Nations, General Assembly, Fifth Committee, *Budget Estimates for the Financial Year 1950*, 21 Sept. 1949 (A/C.5/298: UNGAOR. 4th sess., Annex, v.1. Agenda item 39 [a]), p.43.

[90]UNGAOR, 4th sess., Fifth Committee, 197th Meeting, 13 Oct. 1949, p.70.

[91]United Nations, Library, "Departmental Libraries," Dec. 1949 (UNA: RG 15, A/122, box 26), p.1–2.

[92]Memorandum from Carl H. Milam to Te-Lou Tchang, Department of Social Affairs, and Sturgis B. Shields, Department of Economic Affairs, dated 10 May 1949 (UNA: RG 1, box 509).

[93]United Nations, Library, "United Nations Departmental Libraries," 7 July 1949 (UNA: RG 18, A/193, box 4), p.1.

[94]Ibid., p.2.

[95]Ibid.

[96]United Nations, Library, "Secretariat Building: Departmental Branch Libraries," 22 June 1950 (UNA: RG 15, A/122, box 26).

[97]United Nations, General Assembly, Advisory Committee on Administrative and Budgetary Questions, *Second Report of 1950 to the General Assembly*, 1950 (A/1312: UNGAOR, 5th sess., Suppl. no.7), p.23.

[98]PALC, Minutes of Meeting, 13 Sept. 1950 (UNA: RG 15, A/122, box 26).

[99]Memorandum from Edouard Reitman to Members of the Library Advisory Committee, dated 3 Oct. 1950, with attachment: Final Draft for A/C.5 Document on the Departmental Libraries (UNA: RG 15, A/122, box 26), p.4.

[100]United Nations, General Assembly, Advisory Committee on Administrative and Budgetary Questions, *Second Report of 1951 to the General Assembly*, 1951 (A/1853: UNGAOR, 6th sess., Suppl. no.7), p.21.

[101]PALC, Minutes of Meeting on Matters Concerning Departmental Libraries, 5 Oct. 1951 (UNA: RG 15, A/122, box 26).

[102]United Nations, Library, "History and Functions of the Departmental Branch Libraries," 12 Oct. 1951 (UNA: RG 15, A/122, box 26).

[103]United Nations, General Assembly, Advisory Committee on Administrative and Budgetary Questions, *First Report to the Seventh Session of the General Assembly*, 1952 (A/2157: UNGAOR, 7th sess., Suppl. no.7), p.23.

[104]Letter from Edouard Reitman to Carl H. Milam, dated 9 Jan. 1952 (UNA: RG 21, A/428, box 1).

[105]Verner W. Clapp, "The United Nations Library: Organization –Work–Utilization of Staff," 20 May 1952 (in the files of Mr. Clapp), p.47. Also published as an attachment to United Nations, General Assembly, Fifth Committee: Budget Estimates for the Financial Year 1953 (A/C.5/L.177: 23 Oct. 1952).

[106]Memorandum from R. Borba de Moraes, to Andrew W. Cordier, dated 8 Apr. 1954 (UNA: RG 21, A/428, box 1).

Chapter 3

[1]A/65, p.66.

[2]Meyer Berger, "Multi-Lingual UNO Sounds like Babel," *New York Times*, 26 Mar. 1946.

[3]Tom O'Hara, "Staff of U.N.O. Keeps Busy at Routine Tasks," *New York Herald Tribune*, 26 Mar. 1946.

[4]Letter from Albert C. Gerould to the writer, dated 18 Mar. 1968.

[5]Leonard Lyons, "The Lyons Den," *New York Post*, 21 June 1946.

[6]Rasmussen, [Notes for a History], p.2.

[7]PALC, Summary of the 1st Meeting, 3 Mar. 1947 (UNA: RG 15, A/122, box 26), p.1.

[8]PALC, Special Meeting, 9 Sept. 1947 (UNA: RG 15, A/122, box 26), p.1.

[9]PALC, Special Meeting, 12 Sept. 1947 (UNA: RG 15, A/122, box 26), p.5–6.

[10]A/C.5/222, p.9.

[11]Ibid., p.10.

[12]Letter from Carl H. Milam to Angus S. Macdonald, President, Snead and Company, dated 3 Sept. 1948 (UNA: RG 1, box 509).

[13]William Farrell, "Housing Authority Joins Rest of Us," *New York Times*, 19 Apr. 1947.

[14]"U.N. Offices to Move to Headquarters," *New York Times*, 16 Aug. 1947.

[15]Carl H. Milam, "Preparations for Moving Library to Manhattan," 15 Mar. 1949 (UNA: RG 15, A/122, box 26), p.1–6.

[16]PALC, Minutes of Meeting, 16 Mar. 1949 (UNA: RG 15, A/122, box 26), p.9–10.

[17]Memorandum from Carl H. Milam to Benjamin Cohen, dated 23 Mar. 1949 (UNA: RG 15, A/122, box 26).

[18]Letter from Carl H. Milam to Joseph L. Wheeler, dated 7 June 1949 (UNA: RG 1, box 509).

[19]Letter from Carl H. Milam to Joseph L. Wheeler, dated 23 June 1949 (UNA: RG 1, box 509).

[20]United Nations, Library, "Headquarters Library," 22 June 1950 (UNA: RG 15, A/122, box 26); idem, Plans for the Library Building in Manhattan, ca. 22 June 1950 (UNA: RG 21, A/428, box 1).

[21]UNGAOR, 5th sess., Fifth Committee, 238th Meeting, 3 Oct. 1950, and 239th Meeting, 3 Oct. 1950, p.11 and 19.

[22]United Nations, General Assembly, *Headquarters of the United Nations: Report of the Fifth Committee*, 6 Dec. 1950 (A/1634: UNGAOR, 5th sess., Annexes, v.2, Agenda item 36), p.9–10.

[23]United Nations, Library, *The United Nations Headquarters Library, 1 July 1950–30 June 1951*, p.3.

[24]Ibid., 1 July 1951–31 Dec. 1951, p.2.

[25]UNGAOR, 11th sess., Fifth Committee, 593rd Meeting, 20 Feb. 1957, p.347.

[26]United Nations, Library, *Report of the Headquarters Library and the Geneva Library, 1959 and 1960* (ST/LIB/8: 9 Nov. 1961), p.3.

[27]Memorandum from Byron Price to Edouard Reitman, dated 6 Nov. 1950 (UNA: RG 21, A/428, box 1).

[28]Andrew D. Osborn, "The United Nations Library," 21 Nov. 1950 (UNA: RG 21, A/428, box 1), p.3.

[29]Ibid., p.3–4.

[30][Carl H. Milam], "Program for a Permanent Library Building," 8 May 1951 (UNA: RG 21, A/428, box 1).

[31]Memorandum from Carl H. Milam to Andrew W. Cordier, dated 1 Mar. 1951 (UNA: RG 21, A/428, box 1), p.5.

[32]Ibid., p.1–6.

[33]Memorandum from Carl H. Milam to Andrew W. Cordier, dated 9

May 1951 (UNA: RG 21, A/428, box 1).

[34]Carl H. Milam, "The United Nations Headquarters Library: Its Character, Services and Needs," 1 Oct. 1951 (UNA: RG 21, A/428, box 1).

[35]Memorandum from Carl H. Milam to Andrew W. Cordier, dated 2 Oct. 1951 (UNA: RG 21, A/428, box 1).

[36]Letter from Carl H. Milam to Andrew W. Cordier, dated 3 Dec. 1951 (UNA: RG 21, A/428, box 1), p.1.

[37]Ibid., p.3.

[38]Letter from Carl H. Milam to Andrew W. Cordier, dated 24 Jan. 1952 (UNA: RG 21, A/428, box 1).

[39]Letter from Andrew W. Cordier to Carl H. Milam, dated 20 Sept. 1952 (in the files of Mr. Milam).

[40]United Nations, *United Nations Library*, n.d., ca. 1952 (in the files of Mr. Milam), p.6.

[41]Letter from H. Rowan Gaither, Jr. (President of the Ford Foundation) to Andrew Cordier, dated 13 May 1956; and letter from Henry T. Heald (President of the Ford Foundation) to Dag Hammarskjöld, dated 18 Dec. 1958 (in the files of the Ford Foundation).

[42]On 16 April 1963, a check for $131,340.03, representing "the unencumbered balance of the initial grant, plus accumulated income," was returned to the Ford Foundation. The total amount of the grant therefore amounted to $6,068,659.97. See letter from U Thant to Henry T. Heald, dated 16 Apr. 1963 (UNA: Registry File FI 322 [1]).

[43]United Nations, General Assembly, *The United Nations Library: Gift of the Ford Foundation*, 29 Sept. 1959 (A/4231: UNGAOR, 14th sess., Annexes, Agenda item 72), p.1.

[44]United Nations, General Assembly, *The United Nations Library: Gift of the Ford Foundation*, Res. 1354 (XIV), 3 Nov. 1959 (A/4354: UNGAOR, 14th sess. Suppl. no.16), p.42.

[45]United Nations, General Assembly, *Report to the General Assembly of the United Nations by the Secretary-General on the Permanent Headquarters of the United Nations* (A/311: July 1947), p.22.

[46]Memorandum from Edouard Reitman to Wallace K. Harrison, dated 3 Jan. 1951 (UNA: RG 21, A/428, box 1), p.1–2.

[47]Memorandum from Carl H. Milam to Wallace K. Harrison, dated 27 Feb. 1951 (revision of memorandum dated 3 Jan. 1951) (UNA: RG 21, A/428, box 1).

[48]United Nations, Library, Minutes of Meeting Held at Headquarters Planning Office on Proposed New Library Building, 8 May 1951 (UNA: RG 21, A/428, box 1), p.1.

[49]Carl H. Milam, "Notes on Space Requirements for Permanent United Nations Library Building," 8 May 1951 (UNA:RG 21, A/428, box 1), p.2.

[50]Memorandum from W. A. Heaps for the Record, dated 2 Oct. 1951 (UNA: RG 21, A/428, box 1).

[51]A/4231, p.2.

[52]Ibid., p.4–5.

[53]A/4354, p.42.

[54]United Nations, Office of General Services, "United Nations Library,

Progress Report," no.1, 6 Nov. 1959; ibid., no.15, 15 Feb. 1960 (UNA: RG 22, A/426, box 1).

[55] Ibid., no.31, 6 June 1950.

[56] United Nations, Library, *Notes on Its Construction and Furnishing*, p.1–3.

[57] Harrison, Abramovitz and Harris, Architects, "Rare Woods from Three Continents for the UN's Dag Hammarskjöld Library," *Interiors*, 122:102–107 (Apr. 1963).

[58] United Nations, Office of Public Information, *The Library Building* (Press Release HQC/198: 14 Nov. 1961), p.2.

[59] "New Mural for U.N.: Swedish Artist Is Working in Hammarskjöld Library," *New York Times*, 9 Nov. 1961.

[60] Michael Harris, "Designing the New Library in Terms of Function," in United Nations, Library, *The Dag Hammarskjöld Library: Gift of the Ford Foundation*, p.69.

[61] Ibid., p.68.

[62] Ibid.

[63] Letter from Dag Hammarskjöld to Carl H. Milam, dated 1 Sept. 1961 (in the files of Mr. Milam).

[64] United Nations, General Assembly, *United Nations Library: Memorial to the Late Dag Hammarskjöld*. 3 Oct. 1961 (A/4908: UNGAOR, 16th sess., Annexes, Agenda item 68), p.1.

[65] United Nations, General Assembly, *Memorial to the Late Dag Hammarskjöld*, Res. 1625 (XVI), 16 Oct. 1961 (A/5100: UNGAOR, 16th sess., Suppl. no.17), p.46.

[66] United Nations, Library, *Dedication of the Dag Hammarskjöld Library, United Nations, 16–18 November, 1961: Programme*, p.125–27.

[67] United Nations, Library, *The Dag Hammarskjöld Library: Gift of the Ford Foundation*, p.44.

[68] Ibid., p.47.

[69] Ibid., p.47.

[70] Ibid., p.49.

[71] Ibid., p.39–43.

[72] Ibid., p. 50–124.

[73] Ibid., p.121.

[74] Ibid., p. 122–23.

[75] Letter from Arthur E. Gropp to Josef Stummvoll, dated 22 Nov. 1961 (UNA: RG 21, A/428, box 2).

[76] Letter from C. Wormann to Andrew W. Cordier, dated 19 Dec. 1961 (UNA: RG 21, A/428, box 2).

[77] Letter from Arthur Sweetser to Andrew W. Cordier, dated 9 Dec. 1961 (UNA: RG 21, A/428, box 2).

Chapter 4

[1] Memorandum from David Vaughan to Albert Gerould, et al., dated

16 Apr. 1946 (UNA: RG 18, A/193, box 4).

²Letter from Albert C. Gerould to the writer, dated 18 Mar. 1968.

³Memorandum from the secretary-general to Adrian Pelt, dated 26 Aug. 1946 (UNA: RG 19, A/369, box 1).

⁴Ibid.

⁵S. Hartz Rasmussen, "General Plan for the United Nations Library Service," 3 Oct. 1946 (UNA: RG 19, A/369, box 2).

⁶Ibid., p.7.

⁷Cited in Rasmussen, [Notes for a History], p.5. Mr. Rasmussen found the Hadley letter in File 309-15-1 of the United Nations Archives. A letter to the author from Marjan Stopar-Babsek, archivist of the United Nations, dated 29 February 1968 reported that "Central Registry File No. 309-15-1 'Inter-Library Cooperation, General' became integrated with some DPI Registry files some time ago and were disposed in accordance with approved schedules." This letter is also mentioned in [François Stefanini], "Supplementary Report on the United Nations Library," n.d. (UNA: RG 19, A/369, box 1), p.2-3. Mr. Hadley, in a letter to the author dated 9 September 1968, said: "The quotation accords with my recollection of the situation in 1946."

⁸Rasmussen, [Notes for a History], p. 5.

⁹Memorandum from Albert C. Gerould to Adrian Pelt, dated 17 June 1946, entitled Report of Division of Library and Archives (UNA: RG 19, A/369, box 1), p.1.

¹⁰S. Hartz Rasmussen, "Report on the United Nations Library Service," 27 Jan. 1947 (UNA: RG 19, A/369, box 2), p.2.

¹¹[François Stefanini], "Report on the United Nations Library," 5 Feb. 1947 (UNA: RG 19, A/369, box 1), p.3.

¹²[Stefanini], "Supplementary Report," p.3. The role of the New York Public Library in the development of the United Nations Library is not completely clear. The only documentary evidence of this offer to house the United Nations Library in the New York Public Library is the Hadley letter and the reference to it in this report.

¹³Ibid.

¹⁴PALC, Summary of the 1st Meeting, 3 Mar. 1947 (UNA: RG 15, A/122, box 26), p.3.

¹⁵[Shaw], *Library and Documentation Services*, p.8.

¹⁶Letter from S. Hartz Rasmussen to the author, dated 27 Feb. 1968.

¹⁷PALC, Summary of the 2d Meeting, 17 Mar. 1947 (UNA: RG 15, A/122, box 26), p.1.

¹⁸PALC, Summary of the 4th Meeting, 31 Mar. 1947 (UNA: RG 15, A/122, box 26), p.1.

¹⁹Statement by P. Schmidt of the Security Council Department in PALC, Summary of the 7th Meeting, 22 Apr. 1947 (UNA: RG 15, A/122, box 26), p.5.

²⁰Ibid., p.3.

²¹Ibid., p.7, 10.

²²Ibid., p.9-10.

²³Letter from Carl H. Milam to John E. Burchard, dated 9 May 1947 (in the files of Mr. Milam).

[24]United Nations, Library, *The Division of Library Services as of 1 January 1949*, p.2.

[25]PALC, Summary of the 7th Meeting, 22 Apr. 1947 (UNA: RG 15, A/122, box 26), p.11–12.

[26]Ralph A. Beals, Luther H. Evans, Carl H. Milam, and A. C. Breycha-Vauthier, "Report: Planning of United Nations Library," 22–23 Apr. 1947 (in the files of Mr. Milam), p.1.

[27]Ibid., p.3.

[28]Verner W. Clapp, "Quantities of Materials Required by United Nations Library," 3 May 1947 (UNA: RG 19, A/369, box 1), p.9.

[29]Ibid., p.2, 4, 6–8.

[30]John E. Burchard, "Proposal A: Estimate of Space Requirements for UN Library, New York City," 5 May 1947; idem, "Proposal B: Estimate of Space Requirements for UN Library, New York City," 5 May 1947 (UNA: RG 19, A/369, box 1).

[31]PALC, Summary of the 9th Meeting, 19 May 1947 (UNA: RG 15, A/122, box 26), p.1.

[32]Ibid., p.2.

[33]Ibid., p.3.

[34]PALC, Summary of the 10th Meeting, 2 June 1947 (UNA: RG 15, A/122, box 26), p.3.

[35]United Nations, Secretariat, *Management Survey* (ST/SGB/58: 19 Feb. 1947; SGB/58/Rev. 1: 11 July 1947).

[36][Shaw], *Library and Documentation Services*, p.2.

[37]Ibid., p.104.

[38]Ibid., p.105–106.

[39]Ibid., p.107.

[40]Ibid., p.37.

[41]Ibid.

[42]Ibid., p.37–38.

[43]Memorandum from S. Hartz Rasmussen to François Stefanini, dated 10 Oct. 1947 (UNA: RG 19, A/369, box 1), p.1.

[44]Memorandum from S. Hartz Rasmussen to François Stefanini, dated 13 Oct. 1947 (UNA: RG 19, A/369, box 1), p.1.

[45]Milam Diary, entry for 9 Mar. 1948.

[46]United Nations, General Assembly, Fifth Committee, *Report of the Management Survey of United Nations Headquarters* (A/C.5/160: 3 Oct. 1947), p.20–21.

[47]Memorandum from Carl H. Milam to Benjamin Cohen, dated 18 Mar. 1948 (in the files of Mr. Milam), p.2.

[48]Milam Diary, entry dated 12 Feb. 1948.

[49]Letter (dictated by Carl H. Milam) from R. V. Elms, Senior Purchasing Officer, to the New York Public Library, dated 16 Dec. 1948 (in the files of the New York Public Library).

[50]PALC, Special Meeting, 12 Sept. 1947 (UNA: RG 15, A/122, box 26), p.5.

[51]Ibid., p.4.

[52]Memorandum from Benjamin Cohen to V. J. G. Stavridi, dated 22

Sept. 1947 (UNA: RG 18, A/193, box 4).

[53]Letter from Carl H. Milam to Members of Library Staff, dated 18 Mar. 1948 (in the files of Mr. Milam).

[54]Memorandum from Carl H. Milam to Benjamin Cohen, dated 18 Mar. 1948 (in the files of Mr. Milam), p.1.

[55]As cited in United Nations, International Advisory Committee of Library Experts, "Working Paper 1: Library Services, Lake Success and New York," 26 July 1948 (UNA: RG 18, A/193, box 4), p.11.

[56]Several librarians attended the meetings in the capacity of either observers or participants representing the specialized agencies: Miss Janet F. Saunders (International Labour Organisation); Miss Kristine Lomsdal (Food and Agriculture Organization); Theodore Besterman (United Nations Educational, Scientific and Cultural Organization); Alvin Thiessen (International Civil Aviation Organization); Martin Loftus (International Bank for Reconstruction and Development and International Monetary Fund); and G. E. Hill with Miss Elsie Lowenberg as an alternate (World Health Organization). Several other American librarians attended one or more of the meetings as consultants to the committee: Ralph A. Beals (New York Public Library); Thomas P. Fleming (Columbia University); Keyes D. Metcalf (Harvard University); Paul North Rice (New York Public Library); Miss Ruth Savord (Council on Foreign Relations, Inc.); Miss Helen L. Scanlon (Carnegie Endowment for International Peace); Miss Harriet Van Wyck (Woodrow Wilson Foundation); Donald Wasson (Council on Foreign Relations, Inc.); and Jerome K. Wilcox (College of the City of New York).

[57]A/C.5/222, p.5.

[58]Ibid., p.6–7.

[59]As cited in S. R. Ranganathan, *The Five Laws of Library Science*, 2d ed., p.415–16.

[60]UNGAOR, 3d sess., Fifth Committee, 136th Meeting, 20 Oct. 1948, p.402.

[61]A/534; A/598.

[62]A/C.5/298, p.42.

[63]A/C.5/L.177, p.8.

[64]A/1853, p.21.

[65]A/C.5/L.177, p.45.

[66]PALC, Minutes of Meeting, 10 Oct. 1952 (UNA: RG 15, A/122, box 26), p.1.

[67]Frank B. Rogers, "Principles Underlying Types of Special Collections with Particular Reference to the United Nations Library," in United Nations, Library, *The Dag Hammarskjöld Library: Gift of the Ford Foundation*, p.80.

[68]United Nations, International Advisory Committee of Library Experts, "*Working Paper 1*," p.16–23.

[69]Helen E. Wessells, "Report: Notes for a Check List of Projects Under Way or Projected by the United Nations," ca. 1948 (in the files of Mrs. Wessells).

[70]United Nations, Library, *Subjects of Interest to the United Nations Library*.

[71]Rogers, "Principles Underlying Types of Special Collections," p.80.

[72]United Nations, Library, *The United Nations Headquarters Library, 1 January–31 December 1953*, p.6.

[73]United Nations, Library, *The United Nations Headquarters Library, 1 July 1951–31 December 1951*, p.3; idem, *The United Nations Headquarters Library, 1 January–31 December 1952*, p.5.

[74]United Nations, International Advisory Committee of Library Experts, "Working Paper 1," p.22.

[75]A/C.5/298, p.42.

[76]A/C.5/L.177, p.46.

[77]United Nations, Library, *The United Nations Headquarters Library, 1 January–31 December 1953*, p.15.

[78]United Nations, International Advisory Committee of Library Experts, "The Woodrow Wilson Memorial Library: Special Recommendation to the Secretary-General," 8 Sept. 1948 (UNA: RG 18, A/193, box 4).

[79][Carl H. Milam], "The Woodrow Wilson Memorial Library," 6 Apr. 1949 (UNA: RG 18, A/193, box 4; draft copy in the files of Mr. Milam).

[80]Letter from Benjamin Cohen to Mrs. d'Estournelles, dated 18 Jan. 1949 (UNA: RG 18, A/193, box 4).

[81]Ibid.; Letter from Benjamin Cohen to Mrs. d'Estournelles, dated 6 Apr. 1949 (UNA: RG 18, A/193, box 4).

[82]Milam Diary, entry dated 1 July 1949. Mr. Milam gives three reasons why the proposal was not accepted, but it has been impossible to decipher his abbreviations. The records of the Woodrow Wilson Foundation are in storage at Princeton University and are not available for public inspection. See letter from Arthur S. Link, Editor of the Woodrow Wilson Papers, to the author, dated 8 April 1968.

[83]Ibid.. entries dated 23 Feb. 1950 and 8 Mar. 1950.

[84]Ibid., entry dated 25 Mar. 1950. Dr. Eagleton, a professor of government at New York University, was a member of the Council on Foreign Relations. Mr. Fosdick was undersecretary-general for the League of Nations from 1919 to 1920, and was a president and trustee of the Rockefeller Foundation. Mrs. Louise Wright, the wife of Quincy Wright, a well-known professor of international law, had been president of the Woodrow Wilson Foundation and was director of the Chicago Council on Foreign Relations. Mr. Sweetser, who had been a member of the Information Section of the League of Nations from 1918 to 1934 and who had participated in the negotiations for the Rockefeller gift of $2,000,000 to the League Library, was chairman of the United Nations Information Board, 1942–46; president of the Woodrow Wilson Foundation, 1943–45; and had been director of the United Nations Washington Information Office since 1946.

[85]"Old League Records, 100,000 Items, Formally Given to United Nations," *New York Times*, 13 June 1950.

[86]"Woodrow Wilson Library Goes to U.N.," *Library Journal* 76:397 (1 Mar. 1951).

[87]"U.N. Gets Ralston Books," *New York Times*, 25 Aug. 1953; memorandum for record from Joseph Groesbeck, dated 4 Aug. 1953, entitled

Feller Bequest (UNA: RG 21, A/428, box 1); "U.S. Presents Atomic Energy Library to the United Nations," *United States Department of State Bulletin* 34:656–57 (16 Apr. 1956).

[88] PALC, Summary of the 3d Meeting, 24 Mar. 1947 (UNA: RG 15, A/122, box 26), p.1.

[89] United Nations, Library, *The Division of Library Services as of 1 January 1949*, p.5.

[90] Memorandum from S. Hartz Rasmussen to François Stefanini, dated 16 Dec. 1946 (UNA: RG 19, A/369, box 1).

[91] Jerome K. Wilcox, "25 Depository Libraries for U.N. Documents Established," *Library Journal* 72:711 (1 May 1947).

[92] "U.N. Library Chain over World Is Aim," *New York Times*, 7 July 1947.

[93] United Nations, Library, *Report on the 1966 Questionnaire to Depository Libraries* (ST/LIB/20: 4 Jan. 1968), p.1; United Nations, Publications Board, *Principles Governing United Nations Depository Libraries* (ST/PB/4/Rev. 2: 13 Dec. 1967), p.1.

[94] United Nations, Publications Board, *Principles Governing . . . Depository Libraries*, p.2.

[95] Carl H. Milam, "The Depository Library System," *United Nations Bulletin* 6:273 (15 Mar. 1949).

[96] United Nations, Library, *Report on the 1966 Questionnaire*, p.9; United Nations, Library, *Annual Report of the Headquarters Library, the Geneva Library, and the Libraries of the Economic Commissions, 1967* (ST/LIB/21: May 1968), p.15.

[97] United Nations, Library, *Report on the 1966 Questionnaire*, p.2, 4, 7.

Chapter 5

[1] Letter from S. Hartz Rasmussen to Josef Stummvoll, dated 8 Jan. 1962 (in the files of Mr. Rasmussen).

[2] S. Hartz Rasmussen, "Classification System to Be Used in the Library Service," 16 Dec. 1946 (UNA: RG 18, A/363, box 1), p.1.

[3] Ibid., p.3.

[4] Memorandum from Benjamin Cohen to Trygve Lie, dated 11 Apr. 1947 (UNA: RG 1, box 509).

[5] Memorandum from [Carl H. Milam] to Members of the Permanent Advisory Library Committee, dated 6 July 1948 (UNA: RG 15, A/122, box 26), p.1.

[6] For a detailed account of the history of classification systems for government publications, see Doris Cruger Dale, "The Development of Classification Systems for Government Publications," *Library Resources and Technical Services* 13:471–83 (Fall 1969).

[7] Harry N. M. Winton, "United Nations Documents," *Drexel Library Quarterly* 1:35 (Oct. 1965).

[8] William J. Bruce, "The San Francisco *UNCIO* Documents," *American Archivist* 9:6–16 (Jan. 1946).

[9]Lecture by Joseph Groesbeck, Deputy Director, Dag Hammarskjöld Library, United Nations, at Columbia University, 7 Nov. 1966.

[10]Dougall, "The Archives and Documents of the Preparatory Commission," p.33–34.

[11]United Nations, General Assembly, *Outline of Symbols for General Assembly and Other United Nations Documents* (A/1: 3 Jan. 1946; A/1/Corr. 1: 4 Jan. 1946).

[12]United Nations, Library, *Consolidated List of United Nations Document Series Symbols*, preliminary ed. (ST/LIB/SER.D/43: Sept. 1952; Addendum: 14 Sept. 1953).

[13]United Nations, Library, *List of United Nations Document Series Symbols* (ST/LIB/SER.B/5/Rev. 1: 1965).

[14]Brenda Brimmer, et al., *A Guide to the Use of United Nations Documents* (Dobbs Ferry, N.Y.: Oceana Publications, 1962).

[15]Milam, "The United Nations Library," p.276–77.

[16]United Nations, Library, Catalogue Department, *Bulletin*, nos.1–18, 11 July 1949 to 28 Nov. 1949.

[17]United Nations, Library, *Manual of the Cataloguing Unit*, preliminary ed.

[18]Ibid., p.2.

[19]Ibid., p.3–4.

[20]Ibid., p.29–30.

[21]United Nations, Library, [*The United Nations Headquarters Library*], p.5.

[22]Laura C. Colvin, "Serial Checklist: Policy Decisions Affecting Its Reorganization," 31 Aug. 1951 (in the files of Miss Colvin).

[23]Andrew D. Osborn, "The Acquisitions Unit in the United Nations Library: Report on Matters Requiring Action" (in the files of the United Nations Library).

[24]Ibid., p.ii.

[25]Ibid., p.33.

[26]Ibid., p.35–36.

[27]Joseph Groesbeck, "The Osborn Survey," 24 May 1951 (in the files of the United Nations Library), p.10–11.

[28]Ibid., p.12.

[29]*Library Facilities for the United Nations Assembly to Meet on October 23rd, 1946* (UNA: RG 18, A/363, box 1), p.1.

[30]Ibid., p.1.

[31]Ibid., p.2.

[32]Memorandum from S. Hartz Rasmussen to Adrian Pelt, dated 7 Jan. 1947 (UNA: RG 18, A/363, box 1).

[33]United Nations, International Advisory Committee of Library Experts, "Working Paper 1," p.26.

[34]Ibid., p.29.

[35]United Nations, Library, *The Division of Library Services as of 1 January 1949*, p.4.

[36]United Nations, Library, *You Are Invited to Use Your Library*.

[37]United Nations, Library, *The United Nations Headquarters Library*,

January 1950, p.16.

³⁸A/C.5/298, p.1.

³⁹United Nations, Library, *United Nations Library: Policy on Visitors*, 27 Apr. 1951 (UNA: RG 21, A/428, box 1).

⁴⁰United Nations, Library, *United Nations Library: Interpretation of Policy on Use of Library by Public*, 27 Apr. 1951 (UNA: RG 21, A/428, box 1), p.2.

⁴¹United Nations, *Annual Report of the Secretary-General on the Work of the Organization, 16 June 1966–15 June 1967* (A/6701:UNG-AOR. 22d sess., Suppl. no.1), p.201.

⁴²United Nations, Secretariat, *Publications Board* (ST/SGB/60: 4 Mar. 1947).

⁴³Margaret L. Bates and Robert K. Turner, "International Documentation: An Introduction," *International Organization* 1:609 (Nov. 1947).

⁴⁴"News and Notes," *American Political Science Review* 41:1205 (Dec. 1947).

⁴⁵Ibid., p.1205–1206.

⁴⁶United Nations, Advisory Committee of Information Experts, *Report of Session Held at Lake Success, New York, 25 May–3 June [1948]*(Annex I to A/C.5/223: 3 June 1948), p.28.

⁴⁷United Nations, International Advisory Committee of Library Experts, "Working Paper 2: Distribution and Use of United Nations Documents and Departmental Publications," July 1948 (UNA: RG 18, A/193, box 4).

⁴⁸Ibid., p.25.

⁴⁹Harry N. M. Winton, "Documents and Publications of the United Nations," *College and Research Libraries* 9:14 (Jan. 1948).

⁵⁰United Nations, International Advisory Committee of Library Experts, "Working Paper 2," p.26.

⁵¹A/C.5/222, p.11–12.

⁵²S. Briet, "La Conférence de la Dotation Carnegie sur les Documents de L'O.N.U., Paris, 21–22 Novembre 1948," *Revue de la Documentation* 16:6 (1949).

⁵³K. P. R. Menon, "Index and Reference Services (Documents Index Unit, Department of Public Information)," Inspection Service Report no.5, 19 May 1949 (UNA: RG 18, A/193, box 4), p.4.

⁵⁴United Nations, Publications Board, "Weekly Index to Documents and Publications," Paper no.244, 18 Jan. 1949 (UNA: RG 15, A/397, box 2).

⁵⁵K. P. R. Menon, "Notes: Documents Index Unit," 17 Mar. 1949 (UNA: RG 18, A/193, box 4).

⁵⁶Letter from R. B. Eastin to Carl Milam, dated 21 Mar. 1949 (UNA: RG 18, A/193, box 4).

⁵⁷R. B. Eastin, "Conference Concerning Present and Proposed Programs of Documents Index Unit, Division of Library Services, United Nations," 21 Mar. 1949 (UNA: RG 18, A/193, box 4), p.2–4.

⁵⁸Ibid., p.4.

⁵⁹Jerome K. Wilcox, Review of R. B. Eastin, "Conference Concerning Present and Proposed Programs of Documents Index Unit, Division of

Library Services, United Nations," in a letter to Edouard Reitman, dated 8 Apr. 1949 (UNA: RG 18, A/193, box 4).

⁶⁰PALC, Minutes of the Meeting, 27 Apr. 1949 (UNA: RG 15, A/122, box 26), p.1.

⁶¹Ibid., p.6.

⁶²Menon, "Index and Reference Services."

⁶³Ibid., p.24.

⁶⁴United Nations, Publications Board, "Subject: Document Indexing," Paper no.268, 19 May 1949 (UNA: RG 15, A/122, box 26), p.3–4.

⁶⁵Milam Diary, entry dated 23 Feb. 1950.

⁶⁶LeRoy Charles Merritt, Review of *United Nations Documents Index*, in *Library Quarterly* 21:51 (Jan. 1951).

⁶⁷James B. Childs, Review of *United Nations Documents Index*, in *Library of Congress Information Bulletin* 9:11 (27 Feb. 1950).

⁶⁸"Brief of Minutes of General Interest, Association of Research Libraries, July 19, 1950, Cleveland," *College and Research Libraries* 12: 75 (Jan. 1951).

⁶⁹Review of *United Nations Documents Index*, in *Africa* 21:79–80 (Jan. 1951).

⁷⁰United Nations, Library Co-ordinating Committee of the United Nations Organization, Summary Record of 2d Session, 25–27 Sept. 1951 (CO-ORD/LIBRARY/L.21: 12 Nov. 1951), p.3–4.

⁷¹The specialized agencies are separate, autonomous intergovernmental agencies having international responsibilities in economic, social, cultural, educational, health, and related fields. The United Nations Charter provided that these agencies could be brought into a relationship with the United Nations by means of special arrangements. There are now thirteen specialized agencies. In addition to those listed, they include the International Development Association, International Finance Corporation, Universal Postal Union, International Telecommunication Union, World Meteorological Organization, and Inter-Governmental Maritime Consultative Organization.

⁷²United Nations, Library Co-ordinating Committee of the United Nations Organizations, Summary Record of 1st and 2d Meetings, 10 Aug. 1948 (CO-ORD/LIBRARY/1), p.1.

⁷³Ibid., p.7.

⁷⁴United Nations, Library Co-ordinating Committee of the United Nations Organizations, European Members Working Group, Summary of Meetings, 8–9 Sept. 1949 (CO-ORD/LIBRARY/9: 27 Oct. 1949); CO-ORD/LIBRARY/L.21.

⁷⁵ST/LIB/11, p.4–5.

⁷⁶Joseph Groesbeck, "United Nations Documents and Their Accessibility," *Library Resources and Technical Services* 10:317 (Summer 1966).

⁷⁷ST/LIB/14, p.6.

⁷⁸Groesbeck, "United Nations Documents and Their Accessibility," p.318.

⁷⁹"The Standing Committee on Indexing and Documentation," *United*

Nations Libraries Information Bulletin, no.2:1 (May 1968).

[80]Groesbeck, "United Nations Documents and Their Accessibility," p.318.

[81]Joseph Groesbeck, "Two Library Projects," 22 Apr. 1968 (in the files of the United Nations Library), p.1.

[82]United Nations, Office of Conference Services, *Questionnaire on Documentation Needs of the Secretariat and of the Missions and Delegations to the United Nations*, 1966 (in the files of the United Nations Library).

[83]Memorandum from M. Toerien, Chief, Readers' Services Division, through J. Groesbeck, Deputy Director, to L. I. Vladimirov, Director, United Nations Library, dated 13 Mar. 1967, entitled Summary of the Report on the Questionnaire (in the files of the United Nations Library), p.1.

[84]Groesbeck, "Two Library Projects," p.2.

Chapter 6

[1]These figures refer exclusively to the monographic collection of the United Nations Library. According to the author's calculations derived from the *Annual Reports* of the library, the total monographic collection as of 1967 consisted of 238,629 volumes. Compare this with 380,066 documents and serials received in the one year of 1967. See tables 1 and 3.

Bibliography

United Nations Library
New York

Public documents

General Agreement on Tariffs and Trade. *Information Note to Permanent Missions and Delegations: Borrowing of Books from United Nations Library.* INF/93: 9 Nov. 1961.

[Shaw, Ralph]. *Library and Documentation Services of the United Nations.* Lake Success, 12 Sept. 1947.

United Nations. *Annual Report of the Secretary-General on the Work of the Organization,* 14 July 1947. A/315: UNGAOR, 2d sess., Suppl. no.1.

――――. ――――. 1 July 1947–30 June 1948. A/565: UNGAOR, 3d sess., Suppl. no.1.

――――. ――――. 1 July 1948–30 June 1949. A/930: UNGAOR, 4th sess., Suppl. no.1.

――――. ――――. 1 July 1949–30 June 1950. A/1287: UNGAOR, 5th sess., Suppl. no.1.

――――. ――――. 1 July 1950–30 June 1951. A/1844: UNGAOR, 6th sess., Suppl. no.1.

――――. ――――. 1 July 1951–30 June 1952. A/2141: UNGAOR, 7th sess.,

Suppl. no.1.

―――.―――. 1 July 1952 – 30 June 1953. A/2404: UNGAOR, 8th sess., Suppl. no.1.

―――. ―――. 1 July 1953 – 30 June 1954. A/2663: UNGAOR, 9th sess., Suppl. no.1.

―――. ―――. 1 July 1954 – 15 June 1955. A/2911: UNGAOR, 10th sess., Suppl. no.1.

―――. ―――. 16 June 1955 – 15 June 1956. A/3137: UNGAOR, 11th sess., Suppl. no.1.

―――. ―――. 16 June 1956 – 15 June 1957. A/3594: UNGAOR, 12th sess., Suppl. no.1.

―――. ―――. 16 June 1957 – 15 June 1958. A/3844: UNGAOR, 13th sess., Suppl. no.1.

―――. ―――. 16 June 1958 – 15 June 1959. A/4132: UNGAOR, 14th sess., Suppl. no.1.

―――. ―――. 16 June 1959 – 15 June 1960. A/4390: UNGAOR, 15th sess., Suppl. no.1.

―――. ―――. 16 June 1960 – 15 June 1961. A/4800: UNGAOR, 16th sess., Suppl. no.1.

―――. ―――. 16 June 1961 – 15 June 1962. A/5201: UNGAOR, 17th sess., Suppl. no.1.

―――. ―――. 16 June 1962 – 15 June 1963. A/5501: UNGAOR, 18th sess., Suppl. no.1.

―――. ―――. 16 June 1963 – 15 June 1964. A/5801: UNGAOR, 19th sess., Suppl. no.1.

―――. ―――. 16 June 1964 – 15 June 1965. A/6001: UNGAOR, 20th sess., Suppl. no.1.

―――. ―――. 16 June 1965 – 15 June 1966. A/6301: UNGAOR, 21st sess., Suppl. no.1.

―――. ―――. 16 June 1966 – 15 June 1967. A/6701: UNGAOR, 22d sess., Suppl. no.1.

―――. Charter. 24 October 1945.

―――. *International Library:* Memorandum to the Ford Foundation. New York, 1958.

―――. *Organization of the Secretariat.* ST/AFS/2: 2 June 1951.

——. *Organization of the Secretariat:* Report of the Secretary-General's Survey Group. New York, Sept. 1954.

——. *Preliminary Budget Estimates of Expenditure:* First Annual Budget 1946 and Second Annual Budget 1947. Lake Success, Oct. 1946.

——. *Report of the Secretary-General on the Work of the Organization,* 30 June 1946. A/65: UNGAOR, 1st sess., 2d pt., Suppl.

——. *United Nations Library.* New York, n.d., ca. 1952.

——. ——. New York, 1959.

——. Advisory Committee of Information Experts. *Report of Session Held at Lake Success, New York, 25 May – 3 June* [1948]. Annex I to A/C.5/223: 3 June 1948, p.22 – 38.

——. Advisory Group of Experts on Administrative, Personnel, and Budgetary Questions. *Second Report to the Secretary-General of the United Nations.* Lake Success, Oct. 1946.

——. Department of Public Information. *Library Services of the United Nations.* Lake Success, n.d., ca. 1948.

——. ——. Department of Public Information. *United Nations Headquarters Library Busier Than Ever: Over 7,000 Enquiries Handled Each Month.* Press Feature 167 – G, n.d.

——. General Assembly. *Administration of the United Nations:* Explanatory Memorandum by the Secretary-General, 7 Oct. 1952. A/2214: UNGAOR, 7th sess., Annexes, Agenda item 69.

——. ——. *Budget Appropriations for the Financial Year 1950.* Res. 356 (IV), 10 Dec. 1949. A/1251: UNGAOR, 4th sess. Res.

——. ——. ——. 1951. Res. 471(V), 15 Dec. 1950. A/1775: UNGAOR, 5th sess., Suppl. no.20.

——. ——. ——. 1952. Res. 583(VI), 21 Dec. 1951. A/2119: UNGAOR, 6th sess., Suppl. no.20.

——. ——. ——. 1953. Res. 674(VII), 21 Dec. 1952. A/2361: UNGAOR, 7th sess., Suppl. no.20.

——. ——. ——. 1954. Res. 786(VIII), 9 Dec. 1953. A/2630: UNGAOR, 8th sess., Suppl. no.17.

——. ——. ——. 1955. Res. 890(IX), 17 Dec. 1954. A/2890: UNGAOR, 9th sess., Suppl. no.21.

——. ——. ——. 1956. Res. 979(X), 16 Dec. 1955. A/3116: UNGAOR,

10th sess., Suppl. no.19.

———. ———. ———. 1957. Res. 1083(XI), 21 Dec. 1956. A/3572: UNGAOR, 11th sess., Suppl. no.17.

———. ———. ———. 1957. Res. 1100(XI), 27 Feb. 1957. A/3572: UNGAOR, 11th sess., Suppl. no.17.

———. ———. *Budget Estimates for the Financial Year 1950 and Information Annexes*, 1949. A/903: UNGAOR, 4th sess., Suppl. no.5.

———. ———. *Budget Estimates for the Financial Year 1951 and Information Annexes* 1950. A/1267: UNGAOR, 5th sess., Suppl. no.5.

———. ———. *Budget Estimates for the Financial Year 1953:* Report of the Fifth Committee, 20 Dec. 1952. A/2352: UNGAOR, 7th sess., Annexes, v.2, Agenda item 42.

———. ———. *Budgets of the United Nations for the Financial Years 1946 and 1947.* Res. 68(I), 14 Dec. 1946. A/64/Add.1: UNGAOR, 1st sess., 2d pt., Res.

———. ———. ———. 1948. Res. 166(II), 20 Nov. 1947. A/519: UNGAOR, 2d sess., Res.

———. ———. ———. 1949. Res. 252(III), 11 Dec. 1948. A/810: UNGAOR, 3d sess., 1st pt., Res.

———. ———. *Composition of the Secretariat and the Principle of Geographic Distribution*, 2 Sept. 1948. A/652: UNGAOR, 3d sess., pt. 1, Annexes, Agenda item 40.

———. ———. *Fourth Annual Budget and Working Capital Fund of the United Nations:* Report of the Fifth Committee, 10 Dec. 1948. A/798: UNGAOR, 3d sess., Annexes, Agenda item 33(c).

———. ———. *Geographical Distribution of the Staff of the Secretariat.* Res. 1928(XVIII), 11 Dec. 1963. A/5515: UNGAOR, 18th sess., Suppl. no.15.

———. ———. *Handbook: First Session of the General Assembly.* London, 10 Jan. 1946.

———. ———. ———. rev. ed. London, 10 Jan. 1946.

———. ———. *Headquarters of the United Nations:* Report of the Fifth Committee, 6 Dec. 1950. A/1634: UNGAOR, 5th sess., Annexes, v.2, Agenda item 36.

———. ———. *Headquarters of the United Nations:* Report of the Secretary-General, 26 Sept. 1950. A/1392/Rev. 1: UNGAOR, 5th sess., Annexes, v.2, Agenda item 36.

————. ————. *Interim Arrangements for the Library:* Report of the Advisory Committee on Administrative and Budgetary Questions, 5 Nov. 1959. A/4259: UNGAOR, 14th sess., Annexes, Agenda item 44.

————. ————. *Memorial to the Late Dag Hammarskjöld.* Res. 1625 (XVI), 16 Oct. 1961. A/5100: UNGAOR, 16th sess., Suppl. no.17.

————. ————. *Official Records.*

1st sess., 1st pt. 29th Plenary Meeting, 12 Feb. 1946.

2d sess., Fifth Committee. 94th Meeting, 10 Nov. 1947.

3d sess., Fifth Committee. 134th Meeting, 18 Oct. 1948.

3d sess., Fifth Committee. 136th Meeting, 20 Oct. 1948.

4th sess., Fifth Committee. 197th Meeting, 13 Oct. 1949.

4th sess., Fifth Committee. 207th Meeting, 25 Oct. 1949.

4th sess., Fifth Committee. 232d Meeting, 30 Nov. 1949.

5th sess., Fifth Committee. 238th Meeting, 3 Oct. 1950.

5th sess., Fifth Committee. 239th Meeting, 3 Oct. 1950.

7th sess., Fifth Committee. 375th Meeting, 20 Dec. 1952.

11th sess., Fifth Committee. 550th Meeting, 12 Dec. 1956.

11th sess., Fifth Committee. 593d Meeting, 20 Feb. 1957.

14th sess. 826th Plenary Meeting, 12 Oct. 1959.

14th sess. 835th Plenary Meeting, 3 Nov. 1959.

14th sess., Fifth Committee. 711th Meeting, 29 Sept. 1959.

14th sess., Fifth Committee. 732d Meeting, 29 Oct. 1959.

14th sess., Fifth Committee. 742d Meeting, 11 Nov. 1959.

14th sess., General Committee. 124th Meeting, 9 Oct. 1959.

15th sess., Fifth Committee. 794th Meeting, 17 Nov. 1960.

15th sess., Fifth Committee. 811th Meeting, 7 Dec. 1960.

16th sess. 1037th Plenary Meeting, 16 Oct. 1959.

16th sess. 1047th Plenary Meeting, 6 Nov. 1961.

16th sess., Fifth Committee. 852d Meeting, 11 Oct. 1961.

16th sess., Fifth Committee. 868th Meeting, 31 Oct. 1961.

————. ————. *Organization of the Secretariat:* Report of the Secretary-General, 21 Sept. 1954. A/2731: UNGAOR, 9th sess., Annexes, Agenda item 53.

————. ————. *Organization of the Secretariat:* Sixth Report of the Advisory Committee on Administrative and Budgetary Questions, 7 Oct. 1954. A/2745: UNGAOR, 9th sess., Annexes, Agenda item 53.

————. ————. *Outline of Symbols for General Assembly and Other United Nations Documents.* A/1: 3 Jan. 1946; A/1/Corr. 1: 4 Jan. 1946.

————. ————. *Personnel Questions: Composition of the Secretariat:* Report of the Secretary-General, 23 Dec. 1964. A/5841: UNGAOR, 20th sess., Annexes, v.3, Agenda item 84.

————. ————. *Report to the General Assembly of the United Nations by the Secretary-General on the Permanent Headquarters of the United Nations.* A/311: July 1947.

————. ————. *Resolutions Adopted on the Reports of the Fifth Committee,* 1 July 1946. A/64: UNGAOR, 1st sess., 1st pt., Res.

————. ————. *Review of the Activities and Organization of the Secretariat:* Report of the Advisory Committee on Administrative and Budgetary Questions, 29 Sept. 1961. A/4901: UNGAOR, 16th sess., Annexes, Agenda item 61.

————. ————. *Review of the Activities and Organization of the Secretariat:* Report of the Committee of Experts on the Review of the Activities and Organization of the Secretariat, 14 June 1961. A/4776: UNGAOR, 16th sess., Annexes, Agenda item 61.

————.————. *Staff Regulations of the United Nations.* Res. 590(VI), 2 Feb. 1952. A/2119: UNGAOR, 6th sess., Suppl. no.20.

————. ————. *Supplementary Estimates for the Financial Year 1947.* Res. 164(II), 20 Nov. 1947. A/519: UNGAOR, 2d sess., Res.

————. ————. ————. *1948.* Res. 251(III), 11 Dec. 1948 A/810: UNGAOR, 3d sess., 1st pt., Res.

————. ————. ————. *1949.* Res. 354(IV), 9 Dec. 1949. A/1251: UNGAOR, 4th sess., Res.

————. ————. ————. *1950.* Res. 468(V), 15 Dec. 1950. A/1775: UNGAOR, 5th sess., Suppl. no.20.

————. ————. ————. *1951.* Res. 575(VI), 20 Dec. 1951. A/2119: UNGAOR, 6th sess., Suppl. no.20.

———. ———. ———. 1952. Res. 662(VII), 25 Nov. 1952. A/2361: UN-GAOR, 7th sess., Suppl. no.20.

———. ———. ———. 1953. Res. 785(VIII), 9 Dec. 1953. A/2630: UN-GAOR, 8th sess., Suppl. no.17.

———. ———. ———. 1954. Res. 881(IX), 14 Dec. 1954. A/2890: UN-GAOR, 9th sess., Suppl. no.21.

———. ———. ———. 1955. Res. 978(X), 16 Dec. 1955. A/3116: UNGAOR, 10th sess., Suppl. no.19.

———. ———. ———. 1956. Res. 1074(XI), 7 Dec. 1957. A/3572: UN-GAOR, 11th sess., Suppl. no.17.

———. ———. ———. 1957. Res. 1222(XII), 14 Dec. 1957. A/3805: UN-GAOR, 12th sess., Suppl. no.18.

———. ———. *United Nations Library.* Res. 1641(XVI), 6 Nov. 1961. A/5100: UNGAOR, 16th sess., Suppl. no.17.

———. ———. *The United Nations Library: Gift of the Ford Foundation.* Res. 1354(XIV), 3 Nov. 1959. A/4354: UNGAOR, 14th sess., Suppl. no.16.

———. ———. *The United Nations Library: Gift of the Ford Foundation:* Report of the Fifth Committee, 30 Oct. 1959. A/4252: UNGAOR, 14th sess., Annexes, Agenda item 72.

———. ———. *The United Nations Library: Gift of the Ford Foundation:* Report of the Secretary-General, 29 Sept. 1959. A/4231: UNGAOR, 14th sess., Annexes, Agenda item 72.

———. ———. *United Nations Library: Gift of the Ford Foundation: Secretary-General:* Request for the Inclusion of an Additional Item in the Agenda of the Fourteenth Session, 29 Sept. 1959. A/4232: UNGAOR, 14th sess., Annexes, Agenda item 72.

———. ———. *United Nations Library: Memorial to the Late Dag Hammarskjöld:* Letter dated 26 September 1961 from the President of the Ford Foundation to the President of the General Assembly, 3 Oct. 1961. A/4908: UNGAOR, 16th sess., Annexes, Agenda item 68.

———. ———. *United Nations Library: Memorial to the Late Dag Hammarskjöld:* Report of the Fifth Committee, 13 Oct. 1961. A/4922: UNGAOR, 16th sess., Annexes, Agenda item 68.

———. ———. ———. 2 Nov. 1961. A/4952: UNGAOR, 16th sess., Annexes, Agenda item 68.

———. ———. *United Nations Library: Memorial to the Late Dag*

Hammarskjöld: Report of the Secretary-General, 26 Oct. 1961. A/4938: UNGAOR, 16th sess., Annexes, Agenda item 68.

——. ——. *United Nations Library:* Report of the Fifth Committee, 7 Dec. 1960. A/4630: UNGAOR, 15th sess., Annexes, v.2, Agenda item 56.

——. ——. *United Nations Library:* Report of the Secretary-General, 21 Oct. 1960. A/4545: UNGAOR, 15th sess., Annexes, v.2, Agenda item 56.

——. ——. Advisory Committee on Administrative and Budgetary Questions. *First Report of 1948 to the General Assembly*, Apr. 1948. A/534: UNGAOR, 3d sess., Suppl. no.7.

——. ——. ——. *Second Report of 1948 to the General Assembly*, Aug. 1948. A/598: UNGAOR, 3d sess., Suppl. no.7A.

——. ——. ——. *Second Report of 1949 to the General Assembly*, 8 Aug. 1949. A/934: UNGAOR, 4th sess., Suppl. no.7.

——. ——. ——. *Second Report of 1950 to the General Assembly*, 1950. A/1312: UNGAOR, 5th sess., Suppl. no.7.

——. ——. ——. *Second Report of 1951 to the General Assembly*, 1951. A/1853: UNGAOR, 6th sess., Suppl. no.7.

——. ——. ——. *First Report to the Seventh Session of the General Assembly*, 1952. A/2157: UNGAOR, 7th sess., Suppl. no.7.

——. ——. ——. *Second Report to the Ninth Session of the General Assembly*, 1954. A/2688: UNGAOR, 9th sess., Suppl. no.7.

——. ——. ——. *Second Report to the Eleventh Session of the General Assembly*, 1956. A/3160: UNGAOR, 11th sess., Suppl. no.7.

——. ——. ——. *Ninth Report to the General Assembly at Its Sixteenth Session*, 1961. A/4814: UNGAOR, 16th sess., Suppl. no.7.

——. ——. Fifth Committee. *Annual Survey of the Effectiveness of the Programme of Public Information.* A/C.5/223: 18 Sept. 1948.

——. ——. ——. *Budget Estimates for the Financial Year 1948: Library Services of the United Nations:* Report by the Secretary-General, 8 Nov. 1947. A/C.5/210: UNGAOR, 2d sess., Annexes, Annex 67.

——. ——. ——. *Budget Estimates for the Financial Year 1948:* Report by the Secretary General, 2 Oct. 1947. A/C.5/157: UNGAOR, 2d sess., Annexes, Annex 25.

———. ———. ———. *Budget Estimates for the Financial Year 1950. Budget Estimates Prepared by the Secretary General: Section 7a, Library:* Library Policy and Organization, 21 Sept. 1949. A/C.5/298: UNGAOR, 4th sess., Annex, v.1, Agenda item 39(a).

———. ———. ———. *Budget Estimates for the Financial Year 1960:* Statement by the Secretary-General at the 711th Meeting of the Fifth Committee, 29 Sept. 1959. A/C.5/782: UNGAOR, 14th sess., Annexes, Agenda item 44.

———. ———. ———. *Interim Arrangements for the Library:* Report of the Secretary-General, 27 Oct. 1959. A/C.5/796: UNGAOR, 14th sess., Annexes, Agenda item 44.

———. ———. ———. *Report of the Management Survey on United Nations Headquarters.* A/C.5/160: 3 Oct. 1947.

———. ———. ———. *The United Nations Library: Gift of the Ford Foundation:* Draft Resolution Submitted by Forty-Five Delegations. A/C.5/L.577: 23 Oct. 1959; and A/C.5/L.577/Add.1: 27 Oct. 1959.

———. ———. ———. *United Nations Library: Memorial to the Late Dag Hammarskjöld:* Proposal Submitted by Argentina, Ceylon, Denmark, Ireland, Liberia, Mexico, Norway, Tunisia and United Arab Republic, 6 Oct. 1961. A/C.5/885: UNGAOR, 16th sess., Annexes, Agenda item 68.

———. ———. Working Group on the Examination of the Administrative and Budgetary Procedures of the United Nations. *Budgetary and Financial Practices of the United Nations: Note by the Secretary-General.* A/AC.113/1: 21 Jan. 1963.

———. International Advisory Committee of Library Experts. *Report of the Session Held at Lake Success, New York, 2 to 9 August 1948,* 30 Aug. 1948. A/C.5/222 and Corr. 1: UNGAOR, 3d sess., 1st pt., Fifth Committee, Annexes, Agenda item 33(c).

———. Library. *Annual Reports.*

The Division of Library Services as of 1 January 1949. Lake Success, 1 Jan. 1949.

The United Nations Headquarters Library, January 1950. Lake Success, Jan. 1950.

———. Lake Success, 30 June 1950.

———. 1 July 1950–30 June 1951. New York, July 1951.

———. 1 July 1951–31 Dec. 1951. New York, n.d.

———. 1 Jan.–31 Dec. 1952. New York, n.d.

———. 1 Jan.–31 Dec. 1953. New York, n.d.

Report of the Headquarters Library and of the Geneva Library, 1954. ST/LIB/1:6 Apr. 1955.

———. 1955. ST/LIB/2: 6 Apr. 1956.

———. 1956. ST/LIB/3: 23 Apr. 1957.

———. 1957. ST/LIB/5: 26 Mar. 1958.

———. 1958. ST/LIB/7: 1 May 1959.

———. 1959 and 1960. ST/LIB/8: 9 Nov. 1961.

———. 1961. ST/LIB/9: 4 Dec. 1962.

———. 1962. ST/LIB/11: 30 Dec. 1963.

———. 1963. ST/LIB/14: 28 May 1964.

———. 1964. ST/LIB/16: 1 June 1965.

Report of the Headquarters Library, the Geneva Library and the Libraries of the Economic Commissions, 1965, ST/LIB/18: 8 June 1966.

———. 1966. ST/LIB/19: May 1967.

———. 1967. ST/LIB/21: May 1968.

———. ———. *Bibliographical Style Manual.* ST/LIB/SER.B/8: 1963.

———. ———. *Consolidated List of United Nations Document Series Symbols.* Preliminary ed. ST/LIB/SER.D/43: Sept. 1952; and Addendum: 14 Sept. 1953.

———. ———. *The Dag Hammarskjöld Library: Gift of the Ford Foundation.* New York, 1962.

———. ———. *Dedication of the Dag Hammarskjöld Library, United Nations, 16–18 November, 1961: Programme.* New York, 1961.

———. ———. *Government Gazettes:* An Annotated List of Gazettes Held in the Dag Hammarskjöld Library. ST/LIB/SER.B/10: 1964.

———. ———. *Indexes and Checklists of United Nations and Specialized Agency Documents and Publications.* Preliminary list for criticism. CO-ORD/LIBRARY/2: 13 Apr. 1949.

———. ———. *Instructions a l'Intention des Bibliotheques Depositaires des Documents et Publications de l'Organisation des Nations*

188

Unies. ST/LIB/13/Rev.1: 4 Jan. 1968.

———. ———. *The Libraries of the United Nations: A Descriptive Guide.* ST/LIB/17: 1966.

———. ———. *Library Services and Collections.* New York, 13 Dec. 1956.

———. ———. ———. New York, Nov. 1963.

———. ———. *List of Libraries and Information Centres Receiving United Nations Material.* ST/LIB/12/Rev.2: 11 Nov. 1966.

———. ———. *List of Official Gazettes Received.* New York, 1 May 1958.

———. ———. *List of Rules of Procedure.* ST/LIB/SER.D/25: 5 July 1950.

———. ———. *List of United Nations Document Series Symbols.* ST/LIB/SER.B/5/Rev. 1: 1965.

———. ———. *Manual of the Cataloguing Unit.* Preliminary ed. Lake Success, 1950.

———. ———. *Notes on Its Construction and Furnishing.* New York, 1961.

———. ———. *Report on the 1966 Questionnaire to Depository Libraries.* ST/LIB/20: 4 Jan. 1968.

———. ———. *Subject-Index and Lists of Administrative Instructions, Information Circulars, and Secretary-General's Bulletins in Effect, as of 10 August 1950.* ST/LIB/SER.D/31: 28 Aug. 1950.

———. ———. *Subjects of Interest to the United Nations Library.* Preliminary draft for criticism. Lake Success, Apr. 1949.

———. ———. *Suggestions for Filing, Discarding and Binding of United Nations Material.* ST/LIB/6: 24 July 1958.

———. ———. *Summary of Legislative Action Concerning the United Nations Library, with Particular Regard to the Library's Indexing Responsibilities.* New York, May 1968.

———. ———. *United Nations Publications Sales Numbers: A. Explanation of System.* ST/LIB/SER.D/10: 26 Feb. 1948; and Rev. 1: 12 Apr. 1948.

———. ———. *You Are Invited to Use Your Library.* Lake Success, 20 Sept. 1949.

———. ———. Acquisitions Section. *Booksellers outside the United*

States: A List of Dealers Used for the Purchase of Monographs and Serials. New York, July 1956.

——. ——. Catalogue Department. *Bulletin*, nos.1 – 18, 11 July 1949 – 28 Nov. 1949.

——. ——. Co-ordinating Committee of the United Nations Organizations. *Check List of United Nations Documents, 1946 – 1949.* CO-ORD/LIBRARY /L.13: 25 July 1951.

——. ——. ——. *Co-operative Cataloguing.* CO-ORD/LIBRARY/ L.18: 15 Aug. 1951.

——. ——. ——. *Co-ordination of Translations of Legal Texts and Publication of a Catalogue of Newly Translated Texts.* CO-ORD/ LIBRARY/L.16: 31 July 1951.

——. ——. ——. *Distribution of Documents to the United Nations and Specialized Agencies' Libraries.* CO-ORD/LIBRARY/L.11: 1 Sept. 1951.

——. ——. ——. *Exchange of Bibliographies.* CO-ORD/LIBRARY/ L.17: 31 July 1951.

——. ——. ——. *Exchange of Duplicates and Discard Policy.* CO-ORD/LIBRARY/L.19: 26 July 1951.

——. ——. ——. *Library Implications of Technical Assistance Programmes.* CO-ORD/LIBRARY/L.14: 27 Aug. 1951.

——. ——. ——. *Library Implications of Technical Assistance Programmes. UNESCO Library: Documentation for Technical Assistance.* CO-ORD/LIBRARY/L.14/Add.1: 3 Sept. 1951.

——. ——. ——. *Library Implications of Technical Assistance Programmes. WHO Library.* CO-ORD/LIBRARY/L.14/Add.2: 12 Sept. 1951.

——. ——. ——. *Questionnaire to Libraries of Specialized Agencies.* Lake Success, 10 Aug. 1948.

——. ——. ——. *A Reference Guide to the Documents and Publications of the United Nations and the Specialized Agencies.* CO-ORD/ LIBRARY/L.15: 25 July 1951.

——. ——. ——. Summary Record of 1st and 2nd Meetings, 10 Aug. 1948. CO-ORD/LIBRARY/1: 10 Aug. 1948.

——. ——. ——. Summary Record of Second Session, 25 – 27 Sept. 1951. CO-ORD/LIBRARY/L.21: 12 Nov. 1951.

———. ———. ———. *Tentative Agenda for the 1951 Meeting.* CO-ORD/ LIBRARY/L.10: 29 Aug. 1951.

———. ———. ———. *United Nations Documents Index.* CO-ORD/ LIBRARY/L.12 and L.12/Add.1: 1 Aug. 1951.

———. ———. ———. European Members Working Group. *Co-operative Cataloguing.* CO-ORD/LIBRARY/5: 27 Aug. 1949.

———. ———. ———. ———. *Co-ordination of Translations of Legal Texts.* CO-ORD/LIBRARY/8/Add.1: 7 Sept. 1949.

———. ———. ———. ———. *Co-ordination of Translations of Legal Texts and Publication of a Monthly Catalogue of Newly Translated Texts.* CO-ORD/LIBRARY/8: 27 Aug. 1949.

———. ———. ———. ———. *European Sub-Committee.* CO-ORD/ LIBRARY/4: 27 Aug. 1949.

———. ———. ———. ———. *Subject Indexes.* CO-ORD/LIBRARY/6: 27 Aug. 1949.

———. ———. ———. ———. Summary of Meetings, 8–9 Sept. 1949. CO-ORD/LIBRARY/9: 27 Oct. 1949.

———. ———. ———. ———. *Trainees.* CO-ORD/LIBRARY/7: 27 Aug. 1949.

———. ———. ———. ———. *Working Paper Number 1. Technical Assistance to Underdeveloped Countries:* Use of Books and Libraries in the Dissemination of Information. CO-ORD/LIBRARY/3: Aug. 1949.

———. Office of Public Information. *Dedication of the Dag Hammarskjöld Library.* Press Release HQC/196: 14 Nov. 1961.

———. ———. *Everyman's United Nations:* A Complete Handbook of the Activities and Evolution of the United Nations during Its First Twenty Years, 1945–1965. 8th ed. New York, 1968.

———. ———. *The Library Building.* Press Release HQC/198: 14 Nov. 1961.

———. ———. *The Library Symposium.* Press Release HQC/197: 14 Nov. 1961.

———. ———. *Yearbook of the United Nations, 1946–47 to 1966.* Lake Success and New York, 1947–68.

———. Preparatory Commission. *Library Arrangements.* PC/EX/AD/7: 11 Sept. 1945.

———. ———. *Library Arrangements: Additional Information.* PC/

EX/AD/7/Add.1: 24 Sept. 1945.

————. ————. *Memorandum from the Executive Secretary on the Provision of a Library.* PC/EX/18: 28 Aug. 1945.

————. ————. *Memorandum on Interim Library Arrangements.* PC/EX/AD/3: 1 Sept. 1945.

————. ————. *Report of the Preparatory Commission of the United Nations.* PC/20: 23 Dec. 1945.

————. ————. Executive Committee. Summary Record of the Confidential Portion of the 11th Meeting. 30 Aug. 1945. PC/EX/26, pt. 3: 1 Sept. 1945.

————. Publications Board. *Principles Governing United Nations Depository Libraries.* ST/PB/4/Rev. 2: 13 Dec. 1967.

————. Secretariat. *Circulation des Documents des Nations Unies.* ST/SGB/20: 9 May 1946.

————. ————. *Establishment of the Organization for Conference and General Services.* ST/SGB/33: 1 July 1946.

————. ————. *Management Survey.* ST/SGB/58: 19 Feb. 1947; and Rev. 1: 11 July 1947.

————. ————. *Organization of the Secretariat.* ST/SGB/32: 21 June 1946.

————. ————. *Provisional Procurement Rules.* ST/SGB/6/Rev. 1: 27 Feb. 1948.

————. ————. *Publications Board.* ST/SGB/60: 4 Mar. 1947.

————. ————. *Salary and Wage Administration Plan.* ST/SGB/19/Rev. 1: 12 June 1947.

United Nations Conference on International Organization. *Delegates and Officials of the United Nations Conference on International Organization.* San Francisco, 1945.

————. *From Debate to Document thru the International Secretariat.* San Francisco, 1945 (in the files of Mr. Orne).

————. Conference Library. *Short Title Classified Catalog.* San Francisco, 1 June 1945.

United States. National Archives. *Proposal for the Establishment of a United Nations Archives.* Washington, Oct. 1945.

United States Delegation to the General Assembly. *Statement by Mr.*

Albert Bender, Jr., in Committee Five, on the Proposal to Dedicate the United Nations Library as the Dag Hammarskjöld Library. Press Release No. 3793: 11 Oct. 1961.

Archival and unpublished sources

Beals, Ralph A.; Evans, Luther H.; Milam, Carl H.; and Breycha-Vauthier, A. C. "Report: Planning of United Nations Library," 22–23 Apr. 1947 (in the files of Mr. Milam).

Burchard, John E. "Proposal A: Estimate of Space Requirements for UN Library, New York City." 5 May 1947 (UNA: RG 19, A/369, box 1).

———. "Proposal B: Estimate of Space Requirements for UN Library, New York City." 5 May 1947 (UNA: RG 19, A/369, box 1).

Clapp, Verner W. "The Libraries of the United Nations in New York and Geneva," A Comparative Review of Functions, Staff Requirements and Relationships: Report to the Secretary-General. 5 June 1953 (in the files of Mr. Clapp).

———. "Plans for the United Nations Library at the Permanent Site." 17 June 1950 (in the files of Mr. Clapp).

———. "Quantities of Materials Required by United Nations Library." 3 May 1947 (UNA: RG 19, A/369, box 1).

———. "Report on Activities of the Conference Library." 10 July 1945 (in the files of Mr. Clapp).

———. "The United Nations Library: Organization-Work-Utilization of Staff," General Recommendations: Report of a Review Conducted April 28–May 3, 1952. 20 May 1952 (in the files of Mr. Clapp). Also published as an attachment to: United Nations. General Assembly. Fifth Committee. *Budget Estimates for the Financial Year 1953.* A/C.5/L.177: 23 Oct. 1952.

Colvin, Laura C. "Notes for Reorganization of the Serial Checklist." 31 Aug. 1951 (in the files of Miss Colvin).

———. "Procedures for Checklisting Added, Transferred, and Withdrawn Serials." 31 Aug. 1951 (in the files of Miss Colvin).

———. "Procedures for Checklisting Uncatalogued and Unclassified Serials." 31 Aug. 1951 (in the files of Miss Colvin).

———. "Procedures for Serials Received Directly in Departmental Libraries." 31 Aug. 1951 (in the files of Miss Colvin).

193

———. "Serial Checklist: Policy Decisions Affecting Its Reorganization." 31 Aug. 1951 (in the files of Miss Colvin).

Cruger, Doris M. "An Evaluation of the Monographic Resources of the United Nations Library." Unpublished paper prepared for a seminar in Library Resources at Columbia University, School of Library Service, 20 Jan. 1967.

Dale, Doris Cruger. "The Origin and Development of the United Nations Library." D.L.S. dissertation, Columbia University, 1968.

Drake, Dorothy M. "With an International Flavor." Unpublished paper, n.d. (in the files of Mrs. Wessells).

Eastin, R. B. "Conference Concerning Present and Proposed Programs of Documents Index Unit, Division of Library Services, United Nations." 21 Mar. 1949 (UNA: RG 18, A/193, box 4).

Groesbeck, Joseph. "The Osborn Survey." 24 May 1951 (in the files of the United Nations Library).

———. "Two Library Projects." 22 Apr. 1968 (in the files of the United Nations Library).

Johnson, William Harold. "A Notation Scheme for United Nations Documents Issued without Series Symbols." M.S.L.S. thesis, University of North Carolina at Chapel Hill, 1960.

"Library Facilities for the United Nations Assembly to Meet on October 23rd, 1946." (UNA: RG 18, A/363, box 1).

Menon, K. P. R. "Index and Reference Services (Documents Index Unit, Department of Public Information)." Inspection Service Report no.5, 19 May 1949 (UNA: RG 18, A/193, box 4).

———. "Notes: Documents Index Unit." 17 Mar. 1949 (UNA: RG 18, A/193, box 4).

Milam, Carl H. "Diary on U.N." (in the files of Mr. Milam).

———. "Internships, United Nations Library." 7 Sept. 1948 (UNA:RG 1, box 509).

———. "Notes on Space Requirements for Permanent United Nations Library Building." 8 May 1951 (UNA: RG 21, A/428, box 1).

———. "Preparations for Moving Library to Manhattan." 15 Mar. 1949 (UNA: RG 15, A/122, box 26).

[———]. "Program for a Permanent Library Building." 8 May 1951. (UNA: RG 21, A/428, box 1).

———. "Some Facts about Library Services." 11 May 1948 (UNA: RG 15, A/122, box 26).

———. "The United Nations Headquarters Library: Its Character, Services and Needs." 1 Oct. 1951 (UNA: RG 21, A/428, box 1).

———. "The United Nations Library: Its Character, Services and Needs." 9 May 1951 (UNA: RG 21, A/428, box 1).

[———]. "The Woodrow Wilson Memorial Library." 6 Apr. 1949 (UNA: RG 18, A/193, box 4; draft copy in the files of Mr. Milam).

"The Organization and Work of the United Nations Library." Aug. 1960 (in the library of the American Library Assn.).

Orne, Jerrold. "Super-Library Service for an International Conference." Unpublished paper, n.d. (in the files of Mrs. Wessells).

———, and Clapp, Verner W. "Conference Library." 21 May 1945 (in the files of the Library of Congress).

Osborn, Andrew D. "The Acquisition Unit in the United Nations Library: Report on Matters Requiring Action." Unpublished report, Cambridge, Mass., 1951 (in the files of the United Nations Library).

———. "The United Nations Library." 21 Nov. 1950 (UNA: RG 21, A/428, box 1).

Rasmussen, S. Hartz. "Classification System to Be Used in the Library Service." 16 Dec. 1946 (UNA: RG 18, A/363, box 1).

———. "Comments of the Chief of Library Service on the Proposals of Mr. Cohen and Mr. Stavridi for the Administrative Reorganization of the Library and the Redistribution of Personnel." 31 Dec. 1947 (UNA: RG 18, A/193, box 4).

———. "Essential Points Regarding the Library Policy of the United Nations Which May Be of Interest during the Discussion of the 1949 Budget." ca. May 1948 (in the files of Mr. Rasmussen).

———. "Factual Information Related to My Resignation from the Post of Librarian of the United Nations Library." ca. May 1948 (in the files of Mr. Rasmussen).

———. "General Plan for the United Nations Library Service." 3 Oct. 1946 (UNA: RG 19, A/369, box 2).

————. "Memorandum on the United Nations Library." 13 July 1946 (UNA: RG 19, A/369, box 1).

————. [Notes for a History]. n.d. (in the files of Mr. Rasmussen).

————. "Recommendations Regarding the Permanent Building of the United Nations Library in Manhattan." 20 May 1947 (UNA: RG 19, A/369, box 1).

————. "Report on the United Nations Library Service." 27 Jan. 1947 (UNA: RG 19, A/369, box 2).

Reitman, Edouard. "Report on Negotiations with the Library of Congress Concerning Contractual Services." ca. 15 May 1948 (UNA: RG 18, A/193, box 4).

"Role of Libraries in the United Nations." Conference sponsored by the California Library Assn., 20 May 1945 (in the files of Mr. Clapp).

Stavridi, V. J. G. Note on Conversation with New York Public Library. 30 Dec. 1947 (UNA: RG 1, box 509).

[Stefanini, François]. "Report on the United Nations Library." 5 Feb. 1947 (UNA: RG 19, A/369, box 1).

[————]. "Supplementary Report on the United Nations Library." n.d. (UNA: RG 19, A/369, box 1).

Stern, Herman Anthony. "Handbook to the Use of United Nations Documents." M.A. thesis, New York University, 1952.

Stopar-Babsek, Marjan. "Establishment and Organization of United Nations Archives." Prepared as a Working Paper for the 6th Round Table Conference on Archives, Warsaw, May 1961.

Thompson, George K. "United Nations Documents: A Manual for Their Use in the Library." M.S.L.S. thesis, Western Reserve University, 1951.

Toerien, Marie, and Groesbeck, Joseph. "Summary of the Report on the Questionnaire." 13 Mar. 1967 (in the files of the United Nations Library).

United Nations. International Advisory Committee of Library Experts. "The Woodrow Wilson Memorial Library: Special Recommendation to the Secretary-General." 8 Sept. 1948 (UNA: RG 18, A/193, box 4).

————. ————. "Working Paper 1: Library Services, Lake Success and New York." 26 July 1948 (UNA: RG 18, A/193, box 4).

————. ————. "Working Paper 2: Distribution and Use of United Nations

Documents and Departmental Publications." July 1948 (UNA: RG 18, A/193, box 4).

———. ———. "Working Paper 3: Special Considerations." 23 July 1948 (UNA: RG 18, A/193, box 4)

———. Library. "Book Selection Sources." 3 June 1952 (in the files of the United Nations Library).

———. ———. "Departmental Libraries." Dec. 1949 (UNA: RG 15, A/122, box 26).

———. ———. "Determination of a Policy Statement on Branch Libraries in the Substantive Departments." 12 Sept. 1950 (UNA: RG 21, A/428, box 1).

———. ———. "Final Draft for A/C.5 Document on the Departmental Libraries." 3 Oct. 1950 (UNA: RG 15, A/122, box 26).

———. ———. "Headquarters Library." 22 June 1950 (UNA: RG 15, A/122, box 26).

———. ———. "History and Functions of the Departmental Branch Libraries." 12 Oct. 1951 (UNA: RG 15, A/122, box 26).

———. ———. "Interns in the United Nations Headquarters Library." 11 May 1949 (UNA: RG 1, box 509).

———. ———. "Library Policy and Organization." 2 June 1949 (UNA: RG 1, box 509).

———. ———. Minutes of Meeting Held at Headquarters Planning Office on Proposed New Library Building, 8 May 1951 (UNA: RG 21, A/428, box 1).

———. ———. Minutes of Meeting with Section and Unit Chiefs, 6 Oct. 1954 (UNA: Rg 21, A/428, box 2).

———. ———. "National and Trade Bibliographies Checked or Suggested as Book Selection Sources." 22 Jan. 1954 (in the files of the United Nations Library).

———. ———. "Plans for the Library Building in Manhattan." ca. 22 June 1950 (UNA: RG 21, A/428, box 1).

———. ———. "Proposed Status of Departmental Library Collections." 23 Dec. 1947 (UNA: RG 15, A/122, box 26).

———. ———. "Secretariat Building: Departmental Branch Libraries." 22 June 1950 (UNA: RG 15, A/122, box 26).

———. ———. "Subject Periodicals Being Checked for Book Selection, or for Consideration as Selection Sources." 22 Jan. 1954 (in the files of the United Nations Library).

————. ————. "United Nations Departmental Libraries." 7 July 1949 (UNA: RG 15, A/122, box 26).

————. ————. "United Nations Library: Interpretation of Policy on Use of Library by Public." 27 Apr. 1951 (UNA: RG 21, A/428, box 1).

————. ————. "United Nations Library: Policy on Visitors." 27 Apr. 1951 (UNA: RG 21, A/428, box 1).

————. ————. "Working Paper on Current Indexed List of United Nations and Specialized Agency Documents and Publications." 26 Apr. 1949 (UNA: RG 15, A/122, box 26).

————. ————. "Working Paper on Page-Reference Indexing." 26 Apr. 1949 (UNA: RG 15, A/122, box 26).

————. ————. Permanent Advisory Library Committee. Minutes (UNA: RG 15, A/122, box 26).

Summary of the 1st Meeting, 3 Mar. 1947.

Summary of the 2d Meeting, 17 Mar. 1947.

Summary of the 3d Meeting, 24 Mar. 1947.

Summary of the 4th Meeting, 31 Mar. 1947.

Summary of the 5th Meeting, 14 Apr. 1947.

Summary of the 6th Meeting, 21 Apr. 1947.

Summary of the 7th Meeting, 22 Apr. 1947.

Summary of the 8th Meeting, 13 May 1947.

Summary of the 9th Meeting, 19 May 1947.

Summary of the 10th Meeting, 2 June 1947.

Special Meeting, 9 Sept. 1947.

Special Meeting, 12 Sept. 1947.

Summary of Meeting, 26 Nov. 1947.

Summary of Meeting, 3 Dec. 1947.

Summary of Meeting, 23 Dec. 1947.

Summary of Meeting, 12 Mar. 1948.

Summary of Meeting, 7 July 1948.

Minutes of the Meeting, 2 Mar. 1949.

Minutes of the Meeting, 16 Mar. 1949.

Minutes of the Meeting, 27 Apr. 1949.

Minutes of Meeting, 14 Dec. 1949.

Minutes of the Meeting, 22 June 1950.

Minutes of the Meeting, 30 June 1950.

Minutes of Meeting, 13 Sept. 1950.

Minutes of Meeting on Matters Concerning Departmental Libraries, 5 Oct. 1951.

Minutes of Meeting, 10 Oct. 1952.

————. Office of Conference Services. Questionnaire on Documentation Needs of the Secretariat and of the Missions and Delegations to the United Nations. 1966 (in the files of the United Nations Library).

————. Office of General Services. "United Nations Library, Progress Report." nos. 1–107, 6 Nov. 1959–20 Nov. 1961 (UNA: RG 22, A/426, box 1).

————. Publications Board. "Subject: Document Indexing." Paper no. 268, 19 May 1949 (UNA: RG 15, A/122, box 26).

————. ————. "Weekly Index to Documents and Publications." Paper no.244, 18 Jan. 1949 (UNA: RG 15, A/397, box 2).

Wessells, Helen E. "Report: Notes for a Check List of Projects Under Way or Projected by the United Nations: To Be Evaluated to Determine the Implications for Library Services." ca. 1948 (in the files of Mrs. Wessells).

Wilcox, Jerome K. Review of "Conference Concerning Present and Proposed Programs of Documents Index Unit, Division of Library Services, United Nations," by R. B. Eastin. In a letter to Edouard Reitman, 8 Apr. 1949 (UNA: RG 18, A/193, box 4).

Books, periodicals, and newspapers

Allison, Mary L. "The Most Vital Special Library in the World – The Dag Hammarskjöld Library." *Special Libraries* 53:13–14 (Jan. 1962).

American Library Association. *Minutes of Executive Board Meetings.* v.15 (9–11 Oct. 1943 to 12–14 Oct. 1944) to v.31 (30 Jan. 1961 to 4

Nov. 1961). Chicago, ALA.

"A.L.A. International Activities: Board on International Relations." *ALA Bulletin* 39:353–57 (15 Oct. 1945).

"'And the Trumpets Sounded . . . on the Other Side': Carl Hastings Milam." *Canadian Library* 20:334 (May 1964).

Angelo, Homer G. "Ralston Collection Donated to the United Nations." *American Journal of International Law* 48:493–94 (July 1954).

Bailey, Sydney D. *The Secretariat of the United Nations.* rev. ed. London: Pall Mall Pr., 1964.

Barnett, Sidney N. "Doctoral Dissertations in American Universities Concerning the United Nations, 1943–1961." *International Organization* 16:668–75 (Summer 1962).

Basu, Purnendu. "The United Nations Archives." *Indian Archives* 5:105–18 (July–Dec. 1951).

Bates, Margaret L., and Turner, Robert K. "International Documentation: An Introduction." *International Organization* 1:607–18 (Nov. 1947).

Berger, Meyer. "Multi-Lingual UNO Sounds like Babel." *New York Times* (late city ed.) 26 Mar. 1946, p.13.

Berry, John N. "'International by Definition'." *Library Journal* 89:4469–72 (15 Nov. 1964).

Bishop, William Warner. "Twenty-Five Years." *ALA Bulletin* 39:131–32 (Apr. 1945).

"Borba de Moraes, Rubens." In *Who's Who in the United Nations*, p.58–59. Yonkers-on-Hudson, N.Y.: Christian E. Burckel, 1951.

Bracker, Milton. "Library Facilities of U.N. Restricted." *New York Times* (late city ed.) 21 Dec. 1952, p.6.

"Brief of Minutes, Association of Research Libraries, Jan. 26, 1950, Chicago." *College and Research Libraries* 11:265–70 (July 1950).

"Brief of Minutes of General Interest, Association of Research Libraries, July 19, 1950, Cleveland." *College and Research Libraries* 12:71–75, 78 (Jan. 1951).

Briet, S. "La Conférence de la Dotation Carnegie sur les Documents de L'O.N.U., Paris, 21–22 Novembre 1948." *Revue de la Documentation* 16:5–7 (1949).

Brimmer, Brenda, et al. *A Guide to the Use of United Nations Documents*. Dobbs Ferry, N.Y.: Oceana, 1962.

Brown, Karl. "Carl Hastings Milam: 1884–1963." *Library Journal* 88: 3586 (1 Oct. 1963).

Bruce, William J. "The San Francisco *UNCIO* Documents." *American Archivist* 9:6–16 (Jan. 1946).

"By the Foot." *The New Yorker* 27:26–28 (3 Nov. 1951).

Caballero-Marsal, Fernando; Nielsen, Jorgen K.; and Winton, Harry N. M. "United Nations Documents in the United Nations Library: Organization and Servicing." *Journal of Cataloging and Classification* 7:65–72 (Summer 1951).

Cabeen, Violet Abbott, and Cook, C. Donald. "Organization of Serials and Documents." *Library Trends* 2:196–216 (Oct. 1953).

Campbell, H. C. "The Role of the United Nations and Specialized Agencies in Bibliographical Development." *College and Research Libraries* 10:326–28 (Oct. 1949).

"Carl H. Milam Is New U.N. Director of Libraries." *Library Journal* 73: 571 (1 Apr. 1948).

"Carl Milam." *ALA Bulletin* 57:805 (Oct. 1963).

"Carl Milam Becomes Director of Libraries for U.N." *Publishers' Weekly* 153:1812 (24 Apr. 1948).

"Carl Milam, 78, Librarian, Dead." *New York Times* (late city ed.) 28 Aug. 1963, p.33.

Carroll, Marie J. "League of Nations Documents and Publications Comparable with or Continued in United Nations Publications." *College and Research Libraries* 13:44–52, 64 (Jan. 1952).

Cassidy, Thomas R. "United Nations Documents in the Medium-Sized University—Nuisance or Necessity?" *College and Research Libraries* 13:107–10 (Apr. 1952).

"Cataloging Zip." *Library Journal* 74:1739 (15 Nov. 1949).

Chamberlin, Waldo; Hovet, Thomas, Jr.; and Hovet, Erica. *A Chronology and Fact Book of the United Nations 1941–1964*. Dobbs Ferry, N.Y.: Oceana, 1964.

———, and Moor, Carl Carter. "The United Nations Documents Collection at New York University." *College and Research Libraries* 12: 52–61 (Jan. 1951).

Childs, James B. "Current Bibliographical Control of International Intergovernmental Documents." *Library Resources and Technical Services* 10:319–31 (Summer 1966).

——. Review of *United Nations Documents Index*. In *Library of Congress Information Bulletin* 9:11–12 (27 Feb. 1950).

——. Review of *United Nations Documents Index*. In *Library of Congress Information Bulletin* 10:3 (9 July 1951).

Chrisney, Judson. "For Library near U.N." *New York Times* (late city ed.) 6 Apr. 1957, p.18 (letter to the editor).

Clapp, Verner W. "Catalog Cards for UN Documents." *Library of Congress Information Bulletin* 12:11 (16 Nov. 1953).

——. "Catalog Cards for UN Publications." *Library of Congress Information Bulletin* 12:10–11 (13 Apr. 1953).

——. "League of Nations Documents at the Woodrow Wilson Memorial Library." *Library of Congress Information Bulletin* 12:12 (2 Feb. 1953).

——. "League of Nations Documents to UN." *Library of Congress Information Bulletin* 9:16 (19 June 1950).

——. "The Library of the United Nations Conference on International Organization, San Francisco, 1945." *Library Journal* 70:871–78 (1 Oct. 1945).

——. "Type Is Tanglefoot." *Library Journal* 80:1747–53 (1 Sept. 1955).

——. "United Nations Documents Check Lists." *Library of Congress Information Bulletin* 11:3 (11 Feb. 1952).

——. "The UN Library." *Library of Congress Information Bulletin* 8:14–15 (15–21 Feb. 1949).

——. "The United Nations Library." *Library of Congress Information Bulletin* 10:6 (24 Sept. 1951).

——. "The United Nations Library." *Library of Congress Information Bulletin* 11:13–14 (15 Sept. 1952).

——. "The United Nations Library: 1945–1961." *Libri* 12:111–21 (1962).

"Clapp, Verner W(arren)." In *Current Biography 1959*, p.67–68. New York: Wilson, 1959.

Claus, Robert. "The Archives Program of the United Nations." *Ameri-*

can Archivist 11:195–202 (July 1948).

———. "The United Nations Archives." *American Archivist* 10:129–32 (Apr. 1947).

———. "The United Nations Archives." *Archivum* (Paris) 2:11–15 (1952).

Clift, David H. "Carl Hastings Milam: 1884–1963." *ALA Bulletin* 57: 812 (Oct. 1963).

Cohnen, Ilse Valerie. "Die Bibliothek der Vereinten Nationen in New York." *Zeitschrift für Bibliothekwesen und Bibliographie* 11:362 (1964).

Compton, Charles H. "Carl Milam." *Library Journal* 70:348 (15 Apr. 1945).

"The Conference Library." *The Evening Star* (Washington, D.C.) 13 July 1945.

"The Conference Library." *United Nations Conference on International Organization Cultural Activities Bulletin* no.7:1–2 (13 May 1945).

"The Conference Library." *United Nations Conference on International Organization Journal* no.1:4 (25 Apr. 1945).

"The Contributors to This Issue: Carl H. Milam." *Library Quarterly* 23: 297 (Oct. 1953).

"The Contributors to This Issue: Josef Stummvoll." *Library Quarterly* 20:44 (Jan. 1950).

Crabtree, Jean E. "ALA and the UN." *ALA Bulletin* 49: 498–500 (Oct. 1955).

"Crisis in UNO Near, Yugoslav Asserts." *New York Times* (late city ed.) 6 Mar. 1946, p.7.

"The Dag Hammarskjöld Library." *College and Research Libraries* 23: 32 (Jan. 1962).

"The Dag Hammarskjöld Library." *Library of Congress Information Bulletin* 20: 714–18 (27 Nov. 1961).

"The Dag Hammarskjöld Library." *United Nations Libraries Information Bulletin* no.1:1–4 (Apr. 1967).

"The Dag Hammarskjöld Library." *United Nations Libraries Information Bulletin* no.2:2–10 (May 1968).

"Dag Hammarskjöld Library Dedicated." *United Nations Review* 8:21, 39 (Dec. 1961).

"Dag Hammarskjöld Library Dedication." *Wilson Library Bulletin* 36: 348, 350 (Jan. 1962).

"The Dag Hammarskjöld Library, United Nations." *UNESCO Bulletin for Libraries* 16:152 (May–June 1962).

"Dag Hammarskjöld Library's Fifth Year Observed." *Wilson Library Bulletin* 41:463 (Jan. 1967).

Dale, Doris Cruger. "The Development of Classification Systems for Government Publications." *Library Resources and Technical Services* 13:471–83 (Fall 1969).

Danton, Emily Miller, "Mr. ALA: Carl Hastings Milam." *ALA Bulletin* 53:753–62 (Oct. 1959).

———. "Mr. ALA–Carl Hastings Milam." In *An American Library History Reader: Contributions to Library Literature,* ed. by John David Marshall, p.428–44. Hamden, Conn.: Shoe String, 1960.

Das Gupta, S. Review of *Library Services of the United Nations.* In *Abgila* (Delhi) 1:B31–B32 (June 1949).

Davies, Lawrence E. "Delegates' Leisure a Parley Problem." *New York Times* (late city ed.) 25 Mar. 1945, p.28.

"Dedication of the Dag Hammarskjöld Library." *Library of Congress Information Bulletin* 20:695–700 (20 Nov. 1961).

"Depository Libraries for Unesco and United Nations Documents," *UNESCO Bulletin for Libraries* 4:564–78 (Mar. 1950).

DeWalt, Daniel D. "Distribution of Documents." In *Annual Review of United Nations Affairs 1953,* p.111–19. New York: New York Univ. Pr., 1954.

Divekar, V. D. "United Nations Documents: Problems in Their Arrangement." *Library Herald* (Delhi) 2:98–103 (Oct. 1959).

"Document Office Snarl Postpones UNO Sessions." *New York Times* (late city ed.) 31 Jan. 1946, p.4.

Documents of International Organizations: A Selected Bibliography. v.1–3, Nov. 1947–Sept. 1950. Boston: World Peace Foundation, 1947–50.

Dougall, Richardson. "The Archives and Documents of the Preparatory Commission of the United Nations." *American Archivist* 10:25–34 (Jan. 1947).

Duhrsen, Lowell R. "Classification of United Nations Documents Using the JX Schedule and Document Numbers." *Library Resources and Technical Services* 14:84–97 (Winter 1970).

Evans, Luther H. "Meeting of the Advisory Committee on the United Nations Library." *Library of Congress Information Bulletin* 7:8–10 (10–16 Aug. 1948).

"Every Language in U.N.'s Library." *New York Times* (late city ed.) 4 Dec. 1955, p.143.

"Expanding U.N. City." *New York Herald Tribune* 5 Oct. 1959 (editorial).

"Experts Called to Discuss U.N. Library Problems." *Library Journal* 73:1163 (1 Sept. 1948).

" 'Far Must Thy Researches Go Wouldst Thou Learn the World to Know'." *United Nations Bulletin* 15:157–59 (15 Aug. 1953).

Farquhar, Samuel T. "Binding the Atlantic Charter." *Publishers' Weekly* 148:122–24 (14 July 1945).

———. "Printing the United Nations Charter." *Publishers' Weekly* 148:51–52 (7 July 1945).

Farrell, William. "Housing Authority Joins Rest of Us." *New York Times* (late city ed.) 19 Apr. 1947, p.3.

"Florida State University to be UN Depository." *Library Journal* 93:500 (1 Feb. 1968).

"Ford Foundation Gives UN $6,200,000 for New Library." *Antiquarian Bookman* 24:1223 (12 Oct. 1959).

"Former League of Nations Librarian Assumes Same Post at U.N." *Library Journal* 72:1740 (15 Dec. 1947).

Gerould, Albert C. "Fit the Bindings to the Use." *Library Journal* 72:880 (1 June 1947).

Gomez de Silva, Guido. "Library Services of the United Nations." *Library Journal* 74:1297–99 (15 Sept. 1949).

———. "The United Nations Headquarters Library." *Illinois Libraries* 32:667–68 (Dec. 1950).

Goodrich, Leland M. "Geographical Distribution of the Staff of the UN Secretariat." *International Organization* 16:465–82 (Summer 1962).

Gordenker, Leon. "Policy-Making and Secretariat Influence in the U.N.

General Assembly: The Case of Public Information." *American Political Science Review* 54:359–73 (June 1960).

Groesbeck, Joseph. "The Dag Hammarskjöld Library." *Stechert-Hafner Book News* 16:43–44 (Dec. 1961).

———. "United Nations Documents and Their Accessibility," *Library Resources and Technical Services* 10:313–18 (Summer 1966).

———. "The United Nations Headquarters Library." *Revue de la Documentation* 25:33–36 (May 1958).

Gropp, Arthur E. "Personnel: Dr. Rubens Borba Alves de Moraes." *College and Research Libraries* 16:98 (Jan. 1955).

"Hammarskjöld Library Dedicated." *New York Times* (late city ed.) 17 Nov. 1961, p.5.

"Hammarskjöld's Name Backed for U.N. Library." *New York Times* (late city ed.) 12 Oct. 1961, p.9.

Harris, Alfred G. "Organizing the United Nations Documents Collection." *American Documentation* 2:141–49 (Aug. 1951).

Harrison, Abramovitz and Harris, Architects. "Rare Woods from Three Continents for the UN's Dag Hammarskjöld Library." *Interiors* 122:102–107 (Apr. 1963).

Heaps, Willard A. "A Collection on the U.N." *Library Journal* 80:1753–58 (1 Sept. 1955).

Heuline, Simone. "The Legal Collections of the United Nations Library." *Law Library Journal* 49:244–49 (Aug. 1956).

"High Speed Marks Translation Work." *New York Times* (late city ed.) 26 Mar. 1946, p.11.

"History of U.N. Library: Special Presentation Volume Is in Limited Edition." *New York Times* (late city ed.) 25 Feb. 1962, p.7.

"Housing Heads Get a Vicarious Thrill." *New York Times* (late city ed.) 20 June 1947, p.13.

Hove, Julien van. "Compte Rendu de la Conférence sur la Documentation de l'Organisation des Nations-Unies et des Institutions Spécialisées, Tenue à Paris, sous les Auspices de la Fondation Carnegie pour la Paix Internationale, les 21 et 22 Nov. 1948." *Archives, Bibliothèques et Musées de Belgique* 20:75–78 (1949).

"The Inside Story." *Secretariat News* 16:6–7 (30 Mar. 1962).

"International Library Conference Studies Documentation Questions." *United Nations Bulletin* 6:25 (1 Jan. 1949).

Jackson, Isabel H., ed. *Acquisition of Special Materials*. San Francisco: Special Libraries Assn., San Francisco Bay Region Chapter, 1966.

Jackson, Joseph Henry. "Library of 3000 Reference Books for Delegates." *San Francisco Chronicle: The World of Books* 22 Apr. 1945.

Kahn, Dorothea. "UN to Get Real Library Service: Portrait of a Bibliophile." *Christian Science Monitor* (central ed.) 24 Apr. 1948.

Kennedy, Paul P. "U.N. Publications End Busiest Year." *New York Times* (late city ed.) 1 Jan. 1967, p.19.

Kent, F. L. "University and Research Library Notes." *The Library Association Record* 54:406–408 (Dec. 1952).

Kruse, Paul. "A Special Library at the Conference." *Special Libraries* 36:431–35 (Nov. 1945).

Kyle, Barbara. Review of *United Nations Documents Index*. In *International Affairs* (London) 26:591 (Oct. 1950).

Lamb, Beatrice Pitney. "Documents of the United Nations. *American Journal of International Law* 41:140–45 (Jan. 1947).

"Large International Gathering for UN Library Dedication." *Library Journal* 86:4254 (15 Dec. 1961).

"League of Nations Documents Transferred to the United Nations Library." *UNESCO Bulletin for Libraries* 4:912, 914 (Dec. 1950).

Leube, Sigrid, and Chamberlin, Waldo. *How to Cite United Nations Documents: Footnotes, Bibliographies*. New York University Conference on United Nations Documents Paper no.2. New York; New York University, 1952.

"Libraries and United Nations Publications." *UNESCO Bulletin for Libraries* 8:E31–E36 (Feb.–Mar. 1954).

"Libraries Supply U.N. with Needed Books." *New York Times* 7 Oct. 1946, p.29.

"Library Aids Delegates." *New York Times* (late city ed.) 3 Apr. 1946, p.4.

"Library Browsing Room." *Secretariat News* 6:2 (15 Feb. 1952).

"Library Fire Adds to U.N.'s Problems." *New York Times* (late city ed.) 30 July 1961, p.71.

"Library Gift." *Secretariat News* 4:6 (28 June 1950).

"Library Gift." *United Nations Reporter* 3:8 (July 1950).

"Library of the United Nations." *Special Libraries* 43:127–28 (Apr. 1952).

"Lithuanian Gets U.N. Post." *New York Times* (late city ed.) 19 June 1964, p.28.

Lloyd, Gwendolyn. "Are You Stymied by U.N. Documents?" *Library Journal* 72:1337, 1350–51 (1 Oct. 1947); 72:1453, 1460–61 (15 Oct. 1947); 72:1529–31 (1 Nov. 1947); and 72:1585, 1603–1604 (15 Nov. 1947).

————. "Sources for Biographical Data on United Nations Personnel." *Special Libraries* 38:219 (Sept. 1947).

Luce, Helen. "Library Service for the United Nations Conference." *California Library Association Bulletin* 6:138, 193 (June 1945).

Lydenberg, H. M. "Carl H. Milam, Internationalist." *Library Journal* 70:334–35 (15 Apr. 1945).

————. "Milam, the Internationalist." *ALA Bulletin* 42:P5–P6 (15 Sept. 1948).

Lyons, Leonard. "The Lyons Den." *New York Post* 21 June 1946, p.30.

Maass, Ernest. "Interlibrary Loan Work at the United Nations." *Special Libraries* 54:517–21 (Oct. 1963).

MacBride, James H. "A Subject Approach to United Nations Documents." *College and Research Libraries* 15:42–46 (Jan. 1954).

McDiarmid, Errett W. "Personnel: Carl H. Milam." *College and Research Libraries* 9:257 (July 1948).

Merritt, LeRoy Charles. Review of *United Nations Documents Index.* In *Library Quarterly* 21:51 (Jan. 1951).

Meyer, José. "Publications of the United Nations." *College and Research Libraries* 7:311–18 (Oct. 1946).

————. "Significant Early Documents of the Specialized Agencies Related to the United Nations." *College and Research Libraries* 8:142–46 (Apr. 1947).

————. "United Nations Information Board and Its Library." *Library Journal* 69:7–10 (1 Jan. 1944).

Milam, Carl H. "The Depository Library System." *United Nations Bulletin* 6:273–75 (15 Mar. 1949).

———. "From the Corner Office." *ALA Bulletin* 42:201 (May 1948).

———. "Libraries, Scholars, and the War." *Annals of the American Academy of Political and Social Science* 235:100–106 (Sept. 1944).

———. "The United Nations Library."*Library Quarterly* 23:267–80 (Oct. 1953).

———. "Work of Library Committee." *United Nations Bulletin* 5:681–82 (1 Sept. 1948).

"Milam Announces Reorganization of United Nations Library." *Library Journal* 73:933 (15 June 1948).

"Milam, Carl H(astings)." In *Current Biography 1945*, p.402–404; and in *Current Biography 1963*, p.268. New York: Wilson, 1946, 1964.

"Milam, Carl H(astings)." In *Who's Who in Library Service*. 3d ed., p.332. New York: Grolier, 1955.

"Milam Heads UN Library." *Chicago Sunday Sun and Times* 7 Mar. 1948.

Molleson, John. "Ford Foundation to Give U.N. $6-Million Library." *New York Herald Tribune* 30 Sept. 1959, p.1.

Monk, Richard C. "United Nations Library: Gift of the Ford Foundation." *External Affairs* (Ottawa) 12:626–28 (May 1960).

Moor, Carol Carter, and Chamberlin, Waldo. *How to Use United Nations Documents*. New York University Conference on United Nations Documents Paper no.1. New York: New York University, 1952.

———, and ———. *How to Use United Nations Documents*. New York University Libraries Occasional Paper no.1. New York: New York Univ. Pr., 1952.

"Moraes, Rubens Borba Alves de." In *Who's Who in Latin America*, p.338–39. Stanford, Calif.: Stanford Univ. Pr., 1940.

Munn, Ralph. "Carl Milam—The Administrator." *ALA Bulletin* 42 P3–P4 (15 Sept. 1948).

Murra, Kathrine O. "UN Bibliographies and Indexes." *Library of Congress Information Bulletin* 12:2 (23 Mar. 1953).

"Name Carl H. Milam, Evanston, as Head of U.N. Libraries." *Chicago Sunday Tribune* 7 Mar. 1948.

Neuberger, Richard L. "Marginal Notes at San Francisco: Off-Stage Sights and Sounds at the Security Conference." *Saturday Review of Literature* 28:5–7 (26 May 1945).

"New Building for the United Nations Library." *UNESCO Bulletin for Libraries* 14:76–79 (Mar.–Apr. 1960).

"The New Dag Hammarskjöld Memorial Library . . . ." *The Times* (London), (royal ed.) 21 Nov. 1961, p.20.

"New Library for the United Nations." *Library of Congress Information Bulletin* 18:700–701 (23 Nov. 1959).

"New Mural for U.N.: Swedish Artist Is Working in Hammarskjöld Library." *New York Times* (late city ed.) 9 Nov. 1961, p.31.

"New UN Library Needed." *Library Journal* 78:428 (1 Mar. 1953).

"New U.N. Library Planned." *New York Times* (late city ed.) 30 Oct. 1952, p.9.

"New UN Library Planned with $6-Million Ford Gift." *Publishers' Weekly* 176:32–34 (26 Oct. 1959).

New York Public Library. *National and Local Gazettes Microfilming Program*. New York, Dec. 1961.

"News and Notes." *American Political Science Review* 41:1205–1206 (Dec. 1947).

"News Briefs: UN Depository." *Library Journal* 93:2786, 2789 (Aug. 1968).

Nixon, Emily O., and Chamberlin, Waldo. *How to Catalogue United Nations Documents*. New York University Conference on United Nations Documents Paper no.3. New York: New York University, 1952.

"Obituary Notes: Carl Hastings Milam." *Publishers' Weekly* 184:47 (9 Sept. 1963).

O'Hara, Tom. "Staff of U.N.O. Keeps Busy at Routine Tasks." *New York Herald Tribune* 26 Mar. 1946, p.6.

"Old League Records, 100,000 Items, Formally Given to United Nations." *New York Times* (late city ed.) 13 June 1950, p.29.

Osborn, Andrew D. "Publications of the League of Nations, United Nations, and Organization of American States." In his *Serial Publications: Their Place and Treatment in Libraries*, p.262–71. Chicago: American Library Assn., 1955.

Patch, William H. *The Use of United Nations Documents*. Occasional Papers no.64. Urbana, Ill.: University of Illinois Graduate School of Library Science, 1962.

Penn, William. *An Essay towards the Present and Future Peace of Europe*. Boston: American Peace Society, 1897.

"People: Carl Hastings Milam." *Wilson Library Bulletin* 38:113 (Oct. 1963).

Perry, James W. "The United Nations Library, Lake Success." *South African Libraries* 17:148–55 (Apr. 1950).

"Plans Close Integration of U.N. Library Activities." *Library Journal* 73:772 (15 May 1948).

"Plans for United Nations Library." *UNESCO Bulletin for Libraries* 1: 52 (June 1947).

"Position with U.N." *Recreation* 42:323 (Oct. 1948).

Poste, Leslie I. "No Top Brass in A.L.A." *Library Journal* 74:333–37 (1 Mar. 1949).

"Power Failure at U.N.; World Body Perspires." *New York Times* (late city ed.) 9 May 1964, p.15.

"Publication of Documentation of the Conference." *United Nations Conference on International Organization Journal* no.52:1 (23 June 1945).

Ranganathan, S. R. *The Five Laws of Library Science*. 2d ed. Bombay: Asia Publishing House, 1963.

"Rasmussen, S(igurd) Hartz." In *Who's Who in Library Service*. 3d ed., p.339–40. New York: Grolier, 1955.

Ravage, Denise. "La Bibliothèque des Nations Unies à Lake Success." *Revue de la Documentation* 17:124–33 (Sept. 1950).

"Reference Centre Facilities." *Journal of the United Nations* no.27: 176–77 (9 Nov. 1946).

"Reference Library Established for Research Work of Delegates." *New York Times* (late city ed.) 29 Apr. 1945, p.29.

"Retirement of Dr. Stummvoll from the Austrian National Library." *Library of Congress Information Bulletin* 27:104–105 (21 Feb. 1968).

Review of *United Nations Documents Index*. In *Africa*, 21:79–80 (Jan. 1951).

Rice, Paul North. "Resignation of Carl H. Milam." *ALA Bulletin* 42:155 (Apr. 1948).

Roberts, A. D. "The Documents and Publications of International Organizations." *Revue de la Documentation* 17:3-17 (1950).

——. "United Nations and Its Specialized Agencies: Documents and Publications." *College and Research Libraries* 12:166-70 (Apr. 1951).

Robinson, E. S. "Carl Milam—A Man's Man." *ALA Bulletin* 42:P7 (15 Sept. 1948).

Ronquillo, E. M. "Acquiring Publications of the United Nations and Its Agencies." *Library Herald* (Delhi) 8:64-81 (Apr. and July 1965).

Rosenthal, A. M. "U.N. Curiosa Hide in Archives' Files." *New York Times* (late city ed.) 12 Aug. 1951, p.30.

Russell, Francis H. "United Nations Source Material." In *Proceedings of the Eighth Conference of Teachers of International Law and Related Subjects, Held at Washington, D.C., April 24-25, 1946,* p.103-18. Washington, D.C.: Carnegie Endowment for International Peace, 1946.

Salkeld, J. "United Nations Publications: A Brief Guide." *Manchester Review* 9:242-50 (Spring 1962).

Saunders, Janet F. "Libraries and the Publications of the UN Specialized Agencies." *UNESCO Bulletin for Libraries* 8:E102-E108 (Aug.-Sept. 1954).

"Sechs-Millionen-Dollar-Stiftung für den Neubau der Bibliothek der Vereinten Nationen in New York." *Biblos* 8:121-23 (1959).

Shores, Louis. *Around the Library World in 76 Days: An Essay in Comparative Librarianship.* Berkeley, Calif.: Peacock Pr., 1967.

——. "Epitome." *Journal of Library History,* 1:206-208, 233 (Oct. 1966).

Signor, Nelle. "The San Francisco Conference—Its Structure and Documentation." *Special Libraries* 37:3-6 (Jan. 1946).

——. "United Nations *versus* League of Nations Documentation." *Special Libraries* 43:62-64, 70 (Feb. 1952).

"Speaking of Libraries: The United Nations Library." *Indian Librarian* 14:85-87 (Sept. 1959).

"The Standing Committee on Indexing and Documentation." *United*

Nations Libraries Information Bulletin no.2:1–2 (May 1968).

"Statement on Distribution of UNCIO Documents." *Library Journal* 70:540 (15 June 1945).

Stummvoll, Josef. "Als Bibliotheksdirektor bei den Vereinten Nationen: Tagebuchnotizen, 1. Teil." *Biblos* 8:53–59 (1959).

———. "Als Bibliotheksdirektor bei den Vereinten Nationen: Tagebuchnotizen, 2. Teil." *Biblos* 8:124–45 (1959).

———. "Als Bibliotheksdirector bei den Vereinten Nationen: Tagebuchnotizen, 3. Teil." *Biblos* 9:57–76 (1960).

———. "Als Bibliotheksdirektor bei den Vereinten Nationen. 4. Teil. Die 'Dag Hammarskjöld Bibliothek' in New York." *Biblos* 12:87–96 (1963).

———. "Die 'Dag Hammarskjöld Bibliothek' der Vereinten Nationen in New York." *Libri* 12:97–110 (1962).

"Stummvoll, Josef (Leopold)." In *Current Biography 1960*, p.410–12. New York: Wilson, 1961.

"Stummvoll, Josef Leopold." In *The International Who's Who 1964–65*, 28th ed., p.1050. London: Europa Publications, 1964.

Suttey, Rose C. "San Francisco Public Library Makes Twofold Contribution to Conference." *Library Journal* 70:624–27 (July 1945).

"Thant Gives Lunch for Queen of Greece." *New York Times* (late city ed.) 26 Jan. 1964, p.52.

"U.N. Accepts Ford Aid." *New York Times* (late city ed.) 4 Nov. 1959, p.70.

"U.N. Accepts Gift for Library." *New York Times* (late city ed.) 30 Oct. 1959, p.34.

"United Nations Accepts Gift of Wilson Library." *United Nations Bulletin* 9:39 (1 July 1950).

"U.N. Advisory Committee Made Many Recommendations." *Library Journal* 73:1359 (1 Oct. 1948).

"U.N. Appoints American Director of Its Libraries." *New York Times* (late city ed.) 6 Mar. 1948, p.4.

"U.N. Archivist Chosen." *New York Times* (late city ed.) 6 Oct. 1946, p.34.

"U.N. Book Needs." *Library Journal* 71:1536 (1 Nov. 1946).

"U.N. Building Partly Collapses during Demolition." *New York Times* (late city ed.) 30 Apr. 1960, p.10.

"U.N. Chief Librarian." *UNESCO Bulletin for Libraries* 2:202, 204 (June 1948).

"U.N. Dedicates Room to Abraham Feller." *New York Times* (late city ed.) 7 Oct. 1953, p.5.

"U.N. Gets Historic Papers." *New York Times* (late city ed.) 17 Aug. 1962, p.26.

"U.N. Gets Ralston Books." *New York Times* (late city ed.) 25 Aug. 1953, p.19.

"UN Headquarters Library Report." *Library Journal* 82:2879–83 (15 Nov. 1957).

"U.N. Honors Feller with Reading Room." *New York Times* (late city ed.) 15 Aug. 1953, p.4.

"U.N. Librarian." *Library Journal* 71:1474 (15 Oct. 1946).

United Nations. Library. *The Dag Hammarskjöld Library: Gift of the Ford Foundation*. New York, 1962.

"The United Nations Library." In United Nations, Department of Public Information. *Your United Nations*. Sales no.1952.I.33: Oct. 1952.

"The United Nations Library." In United Nations, Department of Public Information. *Your United Nations: The Official Souvenir Guide Book*. 4th ed. Sales no.1954.I.2: 1954.

"UN Library." *UNESCO Bulletin for Libraries* 2:373 (Oct. 1948).

"The United Nations Library." *UNESCO Bulletin for Libraries* 4:488, 490 (Jan. 1950).

"UN Library Celebrates Its First Five Years." *Library Journal* 92:37–38 (1 Jan. 1967).

"U.N. Library Chain over World Is Aim." *New York Times* (late city ed.) 7 July 1947, p.5.

"The United Nations Library—Gift of the Ford Foundation." *United Nations Review* 6:22–23 (Nov. 1959).

"U.N. Library Head Named." *New York Times* (late city ed.) 15 Nov. 1961, p.32.

"U.N. Library Name Proposed." *New York Times* (late city ed.) 5 Oct. 1961, p.3.

"UN Library Revises 'Documents Index'." *Library Journal* 88:2225 (1 June 1963).

"U.N. Library to Have Repository Branches throughout World." *Library Journal* 72:1174 (1 Sept. 1947).

"U.N. Library Will Get Hammarskjöld's Name." *New York Times* (late city ed.) 17 Oct. 1961, p.20.

"U.N. May Convert a Building on Site," *New York Times* (late city ed.) 7 Jan. 1948, p.6.

"U.N. Names in the News: Adrian Pelt." *United Nations Newsletter* 3: 6 (Jan. 1950).

"U.N. Offices to Move to Headquarters," *New York Times* (late city ed.) 16 Aug. 1947, p.4.

"U.N. Paris Aide Appointed." *New York Times* (late city ed.) 2 Feb. 1954, p.2.

"U.N. Planning New Library on Site at 42nd Street." *New York Times* (late city ed.) 30 Sept. 1959, p.1, 12.

"U.N. Planning to Erect Library Building Here." *New York Herald Tribune* 25 Apr. 1947.

"U.N. Seeking Books for Assembly Use." *New York Times* (late city ed.) 6 July 1946, p.3.

"U.N. to Get Films of League Library." *New York Times* (late city ed.) 15 Aug. 1946, p.3.

"U.N. to Honor Late Legal Chief." *New York Times* (late city ed.) 9 Nov. 1961, p.40.

"U.S. Presents Atomic Energy Library to the United Nations." *United States Department of State Bulletin* 34:656–57 (16 Apr. 1956).

"U.S. to Disclose 'Big 3' Secrets." *New York Times* (late city ed.) 28 Dec. 1946, p.12.

Ulveling, Ralph A. "Carl H. Milam." *ALA Bulletin* 42:203 (May 1948).

Uridge, Margaret D. "At the United Nations Conference." *California Library Association Bulletin* 6:139 (June 1945).

Vashishth, C. P. "UN Depository Libraries in India: Present State and Suggestions for Future Development." *Library Herald* 10:121–36

(July and Oct. 1968).

Vladimirov, Lev I. "The Libraries of the United Nations: Their Goals, Activities and Problems." *Journal of Library History* 1:209–19 (Oct. 1966).

Wasson, Donald. Review of *United Nations Documents Index*. In *Library Journal* 75:702 (15 Apr. 1950).

Wieser, Walter. Review of *The Dag Hammarskjöld Library: Gift of the Ford Foundation*. In *Biblos* 12:75 (1963).

Wilcox, Jerome K. "25 Depository Libraries for U.N. Documents Established." *Library Journal* 72:711 (1 May 1947).

Williams, Elizabeth. "Staff at Conference Library Finds Answers to Big Queries." *Christian Science Monitor* (Atlantic ed.) 14 May 1945.

"Williamstown Conference Stresses International Aspects." *Library Journal* 73:1066–68 (Aug. 1948).

Wilson, Louis R. "Carl H. Milam." *Library Journal* 70:331–33 (15 Apr. 1945).

"Wilson Library Given to U.N. by Foundation." *New York Herald Tribune* 13 June 1950.

Winton, Harry N. M. "Documentation." In *Annual Review of United Nations Affairs 1949*, p.52–68. New York: New York Univ. Pr., 1950.

———. "Documentation." In *Annual Review of United Nations Affairs 1950*, p.193–201. New York: New York Univ. Pr., 1951.

———. "Documentation." In *Annual Review of United Nations Affairs 1951*, p.152–64. New York: New York Univ. Pr., 1952.

———. "Documents and Publications of the United Nations." *College and Research Libraries* 9:6–14 (Jan. 1948).

———. "Information and Documentation." In *Annual Review of United Nations Affairs 1952*, p.50–55. New York: New York Univ. Pr., 1953.

———. "United Nations Documents." *Drexel Library Quarterly* 1:32–41 (Oct. 1965).

"Woodrow Wilson Library Goes to U.N." *Library Journal* 76:397 (1 Mar. 1951).

"Woodrow Wilson Memorial Library Transferred to United Nations." *Special Libraries* 41:264 (Sept. 1950).

"World Archives Unit Asked to Help Peace." *New York Times* (late city ed.) 25 Oct. 1946, p.2.

"World Briefs: United Nations: Library Dedicated." *Christian Science Monitor* (eastern ed.) 17 Nov. 1961.

"World Experts Advise on Library Services: Future of Geneva Library Examined." *United Nations Bulletin* 5:648–49 (15 Aug. 1948).

"World Library Urged: Network to Assist the U.N. Proposed at Panel Here." *New York Times* (late city ed.) 19 Nov. 1961, p.83.

League of Nations Library/United Nations Library, Geneva

Public documents

Field, Norman S. *The United Nations Library at Geneva.* Geneva, n.d.

League of Nations. *Construction of an Assembly Hall, of a New Building for the Secretariat, and of a Library.* A.58.1929: 25 Sept. 1928.

———. ———. A.79.1928 or Gen.1928.7: 22 Sept. 1928.

———. Covenant. 10 Jan. 1920.

———. *Report on the Work of the League 1936/37.* A.6.1937 or Gen.1937.3: 1937.

———. *Rules of Procedure of the Assembly.* C.144.M.92.1937: Apr. 1937.

———. Information Section. *The League of Nations Library.* League of Nations Questions no.10. Geneva, 1938.

United Nations. Economic and Social Council. *Official Records.*

3d yr. 7th sess.. 198th Meeting, 13 Aug. 1948.

8th sess. 233d Meeting, 10 Feb. 1949.

9th sess. 286th Meeting, 6 July 1949.

———. ———. *Plan for the Use of the Central Library at Geneva by the United Nations and Specialized Agencies.* Res. 172(VII), 13 Aug. 1948. E/1065: UNESCOR, 7th sess., Resolutions adopted.

———. ———. *Use of the Central Library at Geneva by the United Na-*

tions and the Specialized Agencies. Res. 205(VIII), 10 Feb. 1949. E/1310: UNESCOR, 8th sess., Res., Suppl. no.1.

———. ———. ———. Res. 260(IX), 6 July 1949. E/1553: UNESCOR, 9th sess., Res., Suppl. no.1.

———. ———. ———. Note by the Secretary-General, 27 Jan. 1949. E/1101: UNESCOR, 4th yr., 8th sess., Annex, Agenda item 35.

———. ———. ———. Note by the Secretary-General, 26 May 1949. E/1358 and E/1358/Corr. 1: UNESCOR, 4th yr., 9th sess., Annex, Agenda item 46.

———. General Assembly. *Official Records.* 1st sess., 1st pt., League of Nations Committee. Summary Record of Meetings, 30 Jan.–1 Feb. 1946.

———. ———. *Transfer of Certain Functions, Activities and Assets of the League of Nations*: Report of the League of Nations Committee to the General Assembly, 12 Feb. 1946. A/28: UNGAOR, 1st sess., 1st pt., Annex 16 to 29th Plenary Meeting.

———. ———. *Transfer to the World Health Organization of Certain Assets of the United Nations.* Res. 129(II), 17 Nov. 1947. A/519: UNGAOR, 2d sess., Resolutions.

———. Office of Public Information. *United Nations Receives $75,000 Grant for League of Nations Archives Project.* Press Release SG/C/2: 31 Jan. 1966.

———. Secretariat. *Rules for the Administration of the Library Endowment Fund.* ST/SGB/76: 28 Nov. 1947.

———. Secretary-General. *Rules Governing Access to the League of Nations.* New York, 23 Aug. 1967.

Archival and unpublished sources

Clapp, Verner W. "The Libraries of the United Nations in New York and Geneva: A Comparative Review of Functions, Staff Requirements and Relationships: Report to the Secretary-General." 5 June 1953 (in the files of Mr. Clapp).

League of Nations. Library Planning Committee. "Preliminary Report to the Secretary-General." Geneva, 1928.

———. ———. "Second Report to the Secretary-General." Geneva, 1928.

———. ———. Third Session Minutes. Geneva, 1929.

———. ———. "Fourth Session Report to the Secretary-General." Geneva, 1932.

———. ———. Fifth Session. Geneva, 1934.

Milam, Carl H. "The Future of the Geneva Library." 10 June 1948 (in the files of Mr. Milam).

———. "The U.N. Library in Geneva." 25 Oct. 1948 (in the files of Mr. Milam).

Wilson, Florence. "The Library: A Report on Its Progress, Aims, Scope, Methods, Details of Work and Personnel." Geneva, 2 Oct. 1922.

———. "The Library of the League of Nations: A Description of Its Functions, Scope and Work." Geneva, Feb. 1923.

———. "The Library of the League of Nations: Statistical Report of Work for Year Ending December, 1922." Geneva, Feb. 1923.

Books, periodicals, and newspapers

Aufricht, Hans. *Guide to League of Nations Publications: A Bibliographical Survey of the Work of the League, 1920–1947.* New York: Columbia Univ. Pr., 1951.

Bishop, William Warner. "International Relations: Fragments of Autobiography." *Library Quarterly* 19:270–384 (Oct. 1949).

———. "The Library of the League of Nations." *American Scholar* 5: 121–22 (Winter 1936).

Breycha-Vauthier, A. C. "La Bibliothèque des Nations Unies de Genève: Centre International de Documentation en Sciences Sociales." *Revue de la Documentation* 24:66–69 (May 1957).

———. *Sources of Information*: A Handbook on the Publications of the League of Nations. New York: Columbia Univ. Pr., 1939.

———. "T. P. Sevensma (1879–1966)." *Libri* 16:312–13 (1966).

———. "The United Nations Library at Geneva." *UNESCO Bulletin for Libraries* 5:81–88 (Mar. 1951).

———. "Vital Problems of International Libraries." *Journal of Documentation* 21:248–51 (Dec. 1965).

"Breycha-Vauthier, Arthur C." In *Who's Who in the United Nations*, p.64–65. Yonkers-on-Hudson, N.Y.: Christian E. Burckel, 1951.

"Call League Unfair to American Women." *New York Times* 24 Jan. 1927.

Carroll, Marie J. *Key to League of Nations Documents Placed on Public Sale, 1920–1929.* Suppl. 1–4, 1930–36. Boston: World Peace Foundation, 1930.

———. "League of Nations Documents and Publications Comparable with or Continued in United Nations Publications." *College and Research Libraries* 13:44–52, 64 (Jan. 1952).

"Catalogue of League of Nations Documents and Publications." *UNESCO Bulletin for Libraries* 4:728, 730 (July–Aug. 1950).

"Cataloguing of League Files." *New York Times* (late city ed.) 1 Feb. 1966, p.2.

Day, Marguerite E. "The Library of the League of Nations." *Library Assistant* 15:212–15 (Nov. 1921).

"Distinguished Foreign Visitors." *Libraries* 33:307–308 (June 1928).

Field, Norman S. "The United Nations Library at Geneva." *UNESCO Bulletin for Libraries* 23:3320–22 (Nov.–Dec. 1969).

"Gift for the Construction and Endowment of a League Library." *Monthly Summary of the League of Nations* 7:305–307 (15 Oct. 1927).

"Gift of $2,000,000 to League of Nations." *New York Times* 11 Sept. 1927.

Gjelsness, Rudolph. "William Warner Bishop Dies." *Library Journal* 80: 621–23 (15 Mar. 1955).

Gordon, Elizabeth L. "Cataloguing League of Nations Publications." *Library Journal* 57:21–22 (1 Jan. 1932).

Hoppes, Muriel. "The Library of the League of Nations at Geneva." *Library Quarterly* 31:257–68 (July 1961).

Hubbard, Ursula Phalla. "The Cooperation of the United States with the League of Nations, 1931–1936." *International Conciliation* no.329:295–468 (Apr. 1937).

"An International Library." *Library Journal* 55:16 (1 Jan. 1930).

"J. D. Rockefeller Jr. Is Donor at Geneva." *New York Times* 13 Sept. 1927.

King, Agnes. "Notes for Librarians: League of Nations Library." *Wisconsin Library Bulletin* 26:186 (June 1930).

Koch, Theodore Wesley. "The Bibliographical Tour of 1928." *Library Journal* 54:101–106 (1 Feb. 1929).

"The League Library." *Monthly Summary of the League of Nations* 8:111–12 (15 Apr. 1928).

"The League Library." *Monthly Summary of the League of Nations* 12:199–200 (June 1932).

"League of Nations Cataloguing Project." *Library of Congress Information Bulletin* 9:18–20 (17 Apr. 1950).

"The League of Nations Library." *Monthly Summary of the League of Nations* 18:68–75 (Mar. 1938).

"League to Seek Here Advice on Library," *New York Times* 27 Sept. 1927.

"League's Librarian Studies Advanced American Methods." *New York Times* 29 Apr. 1928.

"The League's New Buildings." *Monthly Summary of the League of Nations* 16:55–57 (Feb. 1936).

"L.C. Catalog of League of Nations Publications." *Library Journal* 53: 269 (15 Mar. 1928).

"Microfilming League of Nation's Library." *Library Journal* 71:1214 (15 Sept. 1946).

"The New League Buildings." *Monthly Summary of the League of Nations* 8:280–81 (15 Oct. 1928).

"Offer by a Group of American Citizens for the Construction and Endowment of the League of Nations Library." *League of Nations Official Journal* 8:1132–34 (Oct. 1927).

Osborn, Andrew D. "Publications of the League of Nations, United Nations, and Organization of American States." In his *Serial Publications: Their Place and Treatment in Libraries*, p.262–71. Chicago: American Library Assn., 1955.

"Plan for Geneva Library Approved." *United Nations Bulletin* 7:132 (1 Aug. 1949).

"Plans for League of Nations Library." *Library Journal* 53:355 (15 Apr. 1928).

Ranshofen-Wertheimer, Egon F. *The International Secretariat: A Great Experiment in International Administration.* Washington: Carnegie Endowment for International Peace, 1945.

Rasmussen, S. Hartz. "The League of Nations Library during the War." *College and Research Libraries* 5:195–202 (June 1944).

Richardson, Ernest Cushing. "With the League of Nations." *Public Libraries* 26:64–66 (Feb. 1921).

Saunders, Janet F. "Catalog Cards for League of Nations Publications." *Library Journal* 56:14–16 (1 Jan. 1931).

"Says Reich Abused Library of League." *New York Times* 24 Sept. 1941.

Sevensma, T. P. "La Bibliothèque de la Société des Nations." *Revue des Bibliothèques* 40:20–30 (Jan.–July 1930).

————. "The League of Nations Library, I. The Building." *The Library Association Record* 39:472–78 (Sept. 1937).

————. "The League of Nations Library, II. Contents and Organization." *The Library Association Record* 39:521–26 (Oct. 1937).

————. "The Library of the League of Nations." In *Essays Offered to Herbert Putnam by His Colleagues and Friends on His Thirtieth Anniversary as Librarian of Congress, 5 April 1929,* ed. by William Warner Bishop and Andrew Keogh, p.399–408. New Haven: Yale Univ. Pr., 1929.

"Sevensma, Tietse Pieter." In *The International Who's Who.* 17th ed., p.918. London: Europa Publications. 1953.

Signor, Nelle. "League of Nations Publications in the Present Emergency." *College and Research Libraries* 3:326–32 (Sept. 1942).

————. "United Nations *versus* League of Nations Documentation." *Special Libraries* 43:62–64, 70 (Feb. 1952).

Streit, Clarence K. "League Gets $500,000 of Rockefeller Gift." *New York Times* 26 June 1929.

"Text of the Agreement Regarding the Ariana Site." *League of Nations Official Journal,* Special Suppl. no.75:491–92 (1929).

"Topics of the Times: Another Unofficial Adviser." *New York Times* 13 Sept. 1927.

Van Wyck, Harriet. "Documents in Search of a Catalog: League of Nations Collection in Woodrow Wilson Memorial Library." *Library Journal* 71:1177–81 (15 Sept. 1946).

———. *League of Nations Cataloguing Project*: General Over-All Review, 1 Oct. 1945–28 Feb. 1950. New York: Woodrow Wilson Memorial Library, 28 Feb. 1950.

———. *Rockefeller and Wilson Foundations Complete Project with Library of Congress*. New York: Woodrow Wilson Memorial Library, 3 Apr. 1950.

Walton, C. E. "Classifying, Cataloging, and Binding League of Nations Publications." *Library Journal* 55:155–59 (15 Feb. 1930).

Waples, Douglas, and Lasswell, Harold D. *National Libraries and Foreign Scholarship*. Chicago: Univ. of Chicago Pr., 1936.

Wilson, Florence. "The Library of the League of Nations," *Library Journal* 47:1057–61 (15 Dec. 1922).

Wolfsberg, Vernie H. "Three International Libraries." *Minnesota Libraries* 19:103–109 (Dec. 1958).

"Women Assert Rights in League." *New York Times* 23 Jan. 1927.

"World-Wide Library for League of Nations." *New York Times* 10 Dec. 1922.

Index